TUTTLE

DICTIONARY

— OF —

FIRST NAMES

JULIA CRESSWELL

CHARLES E. TUTTLE COMPANY
Boston • Rutland, Vermont • Tokyo

First published in the United States in 1992 by
Charles E. Tuttle Company, Inc. of Rutland, Vermont & Tokyo, Japan,
with editorial offices at 77 Central Street, Boston, Massachusetts 02109.

Library of Congress Cataloging-in-Publication Data

Cresswell, Julia, 1950-
  [Bloomsbury dictionary of first names]
  Tuttle dictionary of first names / Julia Cresswell.
    p.   cm.
  Reprint. Originally published: Bloomsbury dictionary of first
names. London : Bloomsbury, 1990.
  ISBN 0-8048-1780-4 (pbk. : alk. paper)
  1. Names, Personal—Dictionaries. I. Title.
CS2377.C74 1992
929.4'03—dc20   91-67340
                                    CIP

Cover design by Linda Koegel
Book design by Geoff Green
Typeset by Selectmove Ltd.

PRINTED IN THE UNITED STATES

Contents

This book is dedicated to my mother,
Constance,
without whose unfailing help
it would never have been written.

Introduction

Naming names – from Caradoc to Kylie

Throughout the time for which we have records, first names in English show two conflicting trends – one a remarkable conservatism, the other a remarkable fickleness of fashion. Names such as *John* and *James*, *Margaret* and *Mary* have remained in steady use for many hundreds of years, other groups of names have come into fashion and then declined rapidly in popularity or even disappeared altogether. The oldest names still in use in this country are probably the Welsh names *Caradoc*, a descendant of the name *Caractacos*, used by the British chieftain captured by the Romans in AD51, and *Buddug*, a descendant of the name *Boadicea*, the woman who led the revolt against the Romans in c. AD60. At the other end of the scale, *Kylie*, an Australian name popularized by singer and *Neighbours* actress Kylie Minogue, is a new arrival.

Like Caradoc, many other Welsh names are of great antiquity. Some are forms of Latin names which show signs of having been adopted during the Roman occupation of Britain, others are native names which may date from well before this time. There are names found in the earliest surviving Welsh literature and recorded in early saint's lives which are still in use. The other branch of the Celtic language, Irish and Scots Gaelic, also provides many early names recorded in saint's lives. Again these Dark Ages names may well be even older, but we lack written evidence to prove this.

These ancient Celtic names have continued in use amongst the minority of Celtic speaking in Great Britain, and have increased in popularity in modern times. However, for the English-speaking majority the main sources of names have been the traditions of the various Germanic tribes of Northern Europe, and the names introduced by the Church, either the Hebrew names of the Old Testament, or the Greek and Roman names of the New Testament and saints. Truly English names were

1

brought over to England by the invading Anglo-Saxons, a motley collection of peoples from various Germanic tribes, speaking various dialects of what is correctly called Old English, although the terms Anglo-Saxon and Old English have been used more or less interchangeably in this book. These peoples used the Germanic tradition of name-formation, where most names were made up of two elements, each of which has a recognisable meaning, but which do not necessarily make much sense when combined. Thus *Alfred* 'elf-council' and *Alfwine* 'elf-friend' make some sort of recognisable sense, but *Edward* 'fortunate + guard' is a lot more difficult to rationalize. The sense of the name was obviously not the most important aspect of it. What was important was the source of the name, for often the names given to children were coined from name elements used by other members of the family. Alfred the Great was as exceptional in his name as in so much else, being the first bearer of his name in a family which traditionally used 'athel' ('noble') or 'ed' ('fortunate, prosperous, happy') to start names. His father was *Athelwulf*, his three elder brothers *Athelbald*, *Athelbert* and *Athelred* (the second elements of these names meaning 'wolf', 'bold', 'bright', 'council'), his son was *Edward* and his grandsons *Athelstan*, 'noble stone', *Edmund*, 'fortunate protection 'and *Edred*, 'fortunate counsel'. The few names we find that do not fit this pattern tend to be nicknames, often descriptive, or else shortened forms of these double names. This system is found in all those names descended from the northern tribes; not just the obvious names we have inherited or adopted from Germany and Scandinavia, but even in some Italian names which descend from invading Germanic tribes and especially in names brought over by the Normans. It may seem odd that so many of the names introduced by the French-speaking Normans were Germanic, but they were descended from Viking raiders, and the French aristocracy was itself descended from the Franks, another of the Germanic tribes that invaded the crumbling Roman Empire in the Dark Ages.

This pattern of forming names is very marked among the Germanic peoples, but is common throughout Europe, being inherited from our Indo-European ancestors, so it fitted in well with the already established Celtic system, where names could come from nicknames, particularly those associated with complexion or colouring, or were also made up of two elements. This two-part system can been seen in the large number of Welsh names containing the element 'gwen' which means 'white, fair' and so by association with purity, 'blessed'. The two halves of a name are not always as clear in Welsh as in English, for the form changes with the sex of the name so that 'gwen' becomes 'gwyn' in the masculine. In addition, Welsh is one of the languages that has a peculiar system known as lenition, where the initial sound of a word can change to show grammatical function, so that in a name like *Bronwen*, 'breast + white', 'gwen' becomes 'wen'. The same system is found in Gaelic, which explains some of the differences between the original and anglicized forms of the name.

As well as bringing over their own forms of Germanic names which often replaced the Anglo-Saxon forms, the Normans also brought with them the habit of using truly Christian names – those taken from the Bible and the saints. Before 1066 such names are very rare in England, the few examples found being mainly adopted by those taking holy orders. Hebrew names fall into several main categories. There are those that express a particular characteristic or occupation of a person (or that the givers of a name hoped the child would have); those that come from the natural world, some of which may reflect ancient tribal symbols or totems, but many of which show the world-wide desire of parents for their children to emulate certain admired qualities in the natural world; and, very noticeably in those adopted into English, those names containing one of the many elements referring to God, expressing a hoped-for relationship with Him. Many of these names reappear in the New Testament, sometimes in an form altered to fit the Greek in which the Testament was written. Thus the Old Testament name *Simeon* appears in the New both in this form and as the Greek form *Simon*, and *Joshua* becomes *Jesus*. Other names in the New Testament reflect the times when the eastern Mediterranean was heavily influenced by Greek culture overlaid with the influence of the Roman Empire. Thus the names of many early Christians are Greek or Roman. Greek men and women normally had only one name, although nicknames could be added and further identification made by describing someone as the son or daughter of their father. Most Greek names were made up from everyday or 'vocabulary' words, but a good proportion, like the Hebrew names, describe the bearer as having a relationship to a god or goddess. With the coming of Christianity such names remained in use, despite their pagan meanings.

Roman names were rather different. All Roman males had three names: a personal name drawn from a very limited stock that among the aristocracy boiled down to a mere fifteen or so; a clan name; and the name of the family within each clan, although other names could be added on to these three. Women were usually known by the feminine form of the clan name, but this could vary and we do have records of women's personal names. In modern times any of these three names can be used as a first name: *Marcus* is a Roman personal name, *Claud* and *Anthony* derive from clan names and *Adrian* from a family name.

Thus by the early Middle Ages the main sources of British and American first names were established. Since then new names have been added, and old ones have disappeared, but the changes have on the whole been ones of fashion and emphasis. There have always been parents who have wanted to give their children names that are different, and have gone to unusual sources or made up names. As a result, one can never be categorical about when a name was first or last used, or why it has been used, but only deal with general trends. For example, the next main change in names comes with the Renaissance when there is a growth in the use of non-Biblical names from the classical past, but this does not mean that such names were never found in the Middle Ages. *Diana, Lavinia, Leda, Antigone* and *Cassandra* have all been recorded from the late twelfth or early thirteenth centuries. However, such names are found more frequently as a knowledge of Greek spreads. At first it was mainly a literary phenomenon, with authors using names taken from classical literature in their own works, or making up names such as *Pamela* and *Stella*, based on Greek and Latin, for their heroines. As would be expected, this is found again in the late seventeenth and eighteenth centuries, when everything classical was the rage. Literary heroines were given names like *Clarissa* and real-life heroes had names like *Horatio* Nelson. There was also a tendency to use the Latinate form of girl's names, so that *Louisa* became more common than *Louise*. The introduction of classical names has continued since then, although less markedly, and many that were at one time exotic are now so thoroughly naturalized that they hardly seem anything but English. A name like *Penelope*, first used in the mid-sixteenth century with conscious reference to Homer is now so at home that it has lost most of its associations with faithful wifehood, and become as English as its short form *Penny*.

Even more important than the Renaissance in changing the pattern of naming are the effects of the Reformation. For the majority, naming patterns remained much the same, with the perennial *William, John* and *Thomas* still the most common names for boys, and *Elizabeth, Mary* and *Anne* for girls, but there was a decline in the use of names more obviously associated with the saints of the Roman Catholic church, and a distinct increase in the use of names taken from the Bible. This trend became even more marked with the rise of the Puritans who sometimes wished to mark their rejection of past ways by cutting their children off from the associations of well-established names. Thus they would seek out the more obscure biblical names such as *Malachy* and *Shobael*, and also use vocabulary words as first names. Some of these such as *Hope* and *Patience* have survived, but the more astonishing such as *Tribulation*, *Ashes* or *More Trial* had only a brief fashion, although writers on names have tended to over-emphasise this trend, as it is so striking.

American names

The pilgrim Fathers took these new trends with them when they moved across the Atlantic. Politics and fashion led to a rapid decline in such names in Britain, but they remained in use for longer in the new continent, and so entered the main stream of American names, many of the biblical names remaining in use to this day and once more becoming fashionable. It is important not to exaggerate this trend. Studies of American names in the seventeenth century have shown that while Biblical names were in use and names such as *Jered*, *Lemuel* and *Zeruiah* can be found, the majority had well-established names, and certainly no more than fifteen per cent bore vocabulary names such as *Mourning*, *Free-Grace* and *Wrestling*. Moreover we can also find pagan names such as *Atlanta* and *Lucrecia* (although one must be careful with names such as *Phoebe*, which are in fact found in the New Testament) as well as non-religious vocabulary names such as *Lady*.

However, there is no doubt that naming in north America started out with a desire to break away from some of the old traditions, and that ever since there has been a freer attitude to choosing a child's name. There have been a number of contributory factors to this. One is the large number of different ethnic groups that have made up the population. Thus the people from the old French territories followed French patterns of naming, using both French forms of names and from the early nineteenth century following the French fashion for classical names. These naming-habits have remained in use to this day, although they are now less marked. Later on, Scandinavian, German and Jewish immigrants brought their name-forms and preferences with them, and more recently Spanish names have had their influence. All this has made the pool of names that can be drawn on much greater, and the variety available to parents must have helped to form a much less rigid attitude to what constitutes a 'normal' name. In 1959 Thomas Pyles formulated another theory about American naming habits, in an article which he gave the tongue-in-cheek title of 'Bible Belt Onomastics or Some Curiosities of Anti-Pedobaptist Nomenclature'. Here he pointed out that a quarter of American Christians belong to sects that practice adult baptism (Pyles's 'anti-pedobaptism'), and that therefore the conservative influence of a clergyman does not affect the choice of a child's name. 'Where name-giving is no part of the sacrament of baptism, and where consequently a clergyman with some sense of traditional onomastic decorum has no say, individual taste and fancy may run riot – and usually do.' The family he cites where the women were called *Hoyette, Norvetta, Yerdith, Arthetta, Marlynne* and *Wilbarine* has become well-known in name studies. It is interesting to note that a number of the names he lists as remarkable – *Leroy, Prince, Amber, Orlando, Kimberly, Kelly, Fawn, Melody, Madonna* and many others, have now become much more widely known. The fertility of invention among American parents and the freedom that their history gives them to choose, means that the United States in the twentieth century has been the major influence in changing patterns of naming in the English-speaking world.

Surnames as first names

This use of surnames as first names goes back to at least the sixteenth century. Initially the most usual reasons for saddling a child with such a name was to preserve a mother's maiden name, or in honour of a godparent (usually, it is to be feared, in the hope that the godparent would reward the child for this compliment). This pattern of naming continued to be used quietly but increasingly. From the eighteenth century onwards another use of surnames as first names becomes more common, that of naming a child for a famous person admired by the parents. The author, for example, has an ancestor who chose to mark his views about English conduct during the American War of Independence by christening his son *Washington Lafayette* (*his* father had done well through being christened after a wealthy godfather). In the nineteenth century this tendency became more general, and aristocratic surnames, with which the bearer had no connections but which sounded grand, became fashionable. Another peculiarity of the nineteenth century was a fashion for giving a child the same first name as his surname, so we find such oddities as a judge called *Sir Cresswell Cresswell*.

6

Surnames as first names were particularly popular in the Southern United States, where it has been calculated that in the mid-nineteenth century ten per cent of names were of this type. Heroes from the Civil War were popular as names, which may explain the spread of *Lee* as a first name. Surnames have always been used as first names for both sexes – *Douglas* for instance is quoted as a woman's name in the seventeenth century, and *Beverly* and *Shirley*, which we now think of primarily as first names, started as surnames – but this trend is again more marked in the southern States which probably explains why so many modern names based on surnames can be used for either sex in the USA.

Another markedly American fashion is to look to the famous and worthy of the past for first names. Some of these such as *Cyrus*, *Darius* and *Myron* cannot be classed as surnames, but *Milton* is a typical American name of this class.

The use of surnames as first names has become very marked in this century. In America and Australia Irish surnames have been particularly popular as first names, presumably a fashion which started with emigrant communities, and many of these are now widely used in the United Kingdom. The fashion is now so firmly established that almost any surname can be used for a first name without raising eyebrows. Consequently it has been impossible to include any but the most popular here, and readers wanting more information on such names should turn to a good dictionary of surnames.

Names in the nineteenth and twentieth centuries

As well as the growth in surnames and the steady increase in Latinate forms, which have already been discussed, certain other trends can be found in the nineteenth and early twentieth centuries. One of these was the interest shown in old names, which led to a revival of many of the Anglo-Saxon names such as *Alfred* and *Edred* that had disappeared with the Norman conquest. This antiquarianism is a good example of the way in which fashions in names reflect the cultural fashions of the times: Gothic names going hand in hand with Victorian Gothic architecture and a general revival of interest in the Middle Ages. Another example of names reflecting current taste is the way in which more recently names that seem to have a Victorian feel – *Victoria* itself, *Emily*, *Charlotte*, *Flora* – became fashionable at the same time as Victorian architecture and furnishing became popular once more.

In the Victorian and Edwardian periods we find four main sources of new names. Naming a child after the place where he or she was born, or with which a parent was particularly associated was long-established, but comparatively unusual until this time. Moreover, once the name came to public attention, it could be adopted by parents who had no association with the place. The most obvious example of this is *Florence*. Florence Nightingale was named after the town in which she was born, just as her elder sister was called *Parthenope* from the old name for her birth-place, Naples. Florence's fame turned a one-off name into a highly popular one which entered the main stock of British names. A study of the obituary columns will throw up more of this sort of name – for example a *Corcyra*, the old name for Corfu, died recently – and this fashion has not entirely died out; witness the recent rise in popularity of the name *India*, as well as one-offs such as *Cluny* seen recently in the local press. (For further information on this subject see under *Kim*.)

Another fashion of this time was for jewel names, with names like *Pearl*, *Beryl* and *Ruby* having a particularly turn-of-the-century feel to them. Again this fashion has not died out, but the jewels chosen have changed, with a distinct leaning towards the semi-precious such as *Amber*, *Jade* and *Topaz* which may well reflect a rise in the use of such stones in jewellery. Flower and plant names were another fashion of this time, with many girls being christened *Violet*, *Rose* and *Ivy*. Once more this fashion did not die out, but changed with new plants such as *Bryony*, *Heather*, *Holly*, *Saffron* coming into use. Some of the old flower names such as *Poppy* and *Daisy* are once again popular with parents, and new ones are always being coined. In the past twelve months the author has found: *Japonica*, *Lavender*, *Briar*, *Moss*, *Sage*, *Tamarisk*, *Clematis* (sister of *Poppy* and *Fleur*) and two *Fuchsias*.

The final new source has been books, and more recently other media. Obviously the Book of Books, the Bible, has been a major source of names for centuries, and for this reason biblical quotations in this book have been taken from the Authorized Version, as the translation that has had most influence on the history of names. Writers and stories had long influenced parents, but the nineteenth century saw the rise of the novel as an important influence, introducing exotic names such as *Mavis*. Moreover, names were taken more freely from older authors, with Shakespeare and Spenser being particularly favoured. Books have continued to be influential. *Gone with the Wind*, among the most influential, is credited with a rise in popularity of a number of names including *Ashley*, *Melanie* and *Tara* as well as the more obvious *Scarlett*. *Gone with the Wind* introduces the influence of the cinema and later television and pop music. Frequently visual adaptations of books have had a greater influence in making a name popular than the written original, while the influence that film and pop stars (as well as idols from sport) have had on parents' choice in recent years is too obvious to need elaboration.

Modern trends

It would be a brave person who confidently predicted what was going to happen next with names. However, certain recent and current trends can be determined, and tentative suggestions made about the future. The mixture of conservatism and innovation we have seen throughout the history of names continues. On the conservative side boy's names like *James, Thomas, William, Edward* and *Henry* which have been around for hundreds of years are still the most common, while the majority of girls have 'old-fashioned' sounding names like *Alice* and *Emma*, or perennials like *Catherine*. On the innovatory side a whole new crop of surnames – *Darren, Dean, Daryl, Ryan, Hayley, Kelly* – have become established as first names. From abroad we have taken the foreign forms of names which already existed in English – *Karen, Marie, Anton* – or feminines of names which were hitherto only masculine – *Michelle* and *Michaela, Danielle* – or adopted new names – *Nathalie, Gemma* – to a greater extent than before. The return of some of the old saints' names may also be due to foreign influence, as names like *Damian* and *Dominic* remained in use in Catholic countries when they died out in Protestant ones. Ireland may have contributed here, for it has certainly been a source of a number of newly popular names in the rest of the English-speaking world. In fact all the Celtic languages have spread outside their old boundaries when names are being chosen. The Scottish *Kirsty* has been particularly popular recently, and Welsh *Glenda* is firmly established as an 'English' name. For boys Welsh *Gareth* has become very popular, and the Irish *Shaun* is also widely used. Shaun is actually an Irish form of the old standard John, for the Celtic languages do not take well to the 'j' sound, and change it to 'sh'.

What about the future? A few guesses can be made about where names are going. As the generation of women who were given Victorian names come to have their own children, there is some indication that some are choosing to revive slightly more recent names from the beginning of this century, such as the currently fashionable flower names listed above. There also seems to be a minor revival of names based on abstract nouns, with *Clemency* and the like occurring surprisingly frequently in

9

the birth announcements. Fashions in names include fashions in sounds, with new names at different times sharing similar sounds. In the last fifty years 'k' has been very popular as the first letter of new names, and 'l' has been very popular in girl's names. There is a little evidence at the moment that 'p' might be a growth area, at least for girls' names, but this may just be an illusion, for these things can only be established in retrospect. What can not be denied is the vast growth in variety of names in recent years. In particular parents have been making new forms of old names (variants), joining together bits of different names (blends) to give names like *Floella*, or simply inventing names. This has made life much more difficult for the writer on names. It is impossible to record all such blends and variants, and no such attempt has been made in this book. In addition double names such as *Mary Lou* have been ignored. With the greater freedom in forming names, it is also much more difficult for a writer to be didactic about a name. If you find a name like *Kerryn*, do you class it as a variant of *Karin* or *Kerry* or as a name in its own right? Is *Tonya* really a short form of *Antonia*, or a variation of *Tanya*? Nowadays it is impossible to draw any strict lines between names.

What is in this book, and how it got there

Since I started writing this book, I have often been asked where the information comes from. The simple answer is that all writers on first names depend to a large extent on the work of others. There are hundreds of books on names, ranging from awesomely academic studies of Anglo-Saxon naming habits to booklets handed out in maternity wards. I have consulted and made use of a good number of these, as well as reading many articles, particularly in the two major journals devoted to names, *Nomina* in England and *Names* in America. In 1863 Charlotte M. Yonge published her *History of Christian Names* which is really the first, and still one of the most readable, of the modern books on names. Although some of what she wrote has now been superseded, most modern books depend heavily on her either directly or indirectly. Another influential work is E. G. Withycombe's *Dictionary of English Christian Names* first published in 1945 and still going strong. This is particularly useful for anyone wanting the history of names in the Middle Ages and the forms they took then. The most prolific of recent writers on first names has been Leslie Dunkling. Of his numerous books, the most useful is his *Dictionary of First Names* written with William Gosling, which probably lists more variants than any other work. Much of the information on Irish names in this book will be found in P. Woulfe's *Irish Names for Children* and R. Coghlan's *Irish Christian Names*, while much of the information on Welsh names comes from T. R. Davies' *A Book of Welsh Names*, updated by more recent works. Dictionaries and a concordance to the Bible give information on where to find out more about Biblical names (if you are looking for the source of a particularly obscure name, it is always worth checking a concordance). Standard classical and literary reference works are another useful source of information. Many of the comments on twentieth-century fashions are based on extensive analysis of entries in the births, deaths and marriage announcements in newspapers and on more informal sources, such as conversations with midwives about naming trends in the local hospitals.

In this book I have tried to show the relationship between different branches of the same name. These have been grouped under one main 'root' form of the name, with each version of the name printed in bold so that it can be picked out for quick reference. These variants have also been listed alphabetically in the book, with where to find them, except where they would appear immediately before or after the root form. Names in small capitals mean that there is an entry under that name, where the reader can find more information. Where an entry covers both male and female names, the headword in usually in the masculine form, unless the feminine is much more common. This is not sexism, but because it is much more common to have a feminine name coined from a masculine that vice versa. Moreover, naming conservatism has been much stronger for boys than girls. Parents have had the feeling that it is better to give a boy a 'safe' name, but that they can look for something more glamourous and exotic for girls, so it has been easier to find a single main form of the masculine than of the feminine.

Finally, I would like to thank some of the people who have helped with this book. I would like to thank my editor Kathy Rooney for waiting so long for the manuscript. Elizabeth Pearce and Jean Buchanan supplied me with valuable information. My husband Philip has also made many useful suggestions and comments on the work, and given me all the help a spouse can give, as well as giving me the benefit of his expertise in computers. Above all, I would like to thank my Mother, who not only read the whole manuscript as it was being written, making many corrections in content, grammar and spelling, but also gave up most of her time to look after my son, Alexander, for the first seven months of his life.

Pronunciation guide

Vowels

a	as in bad, fat
ah	" father, oompah
aw	" saw, awful
ay	" make, hay
e	" bed, head
ee	" sheep, key
eə	" there, hair
i	" ship, lick
ie	" bite, lied
ie.ə	" fire, liar
iə	" here, fear
o	" pot, crop
oh	" note, Joan
oo	" put, cook
ooh	" boot, lute
ooə	" jury, cure
ow	" now, bough
owə	" our, power
oy	" boy, loiter
oyə	" lawyer, sawyer
u	" cut, luck
uh	" bird, absurd
ə	" mother, about

Consonants

b	as in bad
ch	" cheer
d	" day
dh	" they
f	" few
g	" gay
h	" hot
hl	" Welsh ll as in Llewellyn
j	" jump
k	" king
kh	" loch
l	" led
m	" man
n	" sun
ng	" sung
nh	" restaurant
p	" pot
r	" red
s	" soon
sh	" fish
t	" tea
th	" thing
v	" view
w	" wet
y	" yet
z	" zero
zh	" pleasure

A

Aaron

In the Bible Aaron is the brother of MOSES and is traditionally regarded as the founder of the Jewish priesthood. The meaning of the name is not known; we do not even know if it is Hebrew or Egyptian. The plant Aaron's rod is so called from the story that when Moses and Aaron's right to the leadership of the exiled Children of Israel was challenged, Aaron's rod, or staff, budded and blossomed when laid upon the altar, as a sign that he was chosen by God.

Abel

Abel is the name of the second son of ADAM and EVE, killed in a fit of jealousy by his brother **Cain**. As in the case of so many early biblical names, it is difficult to work out the meaning. It has been suggested that the name comes from a word meaning 'son' or perhaps from another word meaning 'breath'.

Abigail

This name means 'father rejoiced'. The biblical Abigail was a wife of King David. It was a popular name in England until the seventeenth century, when it became a term for a lady's maid; this led to its falling out of favour. It was revived in the nineteenth century, and has remained in steady use. **Abby** (**Abbie**) is a short form (see also GABRIEL), and in the past **Nabby** was also used. **Gail** (**Gale, Gayle**), its other short form, is well established as an independent name.

Abraham

Another Hebrew name, Abraham means 'father of a multitude'. In the Bible Abraham was originally called **Abram** ('high father'), but as the patriarch of the nation, his name was changed to fit his role.

13

Abraham Lincoln's nickname 'Honest **Abe**' shows one short form of the name; **Aby** is also used, and **Bram** Stoker, the creator of Count Dracula, illustrates another short form.

Achilles: see HECTOR

Ada, Adah

These two names come from different roots, although in practice they are probably used interchangeably. **Ada** is a short form of the names in the ADELA group and came into used as an independent name in the last century. **Adah** is a Hebrew name meaning 'an ornament', although the biblical Adah's name has also been interpreted as meaning 'brightness' in contrast to her co-wife ZILLAH, ('shadow'). The computer language Ada is named in honour of Byron's daughter Ada, Countess Lovelace (1815–52), who was a gifted mathematician and a patron of Charles Babbage, encouraging him to develop his prototype computer. Ada and Babbage tried to apply their mathematical skills to predicting the outcome of horse races, and Ada died heavily in debt.

Adam

The name of the first man in Judaeo-Christian tradition, Adam comes from the Hebrew word for 'red', referring either to the colour of his skin or to the earth from which he was made. It has been a very popular name in recent years throughout the English-speaking world, but has particularly strong associations with the Celtic areas of Britain. In Scotland its early popularity led to the development of many variants and pet forms, such as **Adie, Edie, Edom** and **Yiddie**. There is also a rare Scots feminine form **Adamina**. The Welsh form of Adam is **Adda**, and the Irish have a subsidiary form of the name, **Adamnan** which means 'little Adam'. This was the name of an Irish saint and bishop of the 7th-8th centuries who was renowned for his work for peace and for his writings, and who also made the earliest recorded 'sighting' of the Loch Ness Monster.

Adela

This Germanic name means 'noble'. The Frankish nobility were keen to stress their daughters' pedigree (and thus marriageability) and were particularly fond of giving them names compounded with Adel-. Thus we find **Adelicia** or **Adeliza** ('noble cheer') the name of the mother of William the Conqueror and of one of his daughters; **Adelina** ('noble manner'); **Adelinde** ('noble snake'), which developed into our 'Sweet **Adeline**' and also a shortened

form, **Aline**; and **Adelaide** ('noble kind'), now also spelt **Adalaide**.
Addie and **Addy** are used as short forms for all these names. **Adèle**
is the French spelling of the name, which became popular in the
nineteenth century. Adela is also spelt **Adella**, which is the source
of the now independent name **Della**. (See also ADA, ALICE, HEIDI.)

Aden: see AIDAN

Adina
The name of an Old Testament chief of the tribe of Reuben in
Chronicles, Adina is now regarded as a feminine name. It is rarely
used, but is saved from obscurity by being the name of a character
in Donizetti's opera *L'Elisir d'amore* and the title of a work by Henry
James.

Adlai
Adlai is another rare biblical man's name from the same root as
ADAH, meaning 'my ornament'; it was made known to the general
public by the American politician Adlai Stevenson (1900–65).

Adolf
This name means 'noble wolf'. It has never been popular in Britain,
and its association with Hitler has done little to improve its
prospects. Its Latinate form **Adolphus**, with its short form **Dolphus**,
was popular in the eighteenth century, when it was given in honour
of the Swedish King Gustavus Adolphus, and it is still occasionally
encountered.

Adrian, Adrienne
The Adriatic Sea probably got its name from the Latin word *ater*,
meaning 'black', possibly from the black sand of its beaches. The
sea in turn gave its name to the town of Adria, and it was
from this town that the family name of the Roman Emperor
Hadrian (Latin *Adrianus*) came. The only English Pope, Nicholas
Breakspear, took the name of Adrian or Hadrian IV, perhaps from
Saint Adrian of Canterbury (d. 710), a man who twice refused to
become Archbishop of Canterbury, preferring to remain in a local
monastery. The French form of the name is **Adrien**, and from
this comes the most common feminine form **Adrienne**. **Adrianne,
Adriane** and **Adriana** are also used.

Aegidia, Aegidius: see GILES

Aelwyn: see ALVIN

Aeneas, Aengus: see ANGUS

Aeron, Aeronwen ['ie.ǝron, ie.ǝ'ronwen]

The meaning of the Welsh name element Aeron is disputed. The word *aeron* in Welsh means 'fruit, berry'; but it has been suggested that the name comes from a place name or from Agrona the ancient Celtic goddess of battle. Aeron is used for both sexes, but there are specifically feminine variants in **Aerona** and **Aeronwy**. Another feminine, **Aeronwen**, is formed from Aeron plus the suffix *gwen* which means both 'white' and 'blessed'.

Affery, Afra: see APHRA

Afric, Africa

These are forms of a woman's name used in Ireland and the Isle of Man for the Celtic name **Aifric**, meaning 'pleasant', and in Scotland for the Celtic name **Oighrig**, of disputed meaning. It is an old name, going back to at least the eleventh century, and has no connection with the name of the continent. It is also found as **Affrica**, while the form **Aphria** may sometimes lead to confusion with APHRA. It has also been confused with the short forms of EUPHEMIA.

Agatha

Agatha comes from the Greek meaning 'good'. St Agatha, a third-century martyr, is the patron saint of bell-founders, owing to misinterpretation of pictures of her martyrdom. One of the tortures that was supposed to have been inflicted on her was to have her breasts cut off, and she is often painted bearing them on a dish. The bell-like shape of these objects led to her association with campanology. **Agate** is the old form of the name.

Agnes

Derived from the Greek word for 'pure', Agnes was early on associated with the Latin word *agnus*, meaning 'a lamb', and the lamb is her symbol in art. St Agnes was an early Christian martyr and her popularity is attested by the various forms her name has taken. The old English forms of the name were **Annis, Annes** or **Annot**, reflecting the medieval pronunciation, and they may be one source of **Nance** or **Nancy**. In Scotland, as well as the common shortening **Aggie** or **Aggy**, **Nessa** and **Nessie** are used as pet forms, whence the use of Nessie for the Loch Ness Monster.

There is also the peculiar development in Scotland in which the name **Senga** is formed by spelling Agnes backwards. In Wales the name became **Nest** or **Nesta**, and one eleventh-century holder of that name became a byword for her beauty. **Agneta** is both a Latin and Scandinavian form of the name and gives a pet form **Netta**; the Spanish form gives us **Inez** or **Ines**.

Aidan, Haydon, Ethne

Aidan ['aydən] is a Celtic masculine name meaning 'little fire', derived from **Aodh** [ee], the old Celtic god of the sun and fire. Aidan was a seventh-century missionary from Ireland who played an important part in the conversion of the pagan north of England. The name can also be found as **Aiden** or **Aden**. The Welsh masculine name **Hayden (Haydn, Haydon)** presents something of a problem. It seems unlikely that even in as musical a country as Wales it comes, as is sometimes said, from the name of the Austrian composer, particularly as it is pronounced ['haydən] rather than ['hiedən]. It could be from a surname meaning 'hay down', but this is English rather than Welsh. It therefore seems most reasonable to accept the view that it is either a form of, or at least strongly influenced by, Aidan.

In the feminine the name has developed a wide variety of forms in Ireland. Aidan itself is occasionally used for women, as is the closely related **Edana**. However, the full feminine version of the name is **Ethne** (the pronunciation of which is shown by the pop singer **Enya**), **Eithne** or **Ethna** ['etnə], with variants **Ena, Etney** and **Aithne**, which can be shortened to **Aine**.

Aifric: see AFRIC

Ailbe, Ailbhe: see ELVIS

Aileen: see HELEN

Ailie: see ALICE

Ailsa

Some authorities have argued that this is a form of the name ELSA and the similarity of sound may have helped its popularity, or of **Ailsie**, sometimes spelt Ailsa, used in Scotland as a pet form of ALICE. However, it is more likely that the main source of the name comes from the island of Ailsa Craig, in the Firth of Clyde. The name was first used in Scotland in the nineteenth century, but has since spread to the rest of the Britain. Quite how the name came into use is a bit of a mystery. The true meaning of the island's name is disputed, but it seems to have been popularly understood as 'Ailsa's rock', so that Ailsa came to be thought of as a first name. Further south, Ailsa Craig became familiar to vegetable growers as the name of popular varieties of tomato and onion. Since Craig is more familiar to southerners as a surname than as a form of the word 'crag', and as many plants are named after people, this may have helped to establish Ailsa's currency as a name.

Ailsie: see ALICE

Aimé: see ESMÉ

Aimée: see AMY

Aine: see AIDAN

Ainsley, Ainslie
This is a surname of unknown meaning which has come to be used as a first name for both sexes.

Aisha [ie'eeshə, ie'ayshə]
Aisha is an Arabic name meaning 'womanly', and was the name of the favourite wife of the prophet Mohammed, in whose arms he died. In the form **Ayesha** it was used by Rider Haggard for the name of She-Who-Must-Be-Obeyed in his novel *She* (1887). **Ayeisha** is also used. The occasionally found **Asia** probably owes as much, if not more, to Aisha as to the name of the continent as it reflects an alternative pronunciation of the name. It is by tradition the name of the wife of the pharoah drowned in the Red Sea when the Children of Israel escaped from Egypt.

Aisling: see ASHLING

Aithne: see AIDAN

Al: see ALBERT, ALEXANDER

Alan
A Celtic name of unknown meaning, Alan is found in early Welsh records. It seems to have died out in Britain until it was re-introduced at the time of the Norman Conquest by Duke William's

18

Breton followers, who used it in honour of a local saint. It is also found in forms such as **Allan, Allen, Alyn, Alleyn**, which probably show the influence of surname spellings. Attempts have been made to distinguish the form **Alun** from other spellings, linking it with a Welsh river name, but in practice only a minority of parents seem likely to be aware of this distinction.

Feminine forms of the name, which have become much more common since the 1950s, include **Alana, Alanah** and **Alanna**, [a'lahnə] or [a'lanə] and the short form **Lana**, given currency by the film star Lana Turner.

Alaric
This was a traditional name for the kings of the Ostrogoths, the most famous of which, Alaric I, sacked Rome in 410. The name means 'noble rule'. For some reason, perhaps as a part of the admiration of things 'Gothic', it was revived in the nineteenth century, and is still used.

Alasdair, Alastair, Alastrina, Alastriona: see ALEXANDER

Alban
St Alban, who gave his name to the town, was the first British martyr, killed about AD 209 for sheltering persecuted Christians. The name comes from Latin, and can be interpreted as meaning either 'white' or 'from the town of Alba', the town's name meaning 'white'. It is also found in the form **Albin**. Feminine names from the same root are **Albinia** and **Albina**.

Alberic: see AUBREY

Albert
This name means 'nobly bright'. The Anglo-Saxon form of the name was **Ethelbert**, which more or less died out after the Norman Conquest until revived in the nineteenth century. Albert was introduced from Germany by Queen Victoria's husband, and by the end of the last century was extremely popular. Short forms are **Al** (particularly in America), **Bert** and **Bertie**. **Alberta** was coined for a goddaughter of Queen Victoria, and other feminine forms such as **Albertine** – familiar as the name of a rose – and **Albertina** are also used.

Albin, Albinia, Albina: see ALBAN

Alby: see ELVIS

Aldous

Derived from a Germanic root meaning 'old', Aldous is an uncommon name given fame by the novelist Aldous Huxley (1894–1964). **Aldis** is an occasional variant.

Aldred: see ELDRED

Aled

Aled is a Welsh name taken from a river and lake in Clwyd. It was used by the poet Tudur Aled (d. *c.* 1526). In the 1980s the boy-singer Aled Jones made the name widely known outside Wales.

Alec, Aleck: see ALEXANDER

Alessandra: see ALEXANDER

Alethea

A woman's name which comes from the Greek word meaning 'truth', Alethea first came into fashion in the seventeenth century. It has a variety of spellings, such as **Alithea, Alithia, Alethia** and **Aletheia**. ALTHEA comes from a different root.

Alewyn: see ALVIN

Alexander, Alexandra

Alexander is a very ancient and widely spread name. The early Greeks said it came from words meaning 'defender of men', and it is generally so interpreted; but there is evidence that it may be an even earlier name coming from the ancient Hittite. The first Greek holder of the name was the Trojan **Paris**, abductor of HELEN; he was nicknamed Alexander by some shepherds whose flocks he defended from robbers. Much later it was adopted by the Macedonian royal family, who followed the Greek custom of alternating pairs of names between generations. Thus PHILIP II of Macedon was the son of an Alexander, and his son was Alexander III, better known as Alexander the Great (356–23 BC), whose conquests of Asia as far as India spread his name in the form **Iskander** through much of that continent (see also OLYMPIA, ROXANA). The fame of Alexander the Great also meant that the name was found throughout medieval Europe, spread by the fictional account of his life in *The Romance of Alexander*. It is found in England from at least the twelfth century, but has special associations with Scotland. Saint Margaret of Scotland (*c.* 1038–93) was the daughter of an exiled Anglo-Saxon prince and a Hungarian princess. She married King Malcolm III of Scotland and one of her sons was christened Alexander, a name that had not been used in the royal family before, but which was popular in Hungary. Alexander I of Scotland reigned for 17 years, and in the following century two more Alexanders succeeded each other; their combined reigns, lasting from 1214 to 1286, firmly established the name in Scotland. Thus it is not surprising that Scotland provides a multitude of pet forms of the name, including **Alec** and **Aleck, Alick, Eck, Ecky, Sander, Sandy, Elshander, Elshender, Elick, Allie** and **Ally**. In Gaelic the name became **Alasdair** (also spelt **Alastair, Alistair, Alister**), which had been adopted by the Lowland Scots by the seventeenth century, and has become popular outside Scotland in this century. Other pet forms are **Al, Alex, Lex, Xan** and, in the North of England, **Sawnie**.

The name also occurs in forms from other countries. Thus the Russian Aleksandr has pet forms **Sasha** or **Sacha** and **Shura**. These are male names in Russia, but because English speakers think of names ending in -a as feminine, they are now often given to girls. The Hungarian **Sandor** is occasionally found. From Russia we also get the related **Alexis**, or **Alexi, Alexei** ('helper'), the name of a popular Greek saint. Again, these are masculine in origin, but now used as feminines.

Alexandra, made popular by the Danish princess who married King Edward VII, is the most widely used female form of the name, but **Alexandria, Alexandrina, Alexandrine**, and **Alexia** are also used. **Alix** and **Alyx** look as if they should also be forms of the name, but historically they are medieval spellings of ALICE. From the Italian **Alessandra** we get **Sandra, Sondra** and **Zandra**, while in France they use **Xandra** and **Xandrine** as pet forms. There are rare Irish feminine forms of Alasdair: **Alastrina** and **Alastriona**.

Alfred

An Anglo-Saxon name meaning 'elf-council', Alfred was made famous by King Alfred the Great (849–901), who was not only an inspiring leader of men and successful general, forcing the invading Danes out of southern England, but also a great patron of learning. Short forms are **Alf, Alfie**, and **Fred**. The name, which had become obsolete, was revived in the nineteenth century, but its very popularity then and in the early part of this century has led to a decline in its use. **Alured** is coinage of the last century, formed from

21

a misunderstanding of the Latin form of the name, the 'u' being a misreading of the 'v' used for the Old English 'f'. **Alfreda**, a feminine version of the name, can be shortened to **Freda**.

Alfwine: see ALVIN

Algernon

Algernon means 'with whiskers' and started life as a nickname; for instance, William de Percy, who took part in the Norman Conquest and founded the PERCY family, was called Algernon on account of his moustache. It has often been described as an aristocratic name, and certainly has aristocratic associations; but recent research has shown that, in the Middle Ages at least, it was used through all strata of society. **Algy** or **Algie** is the short form.

Alice

Alice comes ultimately from the old German name Adelaide (see ADELE) via the French shortening Adaliz, which came over to England as **Aliz**, **Alys**, **Alyx** or **Alix** (see also ALEXANDER). The Latin form of the name gives us **Alicia**, which has recently developed the forms **Alisa, Alissa** and **Alyssa**. Pet forms are **Ali, Allie** and **Ally**. **Alison**, an old pet form, is now regarded as a name in its own right. In Scotland it has pet forms **Ailie, Ellie, Ailsie** (sometimes written AILSA), and this, alongside ELIZABETH, is one of the sources of **Elsie**. **Elke** ['elkə] or **Elkie** is a German pet form of the name.

Alick: see ALEXANDER

Alienor: see ELEANOR

Aline: see ADELA

Alisa, Alison: see ALICE

Alistair, Alister: see ALEXANDER

Alithea, Alithia: see ALETHEA

Alix, Aliz: see ALICE

Allan, Allen, Alleyn: see ALAN

Allegra

This word means 'lively' in Italian. The poet Byron called his illegitimate daughter Allegra, and the name is still used occasionally.

Alli, Ally: see ALEXANDER, ALICE

Alma
Those wanting to use this girl's name can choose from three different sources. The Latin word *alma*, as in the term Alma Mater for ones school or university, means 'loving, nurturing', and is one source of the name. In the sixteenth century Edmund Spenser created a character called Alma for book II of his *Faerie Queene*, deriving the name from the Italian for 'soul'. The name remained rare until after 1854, when the British and their allies defeated the Russians in the Crimean war at the battle of Alma, named after a Crimean river. This third source gave the name a boost which lasted well into this century, but it is now somewhat out of fashion.

Almeric
This Germanic man's name meaning 'work + rule' was introduced at the time of the Norman Conquest. It is also found in the form **Almery**. In Italy the name became Almerigo, then Amerigo, as in Amerigo Vespucci (1451–1512), after whom the continent of America is named. There is a Scots form of the name, **Awly**.

Aloisa, Aloys, Aloyse: see HELOISE, LEWIS, LOIS

Aloysius: see LEWIS

Althea
Althea is a Greek name meaning 'wholesome'. In the form **Althæa** it occurs in Greek mythology as the mother of the hero Meleager, who was told at his birth that he would live as long as a certain log of wood on the fire remained unburned. She kept the wood safe, thus protecting him, until the day he got into a fight and killed her two brothers. In fury she threw the wood on the fire, and her son immediately died. The form Althea was introduced by the Cavalier poet Richard Lovelace as one of his poetic names for Lucy Sacheverell (see LUCASTA).

Alun: see ALAN

Alured: see ALFRED

Alvin, Aylwin
Two Old English names, **Athelwine** ('noble friend') and **Alfwine**

('elf friend') lie behind this name, both taking on the forms **Alwin** or **Alwyn** after the Norman conquest. The name was uncommon until given a boost by the publication of Theodore Watts-Dunton's romantic novel of gypsy life, *Aylwin*, in 1898. **Alvin** is the form of the name most popular in the United States and may show a Dutch influence. Other forms are **Alvyn** and **Alewyn**. A feminine form, **Alvina**, is found in a Flemish legend in which a king's daughter of that name was rejected by her parents for marrying unsuitably. The sound of her crying can still be heard in the howling of strong winds.

The history of the name is complicated by the existence of a group of similar Welsh names—**Aelwyn, Alwen, Alwyn, Eilwyn** and various other forms—which could be from the same Old English source or from a jumble of Welsh sources; the second element means 'white, fair', the first any one of 'great', 'child' or 'brow'.

Alvis: see ELVIS

Alwen, Alwin, Alwyn: see ALVIN

Alyn: see ALAN

Alys, Alyssa, Alyx: see ALICE

Amabel: see AMY, MABEL

Amadea, Amadeus: see THEODORE

Amalia: see AMELIA

Amanda

This name means 'worthy of love', and it is one of a large group of names connected with love, for which see further under AMY. The name probably goes back to the seventeenth century, when descriptive names based on Latin roots were popular. It was much used for literary heroines in the eighteenth century, and it has been particularly popular as given name in the second half of the twentieth, often in its short form, **Mandy**.

Amandine: see AMY

Amaryllis

A name used by pastoral poets of the classical world for a fair country girl, Amaryllis probably derives from a Greek root with the sense 'sparkling of the eyes' or 'darting quick glances'. It was taken up in their pastoral poetry by Spenser and then Milton, who immortalized the name when he wrote of the shepherd's opportunity 'To sport with Amaryllis in the shade' (*Lycidas*). It is only in modern times that Amaryllis has come to be a plant name. The similar-sounding **Amarantha**, another of Lovelace's poetic names (see ALTHEA), is an ancient Greek flower name, the word meaning 'unfading flower'; the botanical genus *Amaranthus* includes love-lies-bleeding and other annuals.

Amata: see AMY

Amber

This name comes from the fossil resin valued as a jewel; the name was used occasionally in the last century, but became popular in the 1960s.

Ambrose

Ambrose means 'belonging to the immortals' and was the name of one of the great scholars of the early Christian church, the fourth-century St Ambrose, bishop of Milan. The name occurs in British history in the fifth century as Ambrosius Aurelianus, traditionally the uncle of King Arthur, and it is from Ambrosius that the Welsh name **Emrys**, now more common that Ambrose, derives.

Amelia

Although **Amelia** looks as if it should derive from the Latin family name of Aemelia, the latter has become EMILY, and Amelia, sometimes found as **Amalia**, actually comes from a Germanic word for 'work'. Emily and its related forms, however, are found as pet forms of Amelia, and may well have influenced the name's development. **Emmeline** (French **Ameline**) is another form of Amelia and the source of the rare name **Emblem**. **Millie** or **Milly** are short forms of these two names as well as of MILLICENT.

Amethyst: see JEWELL

Amice, Amicia: see AMY

Aminta: see ARAMINTA

Amos

This is the name of an Old Testament prophet who foretold the destruction of Judah and Israel if the people did not reform. The name probably means 'bearer of a burden'.

Amy

Amy means 'loved' (from the French name **Aimée**) and is one of a group of names given to children as an expression of their parents' love. In Latin Amy becomes **Amicia**, which in turn became **Amice** in the early Middle Ages, and is still found, if rarely. As well as AMANDA ('worthy to be loved') there is a French name of the same meaning, **Amandine**. **Amata** means 'beloved' and **Amabel**, which became MABEL, means 'loveable'. There were male equivalents of many of these names, but the only one to have survived is **Amyas** ('loved') kept alive by its use by Charles Kingsley for the hero of his *Westward Ho!* (1855).

Amynta, Amyntas, Amyntor: see ARAMINTA

Anaïs [anie'ees]

Anaïs is a French feminine name, derived from the Greek meaning 'fruitful'. It is found as a character in Colette's *Claudine* books, and has a certain notoriety from the French author Anaïs Nin, but is probably best known in this country as the name of a perfume.

Anastasia

The name of a fourth-century martyr, Anastasia was found from the early twelfth-century onwards in England, often in the form **Anstace** or **Anstice**. We now tend to think of it as a Russian name, thanks to the fame of the Russian princess who is rumoured to have survived the massacre of the last Czar and his family. It comes from the Greek word for 'The Resurrection'. Short forms include **Stacey** or **Stacy** (see also EUSTACE) and **Tansy**, although this can also be thought of as a use of the name of the yellow wildflower (*Tanacetum vulgare*).

Anchoret: see ANGHARAD

Andrew, Andrea

These come from the Greek meaning 'manly'. The Apostle Andrew became the patron saint of Scotland, so it is not surprising that there it has developed its own forms **Andra** or **Andro** and **Dand, Dandie** or **Dandy**. Other pet forms are **Andie, Andy** and **Drew**; the last is used as an independent name and can also be derived from a Germanic-French name Drew or **Drogo** meaning 'trusty'. The French form, **André**, has now spread to English-speaking countries as well.

Andrea, the most common of the feminine versions of the name, is from the Italian, which also gives **Andreana**. **Andrée** is the French form. There are also a number of feminine versions which probably started life in Scotland, as they show typical Scots forms, but which are now by no means restricted to Scotland. Included in this group are **Andrina, Andrene, Andrewena, Andrine, Andreena** and their diminutives **Dreena** and **Rena**.

Aneurin, Aneirin [an'ierin]
This name is usually said to derive from the Latin Honorius (see HONORIA), which would mean it was adopted before the end of the Roman occupation of Britain; but it has also been suggested that it derives from Welsh roots giving a meaning of 'little one of pure gold'. It is certainly a very old name, for it was borne by one of the earliest known Welsh poets, who lived in the sixth century. Its short forms are **Nye** and **Neirin**. It is perhaps best known from the Labour statesman Aneurin Bevan (1897–1960), who as Minister of Health was largely responsible for the introduction of the National Health Service after World War II.

Angela
Angela means 'angel', and has pet forms **Ange, Angie** and **Angy**. Variants include **Angelica, Angelina, Angeline, Angelique**. **Angel** is occasionally found for girls; but while it is very common in Spanish-speaking countries as a man's name, it is not felt to be very appropriate here, although we do have the literary character Angel Clare in Thomas Hardy's *Tess of the D'Urbervilles* (1891).

Angharad, Anghared [ang'harəd]
This Welsh name, meaning 'much loved', has been in use since at least the ninth century and is the name of the lady in the medieval Welsh romance *Peredur*. It was out of favour for a while because the element 'an', which in this name is an intensifier, could be understood as a negative, giving a meaning 'unloved'; but it is now firmly back in fashion. It is one of the few Welsh names adopted by the English in the Middle Ages, anglicized to the now rare **Anchoret** or **Ankaret**.

Angie: see ANGELA

Angus

The Scottish form of a Gaelic name, Augus meaning 'one choice'. The Irish form is **Aonghus** or **Aengus** ['enees], which has given the Scots surname **Innes**, occasionally found as a first name. **Aeneas** or **Eneas**, the name of the Trojan founding father of the Roman people, whose name means 'praiseworthy', was used in the past, when Gaelic names were frowned on, as the equivalent of Angus, and is still used in some Scots families. (For a similar use of a Trojan hero, see HECTOR; see also under JULIA.)

Angy: see ANGELA

Anika, Anita: see ANN

Ankaret: see ANGHARAD

Ann, Hannah, Nancy

This disparate-looking group of names derives from the Hebrew **Hannah** ('God has favoured me'). Tradition, rather than the New Testament, makes it the name of the mother of the Virgin Mary, and this tradition led to its spread throughout Europe, where it took many forms. **Anna** is the Greek form of the name, and at the moment it is probably more frequently found in this country than the more traditional **Ann** or **Anne**. **Ana** is also found. The pet form **Annie** is used as an independent name, and leads to other pet forms, such as **Nan, Nanna** and **Nanny**. These in turn are one source of the name **Nancy** and its short form **Nance** (see also AGNES); **Nansi** is the Welsh spelling. Hannah, particularly popular at the moment, was the name of the mother of SAMUEL in the Old Testament.

Many foreign forms of the name have been adopted by British parents. From France we get **Annette** (which in Scotland became **Annot**) and the diminutives **Nanette, Ninette** and **Ninon**. **Anita** (shortened to **Nita**) and **Anya** come from Spain, and **Anneka, Anika** and **Annika** are Scandinavian pet forms. The actress **Anouk** Aimée has made this Russian form better known, and Russia also gives us **Anushka** and **Nina**.

Annabelle (Annabel, Annabella) presents a problem: it is found in Scotland well before Anne, so it is difficult to derive it from the obvious combination Anna-Belle ('fair Anna'). It may be a form of Amabel, the source of MABEL. Its short forms are one of the sources of **Bella** and **Belle**.

Annes, Annis, Annot: see AGNES

Anorah, Annorah, Annora: see ELEANOR, HONORIA

Anouk: see ANN

Anselm

This was the name of a twelfth-century archbishop of Canterbury, canonized for his theological writings. St Anselm was born in Italy but his name is Germanic and means 'divine helmet'.

Anthea

Derived from a Greek word meaning 'flowery', Anthea was an ancient title of Hera, the Greek queen of the gods, and has been in use as a literary name since the fourth century AD. In this country it was taken up and given currency by the poets of the seventeenth century, in particular Herrick, but it has been popular as a given name only since the mid-twentieth century.

Antony, Antonia

These names come from the Roman family name of the Antonii, best known through Julius Caesar's follower Mark Antony (Latin, Marcus Antonius). The meaning of the name is not clear, but the Romans derived it from a word meaning 'inestimable' or else as signifying descent from Antius, one of the sons of the hero-god Hercules. The form **Anthony** arose in the sixteenth century out of an attempt to derive the name from the Greek *anthos* (a flower) as in ANTHEA. **Tony**, and in the past **Nanty**, are pet forms. The name became popular throughout Europe through the fame of two saints, St Antony the Hermit, a third-century saint regarded as the founder of monasticism, and St Antony of Padua, a thirteenth-century saint famous for his preaching, and still one of the best-loved saints of the Roman Catholic church. The French form of the name **Antoine**, and **Anton**, found in both Germany and Russia, have recently become more popular.

   Antonia is the Latin feminine of Antony and is similarly abbreviated to **Tony**, or more commonly **Toni**. **Tonia** and **Tonya** are also used. The French form **Antoinette**, famous from the beheaded Marie Antoinette, is shortened to **Net, Nettie** or **Netty** (See also JANE).

Anushka, Anya: see ANN

Aodh: see AIDAN

Aoife ['eefyə]

Aoife is an ancient Irish name meaning 'beauty' which has come back into favour for Irish girls in the last decade. It is anglicized as EVE.

Aonghus see ANGUS

Aphra

This name comes from a misunderstanding of a biblical passage, when, in the book of Micah I.10, the translators have 'in the house of Aphrah roll thyself in the dust', where the word '**Aphrah**' actually means 'dust'. It is possible that the name is also confused with **Afra**, an obscure early martyr, and with forms of the Irish AFRIC. It was a not uncommon name in the seventeenth century, but its use today is almost entirely due to the fame of Mrs Aphra Behn (1640–89), spy, playwright and author of the first anti-slavery novel in English, who is reputed to be the first Englishwoman to have earned her living by her writing and was nicknamed by her contemporary admirers 'The Incomparable **Astrea**'. Records of her life show her name spelt Afra, Aphra and **Ayfara**. In *Little Dorrit* (1857) Dickens has a character called **Affery** Flintwinch, which illustrates the short form of the name.

Aphrodite: see JULIA

April

Like JUNE, April is the name of a month used as a first name. In Wales the equivalent name is **Ebrilla**, with **Ebrillwen** as a variant. The French form of the name, **Avril**, is also popular in this country, although not much used in France. Avril probably owes something to the name Averil, from the Old English **Everild** or **Everilda** ('boar-battle') the name of a rather obscure Yorkshire saint. Everild became **Averilla** and thence **Averil**. The older forms of are still found today, although rarely, Averil being much more common.

Arabella

This is a Scottish name, probably a form of Annabel (see ANN), although as the name is found in early documents as **Orable** it has been argued that it comes from a Latin word meaning 'easily moved by prayer' or even that it comes from a word meaning 'Arab'; but these are much less likely sources. **Arbel** was a common early form, and **Arabel** seems to be a bit older than the Latinate Arabella. Its pet forms **Bel, Bell, Belle** and **Bella** are one of the sources of this name.

Araminta

This is an elaboration of **Aminta, Amynta**, itself derived from the Macedonian Greek masculine name **Amyntas** ('defender') used by that country's royal family from at least the fourth century BC. The masculine name was used by Spenser in his autobiographical poem *Colin Clout* (1595) and by the Earl of Rochester (1647–80) in 'Phyllis,' and the form **Amyntor** by Beaumont and Fletcher, but the masculine name does not seem to have caught on. The feminine forms have an equally literary pedigree, being poetic names of the seventeenth century; both are used by Sir John Vanbrugh, and Sir Charles Sedley addresses poems to Aminta. Aminta had already been used in the previous century by the Italian poet Tasso. Virginia Woolf's **Minta** Doyle in *To the Lighthouse* (1927) shows one short form of the names, the other being **Minty**.

Archibald

Archibald is a Germanic name meaning 'truly bold'. It has particular associations with Scotland, where the Campbells used it to anglicize the native name **Gillespie** (Gaelic **Gilleasbuig**), meaning 'servant of the bishop'. Short forms of the name are **Arch, Archie, Archy, Baldie** and in Scotland **Erch** and **Erchie**.

Aretha

Given currency by the singer Aretha Franklin, this name comes from the Greek word for 'virtue'. It is also spelt **Areta**. From the same root comes the rarely used **Arethusa**, the nymph who in classical mythology was chased by an amorous river god from Greece to Sicily, where she turned herself into a spring to escape his attentions.

Arfon

A Welsh place name in Gwynedd, Arfon is used as a boy's first name; **Arfona** and **Arfonia** are the female equivalents.

Ariadne [aree'adnee]

In Greek mythology Ariadne is a Cretan princess who falls in love with Theseus and helps him to escape from the Minotaur, only to be abandoned by him. The name means 'the very holy one' and was probably originally used as a title for a goddess. Recently interest

31

has been shown in the French form **Ariane**, perhaps because it has become well known as the name of the European space rocket. The Italian **Arianna** is also found.

Arlene

Also spelt **Arleen** and **Arline**, Arlene seems to be a fairly modern coinage, possibly derived from Charlene (see CHARLES). Similarly **Arlette**, a French name made well known here through the Van der Valk novels of Nicholas Freeling, is thought to be formed from a pet form of Charlotte.

Armand, Arminel, Armine: see HERMAN

Arnold

Arnold is another Germanic name, formed from elements meaning 'eagle' and 'rule'. Its popularity in the Middle Ages is shown by its frequent use as a surname; it later died out, only to be revived, with so many other old names, in the nineteenth century. Short forms are **Arn** and **Arnie**.

Artemis, Artemisia: see DIANA

Arthur

The meaning of this name is much disputed. In one theory it comes from a Celtic root meaning 'bear'; in another it is a form of a Roman name, such as the clan name Artorius. The name is inextricably linked with that of King Arthur, but despite modern interest in Arthur, over-use of the name in the nineteenth century has led to a decline in its popularity in the twentieth. **Art** and **Arty** are its short forms.

Arwel

This is a Welsh masculine name meaning 'prominent'.

Arwyn, Arwen

These Welsh names mean 'fair, fine'; the former is masculine, the latter, with the variant **Arwenna**, feminine.

Asa

Asa is a Hebrew name meaning 'physician', and was the name of one of the Old Testament kings. It is particularly associated with Yorkshire, and is perhaps best known today from the social historian Asa Briggs.

Ashley

This is a surname originally given to someone who lived in an ash wood (or in a clearing in one); it is now used as a first name for both sexes. It is also spelt **Ashleigh**. It has been particularly popular in Australia and the United States. Its spread may owe something to its use by Margaret Mitchell in *Gone with the Wind* for one of her male characters, for this book (1936) and film (1939) has influenced the popularity of several names; but see further EARTHA.

Ashling

Ashling is the phonetic spelling of the Irish feminine name **Aisling**, also found as **Isleen**. It comes from the Celtic meaning 'dream, vision' and has been particularly popular in the past 30 years.

Asia: see AISHA

Astrea: see APHRA

Astrid

A Scandinavian name formed from elements meaning 'god' and 'beauty', Astrid has been used by Scandinavian royal families since at least the tenth century, but only in the twentieth century in this country. Its spread may owe something to the popularity of Queen Astrid of the Belgians (d. 1935).

Atheldreda, Athelthryth: see AUDREY

Athelstan, Athelstane

This is an Old English name meaning 'noble stone'. It suffered the same obscurity after the Norman Conquest as most other Old English names, but was revived in the nineteenth century, and is still occasionally found.

Athelwine: see ALVIN

Athene [a'theenee]

Athene was the patron-goddess of the city of Athens, a warrior goddess, but also the bringer of many skills and crafts and goddess of wisdom. The meaning of her name is not known, but it is thought to go back at least to Mycenean times. Both Athene and the alternative form **Athena** are occasionally used in this century, rather more often than her Roman equivalent **Minerva**.

Athol

This is a Scottish place name and surname of unknown meaning. The form **Athold** is also found.

Aubrey

Aubrey is the Norman French form of the Germanic name **Alberic** ('elf-ruler'), the Scandinavian king of the elves, who plays such an important part in Wagner's *Ring Cycle*. **Auberon** seems to have been a pet form of this name, and had already been used as the name of the king of the fairies before Shakespeare used the name in the form **Oberon** in *A Midsummer Night's Dream*.

Audrey

This is a contraction of the Old English name of St **Etheldreda** or **Ethelthryth** ('noble strength'). The full form of the name is also spelt **Atheldreda, Etheldred,** and **Athelthryth**, and is also one of the sources of the name ETHEL. St Etheldreda was a seventh-century East Anglian princess who founded an abbey at Ely on the site where the cathedral now stands. The name St Audrey was itself contracted to the word 'tawdry', first used to describe the sort of cheap but glittering goods sold at the famous St Audrey's Fair. **Audreen** is a modern variant of the name.

Augustus, Augusta

Augustus, a Latin word meaning 'majesty', was given as a title by the Roman Senate to the first Roman Emperor in 27 BC and adopted by him as a name (see also OCTAVIA). Augusta is the feminine form of the same word. **Gus** and **Gussie** are used as pet forms of these names and of **Augustine**, pronounced [aw'gustin] in Britain but [awgus'teen] in the United States. Augustine was the name of an early saint and one of the great doctors of the Christian Church, and was derived from Augustus. Augustine was also the name of the man sent in 596 to England by Pope GREGORY the Great to convert the heathen Saxons to Christianity. In Medieval England this name was contracted to **Austin** or **Austen**, and used both as a surname and a first name.

Aurelius, Aurelia

These are the masculine and feminine forms of a Roman family name meaning 'golden'. **Aurelian**, the name of one of the Roman emperors, is an alternative masculine form. From Aurelia come the increasingly used **Auriel** and **Auriol**; **Oriel** and **Oriole** are spelling variants of this name. ORLA is the Irish equivalent of this name.

Aure: see DAWN

Aurnia: see ORLA

Aurora, Aurore: see DAWN

Austen, Austin: see AUGUSTUS

Ava
This name is found in the early middle ages, where it is probably a pet form of names beginning 'av-', but then disappears until this century, where it is strongly associated with the film actress Ava Gardner. It may be a form of Eva (see EVE) or a pet form of a name containing 'ava'; but it is just as likely to have been a parental invention.

Aveline: see EVELYN

Averil, Averilla: see APRIL

Avice, Avis
This is an old feminine name of unknown meaning, although the form Avis has led to its association with the Latin for 'bird'. Some French writers associate it with the German name **Hedewig** or **Hedwige** ('combat'), the source of the pet forms found in Ibsen's **Hedda** Gabler and the film star **Hedy** Lamarr.

Avril: see APRIL

Awly: see ALMERIC

Ayeisha, Ayesha: see AISHA

Aylmer: see ELMER

Aylwin: see ALVIN

Aymé: see ESMÉ

B

Babbie, Babs: see BARBARA

Babette: see BARBARA, ELIZABETH

Baldwin, Baldric

The name-element 'bald' has nothing to do with hair loss, but represents the Germanic form of the English 'bold'. Baldric means 'bold-rule' and Baldwin 'bold-friend'. **Baudouin**, the French form of Baldwin, is familiar today from its use by the Belgian royal family.

Balthazar: see JASPER

Bambi: see FAWN

Barbara

This name comes from the Greek word for 'foreign, strange', the same root gives us the word 'barbarian'. It may have started as a name given to a foreign slave. St Barbara, virgin and martyr, was a very popular saint from the ninth century onwards. Her symbol is the brass tower in which her father shut her before executing her for her faith. Since he was punished by being struck down by a thunderbolt, Barbara is invoked against lightning and, by an association of ideas, is also the patron saint of gunners and miners. Her story has elements found in many folk tales, and there is no evidence that she ever existed. Short forms are **Babs, Barbie** (as in the doll), and in Scotland **Babbie, Baubie**. The French pet form **Babette** (also used for ELIZABETH) is sometimes found.

Barnabas

Barnabas is defined in the Bible as meaning 'son of consolation' although a more correct interpretation would be 'son of exhortation'. The biblical St Barnabas, 'a good man, full of the Holy Ghost and of faith' (Acts xi. 24), was closely associated with St Paul in spreading Christianity through Asia Minor. **Barnaby** is an old variant of the name which has been revived in recent years. **Barney** is a short form shared with BERNARD.

Barney: see BARNABAS, BERNARD

Barry

The three main sources of Barry, a Celtic name, have become so confused as to be indistinguishable. There is an Irish name Barry (**Bearach** in Gaelic), which comes from the word for 'spear'. In Wales the name can be a form of the surname 'ap Harry' (son of Harry); but it may also be derived from the place name of Barry Island, in which case it comes from the Welsh word *bar* meaning 'a dune or mound'. In addition Barry can be used in Ireland as a pet form of Finbar 'fair head' (see FINLAY), in which case it is sometimes spelt **Barra**.

Bartholomew

Bartholomew is a Hebrew name meaning 'son of Talmai', Talmai itself meaning 'abounding in furrows'. It is thought that the apostle Bartholomew is probably the same as NATHANIEL, Bartholomew being the equivalent of a surname. **Bart** is a common short form; **Bartlemy** and **Bartly** are less common old shortenings, and **Tolomey** is also found. In Ireland Bartholomew is used to anglicize the Gaelic name **Parthalon** or **Partholon**.

Basil

The Greek word for 'kingly', Basil is thus the equivalent of the Latin REX. It was the name of several saints in the Orthodox Church and is very popular in Slavic countries, usually in a form beginning with a 'v', as in the Russian **Vasilii**. Short forms are **Baz** or **Bas**, and there are rare feminine forms, **Basilia** and **Basilie**.

Bastian, Bastien: see SEBASTIAN

Bathsheba

This Biblical name means 'opulent' or 'voluptuous' – apt for a woman whose naked body, seen while she was bathing, led King David to bring about the death of her husband **Uriah** the Hittite, so that he could marry her. It is nowadays better known as a literary name from Bathsheba Everdene in Thomas Hardy's *Far From the Madding Crowd* (1874) than as a real-life name, but it was popular with the Puritans, presumably more as a warning than as a model for the bearer. The short form **Sheba** is occasionally found, but is also best known in a literary context from the play and film *Come Back, Little Sheba*.

Baubie: see BARBARA

Baudouin: see BALDWIN

Baz: see BASIL

Bearach: see BARRY

Beatrice
'Bringer of joy or blessing', Beatrice has variant forms **Beatrix** and, in Wales, **Bet(t)rice** or **Bet(t)rys**. Short forms include **Bea, Bee, Beatty, Trix, Trixie** and **Triss**. Beatrice is the name of the woman immortalized by Dante (1265–1321) in *The Divine Comedy* and the *Vita nuova*. The choice of the name in 1988 by the Duke and Duchess of York for their first child does not seem to have had an influence on its popularity. **Beata** is from the same Latin root and means 'blessed'.

Beck, Becky: see REBECCA

Bedelia: see BRIDGET

Belinda
Strictly speaking Belinda is an old Germanic name, with an unexplained first element and the '-linda' part meaning 'serpent': a symbol of wisdom. However, most users today probably think of it as a combination of the French 'belle' (as in the name **Bella**, also used as a short form of this name) and of the Spanish 'linda'; both mean 'beautiful'. Alexander Pope seems to have had the connotations of beauty in mind when he gave this name to the heroine of *The Rape of the Lock* (1712–14). The name is one of the sources of LINDA.

Bell, Bella, Belle: see ANN, ARABELLA, BELINDA, ISABELLA

Ben: see BENJAMIN

Benedict

Benedict comes from the Latin meaning 'blessed' and owes its use as a name to St Benedict (490–c. 542), founder of the Benedictine order. **Benedick** is an old variant form of the name, as is the surname **Bennet(t)** once used as a first name. **Benedicta** is an uncommon female form of the name; **Benita** comes from the same root.

Benjamin

An Old Testament name meaning 'son of the right hand' – Benjamin thus represents strength and good fortune. In the Bible Benjamin is the youngest of the twelve sons of JACOB, and the pet of his father and brothers, so the name has sometimes been used to signify a favourite child. Short forms are **Ben, Benjie, Bennie** or **Benny**.

Berenice: see VERONICA

Bernard

This is a Germanic name meaning 'strong or brave as a bear'. **Barney** is a short form used particularly in the United States. The feminine form **Bernadette** (sometimes **Bernardette**) was given popularity by St Bernadette of Lourdes. **Bernardine** is a feminine variant, and **Bernie** is used as a short form for both sexes.

Bernice, Bernie: see VERONICA

Berry: see BERTRAM

Bert, Bertie: see ALBERT, BERTRAM, CUTHBERT, EGBERT, GILBERT, HERBERT, HUBERT, LAMBERT, OSBERT, ROBERT, WILBERT

Bertha

This is an old Germanic name meaning 'bright'. It is found in various forms throughout Europe, and has been used in England since Anglo-Saxon times. Bertha Bigfoot ('Berthe au grand pied'), mother of the emperor Charlemagne (c. 742–814), was an early holder of the name. A less attractive use of the name is Big Bertha, the name given to each of a set of four immense howitzers made by the Krupp armaments firm and used by the Germans to bombard Paris in 1918. They were named after Bertha Krupp, the heiress to the firm, and their range of 76 miles was the greatest of any gun yet made. (See also HERBERT).

Bertram, Bertrand

Strictly, Bertram means 'bright raven' and Bertrand 'bright shield', but these two Germanic names early on came to be regarded as variants of the same name, with Bertrand the French form of Bertram. The commonest short forms are **Bert** and **Bertie**; **Berry** (as in the case of the Dornford Yates character) is sometimes used, although this can also be derived from the surname, which comes from fruit or the French place name.

Beryl

This is one of the gem names popular in the late nineteenth and early twentieth centuries. It came into use rather later in the American Middle West, where it has also been recorded as a man's name.

Bess, Bessie, Bessy, Bet, Beth, Bethan, Bethany, Bethia, Betsy, Bettina, Betty, Bettyn: see ELIZABETH

Betrice, Bettrice, Betrys, Bettrys: see BEATRICE

Beulah: see HEPHZIBAH

Beverly, Beverley

This name comes from a place and surname meaning 'beaver stream'. While it can be used as a name for either sex, it is now rare as a male name, although the journalist Beverley Nichols is a recent example of its masculine use. **Bev** is the short form.

Bevis

An old French name, Bevis was famous in the Middle Ages as the name of the hero of the inordinately long but very popular romance *Sir Bevis of Hamtoun* (i.e. Southampton). Richard Jefferies' successful novel *Bevis: The Story of a Boy* (1882) helped to revive the name.

Bianca, Bibi: see BLANCHE

Biddie, Biddy, Bidelia: see BRIDGET

Bill, Billie, Billy: see WILLIAM

Birgita: see BRIDGET

Blair

Derived from a Scottish surname and place name, Blair means 'marshy plain'.

Blaise

According to one view, Blaise derives from the Greek *basileios* 'royal', but it is more likely to come from a Latin nickname *blaseus* 'stuttering deformed'. In Arthurian legend it is the name of Merlin's secretary, who is supposed to have written down his master's sayings. The name is more popular in France than in English-speaking countries, no doubt due in part to the fame of the natural philosopher Blaise Pascal (1623–62). **Blaze** and **Blase** are variants.

Blake

A surname meaning 'black, dark-complexioned', Blake is also used as a first name. It is usually a masculine name, but feminine uses have been recorded.

Blanche

Occasionally spelt **Blanch**, this is an old name meaning 'white'. A fourteenth-century holder was Blanche, Duchess of Lancaster, the wife of John of Gaunt and heroine of Chaucer's elegy, *The Book of the Duchess* (*c.* 1369). **Bianca** (which can be shortened to **Bibi**) and **Blanca**, the Italian and Spanish forms of the name, are also found.

Blase, Blaze: see BLAISE

Blodwen

This Welsh feminine name is made up of elements meaning 'flower' and 'white' and therefore belongs with the group of flower names (see FLORA). Another Welsh flower name is **Blodeuwedd** ('flower-form'), the name of a woman magically created out of flowers in the medieval Welsh story of *Math, Son of Mathonwy*. She was unfaithful to her husband for whom she had been made, and as a punishment was turned into an owl. The legend has become familiar to modern children through its retelling in Alan Garner's *The Owl Service*. **Blodyn** or **Blodeyn** which simply means 'flower, blossom', is another member of this group.

Blossom: see FLORA

Boadicea: see VICTORIA

41

Bob, Bobbie, Bobby: see ROBERT

Bonny, Bonnie

A Scottish word for 'fine', 'fair', 'comely', Bonny as a first name is a comparatively recent introduction.

Boris

Boris is a Slavic name, meaning 'fight', 'battle'. In early Russia it was frequently used as a royal name. Boris Godonov, Czar of Russia in 1598–1605, is familiar to us as the eponymous hero of Mussorgsky's opera. Its associations are still predominantly Russian, but it is occasionally found in English-speaking countries.

Bradley

A masculine name, Bradley has been particularly popular in Australia and the United States in recent years. It derives from the Old English surname meaning 'broad clearing'. **Brad** is used as a short form.

Bram: see ABRAHAM

Brandan, Brandon: see BRENDAN

Brandy, Brandi

This is a feminine name rare in Britain but now popular in the United States. It would appear to be the drink used as a first name, but may well be used as a feminine echo of the name Brandon (see BRENDAN), which is also very popular in the States.

Branwen: see BRONWEN

Brenda

Sir Walter Scott popularized this as the name of one of the heroines of *The Pirate* (1821). It comes from the Shetland Islands, and is probably a feminine form of the old Norse name **Brand** ('sword'). In Ireland it is used as the feminine of BRENDAN.

Brendan

This is the name of more than one Irish saint, the most famous of which is St Brendan the Navigator (484–577), who sailed his coracle in the Atlantic and whose legend has been interpreted as an account of a pre-Columbian discovery of America. The meaning of the name is disputed but is usually interpreted as the unflattering 'stinking hair'. **Brandon**, used by Charles Kingsley in *The Water Babies* (1863), is often a variant of Brendan, although it can have other sources, including a surname derived from either the Old English meaning '(person from the) broom-covered hill', or from the French for 'sword'. Brendan tends to be the more common form in Great Britain, Brandon (or **Brandan**) in the United States.

Brent
Originally a surname, Brent comes either from an Old English word meaning 'burnt' or from a West Country place name meaning 'hill, high place'.

Bret, Brett
This name comes from the surname meaning 'Briton' or 'Breton'. Its best-known holder is probably the American poet and short story writer Bret Harte (1836–1902), whose work helped give literary form to the legends of the Far West.

Brian
A Celtic name, Brian probably comes from a word for 'hill'. In Ireland it is famous as the name of Brian Boru, High King of Ireland 1002–14, who defeated the Viking invaders. The name was used by Celtic-speaking Bretons, who probably introduced the name to England in the Middle Ages. The common alternative **Bryan** reflects the spelling of the surname. (See also BRYN).

Bridget
An Irish name meaning 'the High One', Bridget seems to have been the title of an ancient Celtic goddess whose name may also be connected with the ancient British tribe of the Brigantes. St Bridget (*c.* 450–*c.* 523) is the greatest of the Irish female saints, but little is known of her for sure, for her legend seems to have attracted stories of the original pagan goddess. **Brigid** is an alternative form, while **Bride**, with its pet forms **Bridie, Biddie** or **Biddy**, reflects the Gaelic pronunciation of the name. **Brigitte**, occasionally **Brigette**, comes from the continental form, and **Bidelia** or **Bedelia** is an Irish gentrification of the name, which has fallen out of favour as it was felt to be over-genteel. **Birgita**, the Swedish form, gives us **Britt** as a short form.

43

Brittany

Although it does not yet seem to have reached this country, Brittany is a girl's name that has become current in the United States. No one has come up with a convincing explanation of why this region of France should be used, but the sounds of both syllables can be found in other names, so the attraction may be the same as in the use of blends.

Broderick: see RODERICK

Bronwen

Bronwen is a Welsh feminine name meaning 'fair or white breast'. The similar-sounding **Branwen**, origin of **Brangwain** or **Brengwain**, the name of ISOLDA'S maid in the TRISTAN legends, means 'fair raven', indicating a dark beauty, and is the name of the heroine of one of the medieval Welsh *Mabinogion* stories. Her name may be of divine origin as the names of her father Llyr and her brother Bran are both those of Celtic gods.

Brooke

A surname meaning 'brook', this has recently come into use for both sexes.

Bruce

The fame of the heroic King Robert the Bruce (1274–1329) is probably the cause of this surname being adopted as a Scottish first name. Despite its Scottish associations, the surname comes from a Norman place-name, but it has since spread throughout the English-speaking world.

Bruno

This name simply means 'brown', and is a common German name which has become popular in this country in recent years, probably via the United States. The rare feminine equivalents, **Brunella** and **Brunetta**, show the influence of Romance languages.

Bryan: see BRIAN

Bryn

A masculine name from the Welsh for 'a hill', Bryn comes from the same root as BRIAN. The elaboration **Brynmor** means 'big hill'. They are both place names which have become first names.

Bryony

Bryony is a plant name introduced as a first name in this century. As the plant is a climber of little distinction, it may owe its use in part to the lack of any real feminine form of BRIAN.

Buddic, Buddig: see VICTORIA

Bunnie, Bunny: see VERONICA

Bunty

Usually a nickname rather than a given name, Bunty probably first became popular in 1911, when there was a successful comedy performed in London called *Bunty Pulls the Strings*. The name comes from the same source as 'bunting' in the nursery song 'Bye, baby bunting', which is a dialect word for a pet or hand-reared lamb, and came to be used as an endearment.

Burt: see ALBERT, BERTRAM, CUTHBERT, EGBERT, GILBERT, HERBERT, HUBERT, LAMBERT, OSBERT, ROBERT, WILBERT

Byron

This name comes from the Romantic poet George Gordon, Lord Byron (1788–1824). The first of this line was created Baron Byron as a reward for his support of Charles I in the Civil War. The meaning of the name ('at the cattle sheds', from the same root as the modern English 'byre') is far from aristocratic; it would have been a name given to a cowman.

C

Caddy: see CHARLES

Cadel, Cadfael, Cadwallader

The Welsh name-element *cad* means 'battle' and is used in a multitude of Welsh masculine names, some of them the names of warriors in our earliest records. **Cadel** or **Cadell**, again meaning 'battle', is both a name in its own right and a pet form of these names. **Cadfael**, a name familiar as the hero of Ellis Peter's medieval whodunnits, means 'battle-metal', a suitable name for an old and experienced soldier. **Cadwallader** (also spelt **Cadwalader** and **Cadwaladr**) means 'battle prince' and is found as early as 681. The most famous holder of this name was a Welsh ruler who led his people against the troops of Henry II and who died in 1172.

Cædmon: see HILDA

Caelia: see CECILIA

Cahir, Cahal: see CATHAL

Caiseal: see CASHEL

Caitlin: see CATHERINE

Caius, Gaius

This is a Roman first name which comes from the Latin *gaudere* (to rejoice). The name seems to have passed into use among the native Britons during the Roman occupation, for it is the source of Sir **Kay** or **Kai**, King Arthur's foster-brother and steward in the legends. His is one of the earliest name associated with King

Arthur and is still used in Wales in the forms **Cai, Caio** and **Caw**.

Callum, Calum: see MALCOLM

Calvin

Calvin came into use as a first name in honour of John Calvin (Jean Cauvin; 1509–64), the French Protestant theologian who gave his name to Calvinism and who was famous for his strict morality, his learning and his support of austerity. The French surname means 'bald'.

Cameron

A Scottish clan name used as a male first name, Cameron comes from the Gaelic for 'crooked nose', a nickname given to an early clansman.

Camilla

Camilla is a figure from Roman legend, whose name, it has been suggested, means 'one who assists at sacrifices to the gods'. In VIRGIL'S *Aeneid* she figures as a warrior queen who fights with Aeneas and is described as so fast a runner that she could run over a field of wheat without bending a blade, or over the sea without getting her feet wet. The French form of the name, **Camille**, can be used for either sex.

Candace, Candice

This name, which was formerly pronounced [kan'daysee] but is now usually ['kandis], is an ancient title of the queen of Ethiopia. It was introduced into the body of European first names through its mention in the Acts of the Apostles. **Candy** is a pet form of the name, shared with CANDIDA.

Candida

This name comes from the Latin for 'white', the same word that gives us 'candid' (originally 'unblemished') and 'candidate' (from the white robes worn by Roman politicians when standing for office). Although it is found as a woman's name in Roman inscriptions, it was not used thereafter until it was 're-invented' by Bernard Shaw for the heroine of his play *Candida* in 1897. He had modelled the name on the hero of Voltaire's allegorical novel *Candide* (1759). The similar-sounding **Candia**, is not, as it would appear, a variant of Candida or of the pet form **Candy**, which

47

it shares with CANDACE, but (according to E.G. Withycombe) a name first given to one Candia Palmer who was born while her father was travelling to Candia, the old name for Heraklion in Crete, and which then passed into use among certain families.

Cara

The word is Italian for 'dear' or 'dear one' used as a girl's name, and therefore the equivalent of the French Chère (See CHERYL). The affectionate diminutives **Carina** and **Carita** are also used. These names are all recent introductions. (See also **Karina** under CATHERINE).

Caradoc, Caradog

This name comes from the Welsh word *cariad* ('love') and is therefore the masculine equivalent of the feminine names found under CERI. It is one of the oldest recorded British names, for it is the same as **Caractacos** (Latin **Caratacus**), the name of the captured British chief taken in chains to Rome in AD 51, whose noble bearing won him his liberty. Caradoc is also the name of a character in the Arthurian legends, chiefly famous for being the only man at the court who came through various magical tests to prove he had a faithful wife.

Cari: see CERI

Carina, Carita: see CARA

Carl, Carla, Carleen, Carlene, Carlina, Carlota, Carlotta, Carly, Carlyn: see CHARLES

Carlton

Carlton is a place and surname meaning 'settlement of the free men or peasants'. **Carleton** is an alternative spelling. The name **Charlton**, as in the actor Charlton Heston, comes from a variant form of this surname.

Carmel

The Hebrew word for 'a garden', Carmel is the name of a mountain in Israel, famous in the Bible for its fruitfulness. A monastery dedicated to the Virgin Mary was established there by Crusaders and the name is given in honour of Our Lady of Mount Carmel. **Carmella** is a diminutive form, and **Carmen**, famous from the Bizet opera (1874), is the Spanish form of the name.

Carol, Carola, Carole, Carolina, Caroline, Carolyn, Carrie: see CHARLES

Caron: see CATHERINE

Carrie: see CHARLES

Carwen, Carwyn: see CERI

Caryn: see CATHERINE

Carys: see CERI

Casey: see CASIMIR

Cashel
An Irish man's name, this comes from the city of Cashel, the ancient capital of the province of Munster. The Irish spelling is **Caiseal**.

Casimir
Traditionally Casimir or **Kasimir** has been interpreted as meaning 'proclamation of peace', but recently scholars have suggested it actually means the opposite and comes from words meaning 'to spoil peace'. It is a Polish name, used here in the nineteenth century among supporters of Polish independence and introduced to the United States by Polish immigrants. **Casey** (now used for both sexes, but formerly only masculine) has been claimed as a diminutive of Casimir, but is more likely to be a use of the Irish surname, meaning 'descendant of the vigilant one'.

Caspar: see JASPER

Cassandra
A character in Greek legend, Cassandra was a Trojan princess and priestess of Apollo, who agreed to let him make love to her in return for the gift of prophecy. However, she reneged on the bargain, and as a punishment the god condemned her to prophesy the truth, but to be believed by no one. Thus she is often used as a symbol of one who foretells unpleasant events, but is ignored. Her name was used to conceal the identity of one of the most famous columnists on the *Daily Mirror*, whose criticisms so annoyed Winston Churchill during World War II.

Despite the unpleasant aspects of her story, Cassandra is one of the earliest classical names found in England, having come into use in the thirteenth century owing to the popularity of the romanticised story of Troy in the Middle Ages. The name is now more commonly used in the United States than in this country. British use may owe something to Jane Austen (1775–1817) having a sister called Cassandra, to whom many of her delightful letters were written. **Cass** and **Cassy** are short forms of the name often used independently.

Castor: see COSMO

Cathal
Cathal is an Irish name meaning 'battle-mighty'; **Cathair**, from the same root, means 'warrior'. They have the anglicised forms **Cahal** and **Cahir**.

Catherine
Although a name of unknown meaning, Catherine was early on associated with the Greek word for 'pure' (an appropriate sense for the name of so many virgin saints) and this is frequently given as its meaning. It is a name spelt in a variety of ways: the original Greek form of the name was Aikaterine, which led to the spellings with 'e' in the middle; but the Greek word for 'pure' is *katharos*, which led to these being 'corrected' to the 'a' spelling. The commonest forms are **Catherine, Catharine, Katherine, Katharine** and more recently, **Kathryn**. A wide variety of forms from other languages has also been adopted by English speakers. **Caterina** and **Catherina** show the Italian form, with the similar **Katerina** being technically from the Swedish. **Karen, Karina** (although this may owe something to Carina: see CARA), **Karin** and ultimately their variants **Caryn** and **Caron**, are other Scandinavian forms of the name. **Katja** or **Katia** is a little-used Russian form. There is an important group of variants from the Celtic areas of Great Britain: **Kathleen** is the Irish form of the name, with **Caitlin** showing its Gaelic form; **Catriona**, given wide currency by R.L.Stevenson's novel of that title (1893), is the Scottish Gaelic form, with **Catrina, Katrina** and **Katrin(e)** as variants; Wales gives us **Catrin, Cadi** and **Cati**. Short forms of these names include **Cathie, Cathy, Kate, Katie, Katy, Kathie, Kathy, Kay** (which can be used for any name beginning with 'K'), **Kit, Kittie, Kitty** and less frequently **Trina**. KERRY is said by some to be an Irish or Irish-American pet form.

Cecilia

The use of this ancient Roman family name (probably derived from a word meaning 'blind') is due to the popularity of the third-century martyr Saint Cecilia, the patron saint of music, whose 'life' is now thought to be largely, if not wholly, mythical. The name was current in England from the early Middle Ages, when it generally took the form **Cecily**. This can be pronounced ['sesilee] or, as was more usual in the past, ['sisilee]. This second pronunciation gave rise to the variants **Cicely** and **Sisley**, and to the short forms **Sis, Cis, Sissy, Sissie, Cissy** or **Cissie**. **Cecile** [se'seel] is the French form of the name, used for both sexes in France, but in the English-speaking world feminine. **Celia** is often used as a short form of Cecilia, but is in fact a separate name. It comes from another Roman family name, that of the Caelii; this was taken to come from the word *coelum* ('heaven') which gave rise to the old spelling **Coelia** as well as to the Latin **Caelia**. This derivation is incorrect, and as the family was supposed to have been founded by an Etruscan it seems probable that the name comes from one of the few Etruscan words we can understand: *celi*, meaning September. Either Cecilia or Celia was the origin of the Irish name **Sile**, anglicized to **Sheila**, also found in a variety of spelling such as **Shiela** and **Sheelagh**.

Cecil, although used as a masculine form of Cecilia, has yet another Latin origin. The Latin name **Sextus**, originally given to a sixth son, developed the form **Sextilius**. This was brought by the Romans to Britain, where it developed into the Old Welsh name **Seisyllt**. This in turn became the family name Cecil, and the surname of this noble family came to be used as a first name.

Cedric

This is a name invented by Sir Walter Scott in his novel *Ivanhoe* (1819) for the father of his hero. Cedric represents all that is good about the old Saxon landowners, in contrast with the rapacious Norman invaders. It used to be thought that the name came from a misreading of Cerdic, a very early Saxon name meaning 'amiable'; others have pointed out that there is a Welsh name **Cedrych**, meaning 'pattern of bounty', and since Scott's other 'Saxon' names are suspiciously Celtic, it seems more likely that Scott got his cultures mixed, and used a form of this Welsh name.

Celeste

This name and its diminutive form **Celestine** come from the Latin word for 'heavenly', and therefore has links with Celia (see CECILIA).

Celia: see CECILIA

Celina, Céline: see SELINA

Cenydd: see KENNETH

Ceri ['keree]

Ceri is one of a large group of Welsh girl's names that come from the word *caru* ('love'), and it is therefore a Welsh equivalent of the English AMY. Ceri and **Carys** are probably the most used, but other forms include **Ceril, Cerys, Cerian, Cari,** and **Caryl**, which is also used as a form of Carol (see CHARLES). Carys should not be confused with CHARIS which, although pronounced in the same way, comes from the Greek. Ceri, particularly in the form **Keri** which is sometimes found, may have contributed to the development and popularity of KERRY. From the same root comes the name **Carwen**, the second element meaning 'white, blessed', with its masculine form **Carwyn**. For other masculines see CARADOC.

Ceridwen [kə'ridwen]

This name is thought to be that of the pagan British goddess of poetic inspiration. Her name is made up of elements meaning 'poetry' and 'white, fair, blessed'. Traditionally she is the mother of TALIESIN, one of the great early bards of the Welsh.

Cerys: see CERI

Chad

This was the name of a sixth-century Anglo-Saxon saint and bishop whose history is told by the Venerable Bede. He was bishop of Lichfield, and the cathedral there is dedicated to him. This kept the name of this rather obscure saint current, at least locally. A slight revival of the name may owe something to the fame of the Rev. Chad Varah who founded the Samaritans. Chad is also the name of a little cartoon figure shown as a bald head, two eyes and a nose peering over a brick wall and associated with the phrase 'Wot, no . . .?' which was created in World War II by the cartoonist Chat as a comment on shortages, and which worked its way into popular culture.

Chae: see CHARLES

Chantal

St Jeanne de Chantal was a seventeenth-century French saint associated with St Francis de Sales. As well as being the grand-mother of Madame de Sévigné (1626–96), she combined a romantic life-story with great worldly wisdom and true piety, and it is not surprising that French parents should want to name a child after her. The name was officially accepted in France as a Christian name in 1913, and spread rapidly thereafter. It arrived more recently in this country, but has already developed variants, including **Chantelle** and even spellings with Sh-. The name ultimately comes from the southern French word *cantal* ('a stone').

Charis ['karis]

Charis is the Greek word for 'grace'. It is tempting to link the increase of its use to the appearance of a character of that name in Georgette Heyer's novel *Frederica* (1965); but it may also be linked with the use of the Welsh name Carys (see CERI), which is pronounced in the same way. **Charissa** is a Latinate form of the name, created by Edmund Spenser for *The Faerie Queene* (1590–6).

Charity

Formed from the same root as CHARIS, Charity is with FAITH and HOPE one of the three great Christian virtues, and all are used for girls' names. **Cherry** started life as a pet form of Charity, rather than being taken from the fruit, but it is now an independent name.

Charles

The Old German word for 'a man' was *carl*, and was a popular name among the Frankish ruling class that dominated Europe in the Dark Ages. The name was Latinized as Carolus, which in turn became Charles in French. These three forms have developed into a vast number of names for both sexes found throughout Europe. The German and Scandinavian forms **Carl** or **Karl**, now popular in this country – probably via their use by Scandinavian immigrants in the United States – reflect the original form of the name. From Carolus comes the eastern European form **Carol** or **Karel** occasionally found in this country, but usually only for those of eastern European descent. The Irish also use the surname **Carroll (Cearbhall)**, meaning 'champion warrior', as a first name. Charles has spawned a large number of diminutives such as **Charlie** or **Charley**, **Chas** from the old abbreviated written form of the name, **Chae** or **Chay** in Scotland, **Chuck** mainly in the United States, while **Chilla** is said to be a form used in Australia.

The feminine forms of the name are even more diverse. **Carla** or **Karla**, with their variants **Carly, Carlyn, Carleen** or **Carlene**, are comparatively recent introductions which reflect the original form of the name. **Carlina** has also been described as a modern coinage, but has been in use in the author's family since at least 1803. **Carlotta** and **Carlota** are the Italian and Spanish versions of the name, with the pet form **Lola** being shared in Spain by Carlota and DOLORES. From the Latin form of the name come **Carol** and **Caroline**, with their variants **Carole, Carola, Carolyn, Carolina** (one of the sources of LINA), **Karol**, and **Karoline**. **Caryl** (see also CERI) is used as a variant. These names give us the pet forms **Carrie, Caddy** and **Caddie**. From Charles come the popular **Charlotte** with its variant **Sharlotte** (in use since the end of the last century, and not a recent form as one might expect) and the Irish forms **Charlot** or **Searlait**. Charlotte gives us the pet forms **Charlie** (pronounced ['chahlee] or ['shahlee]), **Sharley, Chatty** and **Lottie**. **Charlene**, and its variants **Charleen** and **Sharlene**, are modern feminine forms of Charles (see also ARLENE).

Charlton: see CARLTON

Charmaine
This is a name of debated origin, which was widely used in the middle of this century thanks to a popular song. It now has the variant **Sharmaine**. Its origin is often linked to the much older **Charmian**, the Greek for 'joy' and used by Shakespeare for Cleopatra's maid in *Antony and Cleopatra*. This is strictly speaking pronounced ['kahmiən], but the pronunciation with a soft ch- is more often found.

Chas, Chatty: see CHARLES

Chauncey, Chauncy
A masculine name popular in the United States, Chauncey is a surname deriving from a village near the French town of Amiens. It was used as a first name in honour of Charles Chauncey (1592–1672), the second president of Harvard University.

Chay: see CHARLES

Chelsea

The use of this place name as a girl's name presumably owes something to the fame of Chelsea as a glamour spot in the London of the 1960s, although it may equally have been inspired by Chelsea, New York. The name is only just arriving in Great Britain, but has been used for some time in Australia and North America.

Cher, Cheralyn, Chère, Cherida, Cherie: see CHERYL

Cherry: see CHARITY

Cheryl

A modern formation, Cheryl has had currency since the 1920s. It is probably based on the name **Cherry** (see CHARITY) or on the French word **Cherie** ('darling') used as a first name. Cheryl rapidly developed a number of variants, including **Cheralyn** (the most popular) and **Cheryn**. Both Cheryl and Cheralyn are found in a number of different spellings, including forms such as **Sheryl** and **Sheralyn**. **Cher** or **Chère**, the French for 'dear', are also used, and Cherie is also found in the form **Sherry** or **Sherri**. **Cherida** is a rare variant, blending the Spanish and French for 'dear'.

Chester

This is the city name, derived from the Latin *castra* ('a camp'), used as a first name.

Chiara: see CLARE

Chilla: see CHARLES

China: see INDIA

Chloë

This name comes from the Greek for 'a green shoot' and was one of the names for the fertility goddess Demeter (see DEMETRIUS) in her summer aspect (see also MELANIE). Its use in this country is usually ascribed to the name appearing as a minor character in the New Testament, but since early uses are mainly literary it is more likely to be inspired by the Greek pastoral romance, probably from the second or third century AD, of *Daphnis and Chloë*. The name was not very common outside literature until about 30 years ago, when new interest was shown in it. **Chloris**, occasionally **Cloris**, is an unusual name related to Chloë since it comes from the same root and means 'green'.

Christine

This is the most popular of the feminine names meaning **Christian**, which is found as an occasional masculine name along with the pet form **Christy**. **Christy** or **Christie**, along with **Chris** and **Chrissie** are also used as pet forms of Christine, with **Kirsty** or **Kirstie** in Scotland. **Cristyn** is the Welsh version of the name. **Christina** with its pet form **Tina**, are popular variants, and the Scandinavian forms **Kirsten** and **Kersten** have recently come into use. **Christabel** is mainly literary, although it is found in the suffragette Christabel Pankhurst (1880–1958). Other variants include **Christiana**, **Christiane**, **Kristina**, **Krystyna**, **Kirsteen** and **Kirstine**, **Kirsta** and **Kristin**. (See also CRYSTAL.)

Christopher

Christopher means 'Christ carrier': it was the name given to the giant in legend who carried the Christ Child over a river, and thus became the patron saint of travellers. **Kester** is an old pet form now generally replaced by **Chris** or **Kit**, with **Christy** being more common in Ireland. A Scottish form of the name was **Crystal** or **Chrystal**, which is also used in Ireland.

Christmas: see NOEL

Chuck: see CHARLES

Ciara, Ciaran: see KIERAN

Cicely: see CECILIA

Cilla: see PRICILLA

Cillian: see KILLIAN

Cinaed: see KENNETH

Cindy: see CYNTHIA, LUCY

Cis, Cissie, Cissy: see CECILIA

Clare

This name and its French version **Claire** come from the Latin word *clarus* meaning 'bright, clear' but also used in the sense 'famous'. The name owes it popularity to St Clare of Assisi (*c.* 1194–1253), companion of St Francis and foundress of the Poor Clares. Her Italian name would have had the form **Chiara** or **Clara**. **Clarice** is an Italian diminutive of Clara, and featured as a literary name from fifteenth century onwards in various romances. Other literary forms of the name are **Claribel** (masculine in Spenser), **Clarinda**, also found in Spenser, and **Clarissa**, best known as the heroine of Samuel Richardson's novel *Clarissa: or, The History of a young Lady* (1747–9). **Clarry** or **Clarrie**, once almost obsolete, but now familiar to listeners to *The Archers*, is used as a pet form of these names, particularly of Clarice. **Clarence** is the masculine form of the name. This derives from the surname Clare, transferred to the Irish county, from which the dukes of Clarence took their title.

Clark

Clark comes from the surname, and means 'cleric'. It has become well known from the actor Clark Gable and from Clark Kent, *alter ego* of Superman. **Clarke** is also found.

Claudia

This is another name derived from that of a Roman family. The Claudii interpreted their name as coming from the Latin *claudus* ('lame'), from the nickname of an ancestor; but this may be mere folk etymology. **Claudette** and **Claudine**, as in the novels of Colette, are further forms of the name. Claudia has a place in British folk history, for the Claudia found in the New Testament (II Timothy iv. 21) is traditionally held to be the daughter of a British prince, sister of LINUS and wife of Pudens, mentioned in the same verse. The name Pudens has been found on Roman inscriptions at Colchester, and the first-century Roman poet Martial refers to a friend Pudens who has a wife 'Claudia, the foreigner from Britain'. The Welsh name **Gladys** (**Gwladys, Gwladus**) is traditionally said to come from Claudia, but in fact probably comes from a word meaning 'ruler'. The masculine form of the name, **Claud**, once popular, is now rare; even more rare is the full Roman masculine form **Claudius**. The French form of the name **Claude** [clohd] can be used for either sex, but in this country is usually feminine.

Claus: see NICHOLAS

Clayton: see EARTHA

Clementine

This name means 'mild, merciful' and is probably best known from the song 'My Darling Clementine'. **Clementina** is a variant. There has been something of a revival of these names in recent years, including the use of the abstract noun **Clemency**, a name used by the Puritans, along with its counterpart MERCY. **Clement**, the masculine form of the name, popular with Popes, has been less used in this country. The short forms of this group of names can be illustrated from the political world, the prime minister Clement Attlee (1883–1967) being known as **Clem** and Sir Winston Churchill's wife Clementine being called by him **Clemmie**.

Cleo

Cleo is the more frequently used short form of the Graeco-Egyptian name **Cleopatra**, meaning 'glory of her father'. The fame of the first-century AD queen of Egypt has been too strong for the name to be more than quietly used, although there has been a certain usage among black Americans, particularly those wanting to emphasise their African roots. **Clio** [kl'ieoh] is not a variant, but the name of the Greek muse of history.

Clifford

Clifford is a surname used as a first name, originally given to someone living near a cliff and ford. **Cliff** is a common short form.

Clinton

Like CLIFFORD, Clinton is an aristocratic surname used as a first name. Henry de Clinton, founder of the family of the dukes of Newcastle in the twelfth century, held land at Glympton in Oxfordshire and the name is probably a corruption of this place name, meaning 'settlement on the river Glyme'. The actor **Clint** Eastwood has given fame to the short form of the name.

Clio: see CLEO

Clive

Clive is another surname used as a first name, in this case probably in honour of Robert Clive (1725–74), whose exploits in India led to the domination of the sub-continent by the East India Company in the nineteenth century. The surname is an Old English one meaning 'dweller by the cliff'.

Clodagh
This is the name of a river in County Tipperary. It was first used as a girl's name by the family of the marquesses of Waterford. Its use outside Ireland may have spread in the 1960s through the success of the singer Clodagh Rogers.

Cloris: see CHLOË

Clova, Clover, Clovis: see LEWIS

Clyde
Clyde is the Scottish river and surname used as a first name.

Coinneach: see KENNETH

Colin
Although it started life in France as a pet form of NICHOLAS, in Scotland and Ireland Colin has also been associated with a Gaelic word meaning 'pup, cub' and hence 'young man'. The relationship between Colin and Nicholas can be more clearly seen in the feminine **Colette** (sometimes **Collette**) from Nicole, Nicolette. **Colinette** and **Colina** have also been recorded as feminine forms.

Colleen
This is the Irish word for 'a girl' used as a first name. It is rarely found in Ireland itself, but it has been popular in the United States and Australia.

Colm, Colmcille, Columba: see MALCOLM

Conal, Conan, Conchobar: see CONN

Connie: see CONN, CONSTANCE

Conn, Conor, Conan
The Irish name Conn or **Con** means 'high', and is used either as a name in its own right or, with **Connie**, as a short form of a number of names starting with the same element. Thus we have Conor or **Connor**, the anglicized form of the Gaelic **Conchobar** ('high desire') the name of the king of Ulster in the great Irish epic of *The Tain*:

Conal ('high and mighty') and **Conan** (sometimes **Conant**), as in the *Conan the Barbarian* stories, also meaning 'high'. Conan is found as the name of the early dukes of Brittany, and it is possible that it is a Breton name which has since passed into Irish use.

Conrad

This is the English form of the German name **Konrad**, meaning 'bold counsel'. There is an old diminutive, **Conradin**, the name of the last of the Hohenstaufen Holy Roman Emperors; it is also used by 'Saki' (H.H. Munro, 1870–1916) for a character in his short stories. The usual short form now is **Curt** or **Kurt**.

Constance

With its masculine form **Constant**, as in the composer Constant Lambert (1905–51), Constance is a name which celebrates the Christian virtue of steadfastness. **Constancy** has also been recorded as a girl's name. There is a further Christian connection in the related **Constantine**, for it was the name of the Roman emperor who formally brought the empire into the fold of the Church. They all share the short forms **Con** and **Connie**. The Welsh form of Constantine is **Cystennin**.

Cora: see CORINNA

Coral

Coral is one of the gem names introduced in the late nineteenth century. The French form, **Coralie**, dates from some hundred years earlier.

Cordelia

This is one of the less frequently used Shakespearean names, possibly because King Lear's daughter, however admirable, is not the easiest of heroines to warm to. The name may be the same as the Continental **Cordula**, one of the virgins martyred with St URSULA. The name is thought to be connected with the Latin word *cordis* 'a heart'.

Corinna

Corinna was the name of a Greek poetess of the late sixth century BC. Her name probably comes from the Greek *Kore*, 'a maiden', one of the names of the goddess of the underworld, **Persephone**. A less respectable Corinna is the object of the poet's pursuit in Ovid's *Amores* and it is from this source that the seventeenth- and eighteenth-century poets adopted the name for their inamorata, as in Herrick's 'Corinna's going a-maying'. **Corinne** is the French form of the name, made popular by Madame de Staël's novel (1807) of that name. **Cora** is probably an invention of James Fenimore Cooper for a woman in *The Last of the Mohicans* (1826), whence the name's popularity in the United States; but it is thought to be based on the same root. There is a masculine form, **Corin** (also used for women), which is rarely found, but is exemplified in the actor Corin Redgrave.

Cormac

The Gaelic name Cormac was borne by a legendary Irish king. Its meaning is obscure and interpretations include 'charioteer' and 'son of the raven'.

Cornelius

Cornelius, with its short forms **Corney** or **Corny** and **Cornel**, comes from the Roman clan name of the Cornelii, which probably means 'war horn'. The feminine form, **Cornelia**, is more widely used in this country, probably because of Cornelia, mother of the Gracchi, the second-century Roman tribunes. She represented all matronly accomplishments, and devoted herself to the raising of her children. When a visitor showed off her jewels and asked to see her hostess's, Cornelia is said to have produced her sons with the words, 'These are my jewels'. The Romans erected a statue in her honour.

Cosmo

Saints Cosmas and DAMIAN are said to have been twin brothers who practised medicine for free among the poor, and were martyred for their faith. Beyond the fact that they probably existed and belong to the early period of Christianity, little is known of them for sure, and their legend has become heavily adulterated by memories of the pagan heavenly twins **Castor** and **Pollux**, the sons of Zeus. Cosmas (whose name means 'order') and his brother became the patron saints of Milan, and from there the name spread throughout Italy in the form **Cosimo**. Cosmo came to Britain via the dukes of Gordon in the 18th century, who had links with the dukes of Tuscany, and the name became traditional in their family. **Cosima**, the feminine form, is also used occasionally. Its use is probably inspired by the fame of the Cosima who was the daughter of Liszt and wife of Wagner.

Courtney, Courtnay

Another aristocratic surname used as a first name, Courtney was originally a masculine name, but more recently has been used for both sexes. The family came from a Norman village called Courtenay, which would have been named from a Gallo-Roman landlord called Curtenus or Curtius, but from early on the name was thought of and used as a nickname *court nez* ('short nose').

Craig

This word means 'cliff' and is still used in Scotland in that sense (see AILSA). It would have started life as a surname given to someone who lived near a cliff, but came into use as a first name only in this century. It was particularly popular in the 1970s.

Cressida

Considering her history, it is surprising that this attractive-sounding name has come into use. Boccaccio (1313–75) in *Il Filostrato*, told the story of the love of Troilus for Cressida, showing her as a heartless and faithless woman. Chaucer (c. 1340–1400) in *Troilus and Criseyde* gives a rather more sympathetic version of her, showing her as easily led and timid rather than vicious; but by the time that Shakespeare deals with the story she has become a downright wanton, while her uncle's name, Pandarus, became that of the common pander. However, her story must have its attractions as her name has become increasingly popular in recent years, while the virtuous **Troilus** is not generally used, although it has been given to Sir Laurence Olivier's grandson. Cressida has a short form, **Cressy**.

Crisiant: see CRYSTAL

Crispin

Crispin (or **Crispian**) and his brother **Crispinian** are the patron saints of shoemakers. Their name comes from the Latin meaning 'curly-haired'. The use of the name Crispin in this country is probably helped by memories of the speech that Shakespeare gives to Henry V before the battle of Agincourt, where he tells his men:

> And gentlemen of England, now a-bed
> Shall think themselves accurs'd they were not here,
> And hold their manhoods cheap whiles any speaks
> That fought with us upon Saint Crispin's day.

Cristyn: see CHRISTINE

Crystal, Chrystal, Krystal

As a girl's name this belongs with the JEWEL group of names, although it is worth noting that Charlotte Yonge lists **Kristel** as a German form of the name CHRISTINE. The name also exists in a masculine guise, as a Scots pet form of the name CHRISTOPHER. The Welsh name **Crisiant** also means crystal, and has been in use since at least the twelfth century.

Cuddie: see CUTHBERT

Curt: see CONRAD

Curtis

A surname from the French for 'courteous', Curtis is now increasingly popular as a masculine first name.

Cuthbert

St Cuthbert, meaning 'well-known, famous', was a seventh-century bishop of Lindisfarne (Holy Island), whose simple holiness won him great love from the people he ministered to. He was buried in Lindisfarne, but the frequent Viking raids led to his re-burial at Durham. His name was much used in the past in the north of England, where **Cuddie** became a pet form of the name.

Cybill: see SYBIL

Cynan

An old Welsh masculine name meaning 'chief, pre-eminent', Cynan has the variants **Cynin, Cynon** and **Cymon**. **Cynyr** comes from the same root and means 'chief hero'. It was the name of St David's grandfather, who lived *c.* 500 AD.

Cynthia

The goddess of the moon and of hunting Artemis or DIANA had particular associations with the Greek Mount Cynthus, and Cynthia ('of Cynthus') became one of her epithets. It was used as a name in the classical world and was found in this country in the seventeenth or eighteenth century, but it did not become popular until the nineteenth. It shares **Cindy** and **Sindy** as short forms with Lucinda (see LUCY).

Cyprian

St Cyprian was a third-century bishop of Carthage and martyr, famous as a writer and devout Christian and for his gentle good manners and willingness to consult others. The name means 'man from Cyprus' and, although rare, is occasionally used in this country.

Cyril

Cyril comes from the Greek word *Kyrios* ('lord'). St Cyril, from Salonica, was a ninth-century missionary who brought Christianity to Russia; he gave his name to the Russian cyrillic alphabet, devised to write down the gospels. **Syril** is a rare variant. **Kyra** and **Kyrie** have been used as feminine versions of the name.

Cyrus

The name of a number of Persian kings, Cyrus may come from the Persian word for 'throne'. Its use, mainly in the United States, probably owes more to the mention of King Cyrus the Great in the Old Testament than to the rather obscure fourth-century martyr St Cyrus.

Cystennin: see CONSTANCE

D

Daffodil
One of the less common flower names, Daffodil was used when such names were at the height of their popularity, and is still occasionally found.

Dafydd: see DAVID

Dahlia
Another flower name, Dahlia seems to have had more popularity with authors – it is used by George Meredith in *Rhoda Fleming* (1865) and by P. G. Wodehouse for Bertie Wooster's favourite aunt – than with parents, although both Dahlia and **Dalia**, a form also found in France, have been recorded.

Dai: see DAVID

Daisy: see MARGARET

Dale
A surname meaning 'dweller in the dale' used as a first name, Dale was once restricted to men but is now used for both sexes.

Damaris
In the Bible Damaris is the name of an Athenian woman converted by St Paul. As such it was adopted as a name by the Puritans. It seems to have been quite popular at the beginning of the twentieth century, and is still regularly, if quietly, used. It is probably a corruption of the Greek **Damalis** ('a heifer').

Damian
Damian is probably a form of the rather less common **Damon**, an

old Greek name meaning 'to tame, subdue'. The story of Damon and Pythias, proverbial for loyal friendship, dates from the fourth century BC. Damon, an ardent republican, tried to assassinate Dionysius, the tyrant of Syracuse. His friend Pythias volunteered to stand surety for him while Damon went to say goodbye to his family before being executed. Dionysius was so impressed by Pythias's offer and by the fact that Damon returned rather than leave his friend to die in his place, that he pardoned them both. For the legend of St Damian see COSMO. Damon had a certain currency in the first half of this century, and is found in the authors Damon Runyon (1884–1946) and Damon Knight. Damian and its variant **Damien** have been the more popular in the latter part of the present century.

Dan: see DANIEL

Dana

This name when masculine comes from a surname meaning 'a Dane'. As an Irish girl's name it is said to come from Irish word meaning 'bold'. Outside Ireland the feminine form is probably adopted from the Scandinavian pet form of Daniella (see DANIEL).

Danaë

Danaë is a character from Greek mythology. It was prophesied to her father that he would be killed by her son, so to try to avoid this fate he shut her in a tower of brass. However, the god Zeus fell in love with her, visited her in the form of a shower of gold, and she had a son, Perseus, who fulfilled the prophecy.

Dand, Dandie, Dandy: see ANDREW

Daniel

Daniel comes from the Hebrew and means 'God is judge'. Daniel, with his adventures in the lions' den, is one of the most attractive of the Old Testament prophets and it is not surprising that his name was popular from the beginning of the Middle Ages. **Dan** and **Danny** are used as pet forms for both sexes, the feminine forms of the name being the French **Danielle**, the Italian **Daniella**, and more rarely **Danette** and **Danita**. In Wales **Deiniol** or **Deinioel**, meaning 'attractive, charming' and the name of an early Welsh saint, is used as a form of Daniel. (See also SUSAN, DANA.)

Daphne

In the Greek Daphne means 'laurel', and it is therefore the equivalent of LAURA. In mythology Daphne was a nymph with whom the god Apollo fell in love. She fled from his embraces, and when he had all but caught her, her prayers to be saved from him were answered and she was transformed into a laurel tree. Heartbroken, Apollo declared the laurel sacred to him. This story lies behind the use of the laurel wreath as a symbol of honour or achievement in the ancient world.

Darius

This is an ancient Persian royal name meaning 'protector'. There are two pronunciations: [da'rieəs] and ['dareeoos]. The best-known modern holder of the name is probably the French composer Darius Milhaud (1892–1974), and the name is more widely used in France than in this country. There is also a feminine form, **Daria**, although this may owe something to **Darija**, a Russian pet form of DOROTHY.

Darren

A modern name of obscure origin, Darren has been described as an Irish surname, but this is not well documented. Whatever its source, this name and its variants **Darran** and **Darin** became popular throughout the English-speaking world in the middle of this century. Its popularity is often attributed to its use in the 1960s American TV series *Bewitched*.

Daryl

French in origin, Daryl is another surname used as a first name. It comes from 'de Airel', the name of someone from the Norman village of Airel. The village got its name from the Latin word for an open space or courtyard. **Darryl, Darrel** and **Darrell** are variants. The name started out as masculine, but is now used for both sexes.

David

David, the name of the killer of Goliath and the king of Israel, is the Hebrew for 'beloved, friend'. The old short forms **Daw** and **Dawkin** have now been replaced by **Dave, Davie** or **Davy**. The Welsh form of the name is **Dafydd** (anglicized to **Taffy**), the form **Dewi** usually being restricted to the patron saint of Wales; short forms are **Dai, Deio** and **Deian**. **Davina, Davida**, with their short forms **Vina** and **Vida**, are originally Scots feminines. **Davita, Davinia** and **Divina** are also found.

Dawn

A modern name, Dawn was at first strongly associated with fiction and then given wider fame by several actresses. Its use may owe something to the Latin name **Aurora**, the goddess of dawn, which is occasionally used. The forms **Aurore** or **Aure** are well used in France.

Dean

Dean as a surname may be derived from an Old English name meaning 'dweller in a valley', or from the church office of Dean. Its success as a first name may owe something to the romance attached to the film actor James Dean, although it was well established in the United States before he sprang to fame. The feminine name **Dena** may have started as a feminine form of the name.

Deanna, Deanne: see DIANA

Dearbhail, Dearbhla: see DERVIA

Deborah

This is a Hebrew name meaning 'bee'. From the account of the original Deborah in the Old Testament book of Judges she must have been a formidable woman, for at a time when the role of women was very much that of a subordinate she was a prophetess, a judge of the people, and even led the army. **Debra** has become a very popular variant, and **Debora** is also used. **Deb, Debbie** and **Debby** are short forms.

Declan

Declan is the name of an Irish saint associated with the south-east of Ireland who dates from the earliest Christian times in Ireland, even before the coming of St PATRICK. The meaning is not known.

Dee, Dee-Dee

These are pet forms of any name beginning with the letter 'D'. **Deeann** and **Deeanna** are forms of DIANA.

Deinol: see DANIEL

Deirdre

Deirdre was the great romantic and tragic heroine of Irish legend, whose beauty caused the death of several heroes. Its meaning is debated: it has been interpreted as 'the raging one', 'fear', or, most attractively, 'the broken-hearted'. The name was given wider currency by the publication of W.B. Yeats's *Deirdre* (1907) and J.M. Synge's *Deirdre of the Sorrows* (1910), both based on her legend. Variants include **Derdre** and **Deidre**.

Del, Dell

These are used as short forms of any name beginning Del-. A number of these are masculine and represent a fashionable use of place or surname, or of 'blends' – mix of elements from different names. In some cases the sense of 'del' = 'of the' found in Romance languages can still be found. Thus we have **Delmar**, a place and surname ('of the sea'), **Delroy**, a French surname meaning '(servant) of the king', and the blend **Delbert**, 'Del + Bert'. Del has been used as a short form of DEREK. (See also DELYTH.)

Delia

Delia means 'girl from Delos', the Greek island in the Cyclades sacred to Apollo and Artemis. Its use as a first name is adopted from the first-century BC Latin poet Tibullus, who celebrated Delia (a pseudonym for one Plania) in his love poems, and from its use by Virgil for one of his shepherdesses. It was popular in the seventeenth and eighteenth centuries, particularly in literature, and at one time was practically synonymous with 'sweetheart'.

Delia: see ADELA

Delyth

This is a Welsh girl's name meaning 'pretty'. **Del** alone is also used, as is **Delun** ('pretty one') and **Delwen** ('pretty and fair'). This has a masculine form **Delwyn**. **Dilwyn** or **Dillwyn**, also masculine, is not a variant, but comes from the name of a Herefordshire village and means either 'white honeycomb' or 'petal'.

Demelza

A Cornish feminine name, Demelza has reached a wide audience through Winston Graham's *Poldark* novels and the television series made from them. It is a place name, meaning 'the hill-fort of Maeldaf', and is said to be a twentieth-century introduction.

Demetrius

This name has a certain popularity in the United States. It means follower of **Demeter**, the Greek goddess of agriculture and mother of **Persephone** (see CORINNA, CHLOE, MELANIE). Her name means either 'earth mother' or 'corn mother'. Demetrius occurs several times in the Bible, which may in part explain its use. It is also a saint's name, found in the form **Demetrios** in the Greek Church, and as **Dimitri** in Russian. **Demitrius** is another variant.

Dena: see DEAN

Denholm

This surname is made up from the place-name elements 'valley' and 'dry land in a fen'. The similar **Denham**, comes from 'valley' and 'homestead'. The popularity of the actor Denholm Elliott has meant that the name is now well known.

Denis

With its variants **Dennis** or **Denys** and short forms **Den** and **Denny**, **Denis**, is a form of the name **Dionysius**, 'a follower of the god **Dionysos**', the Greek god of wine and poetic inspiration, whose name probably comes from the title 'son of Zeus', the king of the gods. The form Denis is the French corruption of the name of the martyr St Dionysius of Paris, who became the country's patron saint. The Greek form of the name is shortened to **Dion**, a name of growing popularity, which has the feminine **Dionne**, as in the singer Dionne Warwick, and more rarely **Dione** and **Dionysia**. However, **Denise** is still by far the commonest feminine of the name.

Denzil

A Cornish place name of unknown meaning, **Denzil** was first used as a masculine first name in the seventeenth century in a very limited way; it has now spread beyond Cornwall and into more general use.

Derdre: see DEIRDRE

Derek, Derrick, Deryck

This is the English form of the name **Theodoric** ('ruler of the people'), an unstable name since the German form is **Dietrich**, the Dutch **Dirk** and the French **Thierry** (one of the sources of **Terry**). Theodoric the Ostrogoth (*c.* 455–526) was an outstanding figure of his day, ruling northern Italy (by conquest) and parts of what are now Switzerland and Germany. After his death he became a figure in European folklore, which would explain the changes that happened to his name. The word 'derrick' for a crane is said to come from the name of a seventeenth-century hangman at Tyburn, whose name was first applied to the gallows and then used more generally. DEL is occasionally used as a short form.

Dermot

Dermot or **Dermod** (in Irish **Diarmuid** or **Diarmaid**) is the name of a figure from Irish mythology, the lover who eloped with GRAINNE. There were also 11 Irish saints of the name. It occurs in a wide variety of forms, including **Diarmod** and even **Diarmjuid**, and **Kermit** the Frog (from *The Muppets* TV show) owes his name to a regional variant. The name probably means 'free from envy'.

Dervla

This is the most common form of the Irish **Dearbhail**, ('true desire'), which is also found in the forms **Dearbhla, Derval** and **Dervilia**. It is rare outside Ireland, although the travel writer Dervla Murphy has made the name well known.

Désirée

The French for 'desired, longed for', Désirée was used for a long-awaited child from early times, originally in its Latin form, **Desiderata**. **Desiderius** ERASMUS (1466–1536), the Dutch Humanist, bore the masculine form of the name, which is also found as **Desideratus**.

Desmond

Desmond is an Irish surname meaning 'descendant of one from South Munster', used as a first name. **Des** or **Dezzi**, are used as short forms.

Diamond: see JEWELL

Diana

Diana was the Roman goddess of the woods and hunting, and later of the moon. She was equated with the Greek goddess **Artemis**, whose name is also occasionally used as a first name. For example, the grand-daughter of the famous beauty Lady Diana Cooper was christened Artemis with reference to her grandmother. **Artemisia** ('follower of Artemis'), is another rare name, probably used with direct reference either to the queen who fought at the battle of Salamis in 480 BC, or to the Queen of Halicarnassus who built the Mausoleum, one of the Seven Wonders of the ancient world, in memory of her husband. Diana occurs in a number of variants. **Diane** is the French form, which also occurs as **Dianne** or **Dian**. **Deanna** is a form introduced by the film actress Deanna Durbin; and **Deeann, Deanne** and **Deeanna** are now also found, along with **Dyan** and **Dyanna**. Surprisingly, the popularity of the Princess of Wales does not seem to have affected the popularity of the name. Other names linked with Diana as moon-goddess are PHOEBE and CYNTHIA.

Diarmaid, Diarmod, Diarmuid: see DERMOT

Diccon, Dick, Dickie, Dickon, Dicky: see RICHARD

Dietrich: see DEREK

Dieudonné: see THEODORE

Digby
This comes from the place name in Lincolnshire, which means 'farm by the dyke'. As a surname it belonged to a notable family, the most prominent of which was Sir KENELM Digby.

Diggory
Diggory is a corruption of the name of a hero of medieval romance, Sir Degaré, 'the lost one'. The work, highly romantic and full of unlikely events, is not very highly thought of today, but the survival of the name must indicate a different opinion in the past.

Dilwyn, Dillwyn: see DELYTH

Dilys
Dilys is a Welsh word meaning 'certain, genuine'. According to Davies it was first used by William and Jane Davis for their daughter, who was born on 11th June 1857, and they took the word from a Welsh version of the 23rd Psalm. **Dilly** is used as a short form.

Dimitri: see DEMETRIUS

Dinah
Dinah is a separate name from the Greek DIANA, being a Hebrew word meaning 'judgement'. The story of Dinah's abduction and

the revenge taken by her brothers is told in chapter 34 of the Book of Genesis. The name is also found in the form **Dina**.

Dion, Dione, Dionne, Dionysia, Dionysius, Dionysos: see DENIS

Dirk: see DEREK

Divina: see DAVID

Djamila: see JAMILLA

Dod, Doddy: see GEORGE

Dodie, Dodo: see DOROTHY

Dolores
A Spanish name meaning 'sorrow', Dolores is taken from the title of the Virgin Mary as Our Lady of the Sorrows, and was at first used for girls born on 15 September, the feast day of the Seven Sorrows of Mary. Despite the religious nature of the name, the pet forms have gained notoriety, one being attached to the adventuress **Lola** Montez, the other, **Lolita**, inescapably attached to Vladimir Nabokov's novel (1955). Other Spanish names associated with the Virgin Mary are **Mercedes**, ('Our Lady of Mercy'), and **Montserrat** (near Barcelona), a place name meaning 'jagged mountain', where there is a famous monastery with a Black Madonna which is the patron saint of Catalonia.

Dolly, Doll, Dol: see DOROTHY

Dolph, Dolphus: see ADOLPH, RANDOLPH

Domhnall: see DONALD

Dominic
Dominic comes from the Latin meaning 'of the Lord' and therefore has the same root-sense as CYRIL. It may at first have been used for those born on a Sunday, the day of the Lord, but since the thirteenth century it has been associated with Saint Dominic, the founder of the Dominican Order. The old-fashioned spelling **Dominick** is sometimes used, and the name can be shortened to **Dom**. **Dominique**, from the French, is the usual feminine form, although the Latin **Dominica** can also be found.

Donagh: see DUNCAN

Donald

This is the most common form of the Celtic name **Donal (Domhnall, Domnall)**, meaning 'world-mighty'; in eight- and ninth-century Ireland it was regarded as a royal name. **Don** and **Donnie** or **Donny** are the short forms. There is no common feminine form, although **Donelle** and **Donalda** (particularly in Scotland) have been used.

Donata

The Latin masculine form of the name, **Donatus**, means 'given', and is naturalized as **Donat**. The occurrence of this rare name in Ireland may owe something to St Donatus of Fiesole, by tradition a ninth-century Irishman who miraculously became bishop of this town outside Florence. The feminine **Donata** has been recorded more frequently than the masculine, and has also been found in the form **Donate**.

Donna

The Italian for 'lady', Donna is not found as a name before the 1920s. It probably derives from **Madonna**, the Italian for 'My Lady', a title often given to the Virgin Mary. This was rarely found outside the American Middle West until given notoriety by the singer. **Ladonna**, 'the lady' also came into use in the United States in the early part of this century.

Dora: see DOROTHY, THEODORE

Dorcas: see TABITHA

Doreen, Dorinda: see DOROTHY

Doris

This name means 'Dorian woman', the masculine name **Dorian** being 'Dorian man'. The Dorians were an early Greek tribe who gave their name to the Doric order of architecture. The feminine form seems to have come into use at the beginning of the nineteenth century, but became popular only at the end of that century, about the time Oscar Wilde seems to have invented the masculine form for *The Picture of Dorian Gray* (1891). This story of a beautiful but corrupt youth with a portrait in his attic which shows the true ravages of time and vice does not seem to have discouraged use of the name.

Dorothy, Dorothea
This name means 'gift of God'. It has long been popular, as is reflected in the use of the short forms **Doll** and **Dolly** for the toy. Other short forms are **Dora, Dodie, Dodo, Dot, Dorrit** (unusual, but kept alive by Dickens), **Dorrie** and **Thea**. **Doreen** is probably an Irish elaboration of the name (although it has been linked with the Irish word for 'sullen'), and **Dorinda** seems to be a literary elaboration of the eighteenth century. There is no masculine form of the name, but a number of other names have the same meaning, including **Deodatus**, THEODORE and JONATHAN.

Douglas
Douglas with its short forms **Doug, Dougie, Duggie**, is a Scottish surname derived from a river whose Gaelic name means 'blue-black'. During the Renaissance the name was used for both sexes, but it is now exclusively masculine, with **Douglasina** a rare feminine. **Dougal** or **Dugald** comes from the same root, and means 'black(-haired) stranger', a name given to the invading Danish Vikings; the name **Fingal** ('fair stranger') being given to the blonder Norwegians. **Duff** has much the same meaning: 'dark-haired'.

Dreena, Drew, Drogo: see ANDREW

Drusilla
One of the names used by a Roman imperial family. It was first used in its masculine form, **Drusus**, by a man who adopted it from a Gaulish chieftain called Drausus he had killed in battle. This name is said to mean 'firm, rigid'. Its introduction to England does not, however, come from this exalted source, but from a brief mention of a Drusilla in the Acts of the Apostles, thereby giving the name respectability in the eyes of the Puritans who first used it.

Duane, Dwane, Dwayne
This is an Irish surname, probably meaning 'son of the little dark one'. Its great popularity as a first name in recent decades seems to owe much to the success of the pop singer Duane Eddy in the 1950s.

Dudley

This name comes from the town of that name (west of Birmingham), which became an aristocratic surname. The town's name means 'Dudda's clearing or wood'; and Dudda may be an old Saxon nickname for a dumpy man. **Dud** is a short form.

Duff: see DOUGLAS

Dugald: see DOUGLAS

Duke: see MADOC

Dulcie

This is a nineteenth-century feminine name, based on the Latin word *dulcis* ('sweet').

Duncan

Duncan is a pet form of the old Gaelic name **Donagh (Donnchadh)**, which means 'brown warrior'. However, Duncan looks more as if it is derived from the Gaelic words for 'brown head', linking it with the group of names under DOUGLAS, and it is often understood in that way.

Dunstan

St Dunstan, whose name means 'dark hill', is one of the great Anglo-Saxon saints. He was archbishop of Canterbury, adviser to kings and responsible for the revival of monasticism in tenth-century England. The coronation service he devised is still used today.

Dustin

The spread of this surname as a first name owes much to the fame of the actor Dustin Hoffman, although there was an earlier American film actor called Dustin Farman.

Dwane, Dwayne: see DUANE

Dwight

This name has been derived from both an Irish surname and from an English one said to go back ultimately to the name of the Greek god Dionysius, the source of DENIS. America had a prominent family with this surname: Theodore Dwight, a journalist and member of the House of Representatives in the early nineteenth century; his brother Timothy, a clergyman and teacher who became president of Yale, and another Timothy, grandson of the first, who was also president of Yale at the end of the last century. It was not uncommon for Americans to name their children after such academics (see CHAUNCEY) and this is probably how it became a first name, although its greatest fame comes from Dwight D. Eisenhower, general and 34th President of the United States.

Dylan
A Welsh name from heroic legend, Dylan is traditionally understood to mean 'son of the wave'. Its spread is due to the Welsh poet Dylan Thomas, and also to the singer Bob Dylan, who chose this stage surname in honour of the poet. The Welsh pronounce the name ['dulan]; Dylan Thomas preferred the English pronunciation, so elsewhere it is ['dilən].

Dymphna, Dympna
This Irish name probably means 'befitted'. There is a Saint Dympna of Gheel, who is the patron saint of the insane. Little is known of her, and the story of her being an early Irish princess who fled to Belgium to escape the incestuous attentions of her father owes more to folk-tale than to history.

E

Eachann: see HECTOR

Eamon, Eamonn: see EDMOND

Earl

With its variant **Erle**, this is the Old English word for 'a noble', now a title, used as a first name. It is rare in the United Kingdom, but not unusual in the United States.

Earnest: see ERNEST

Eartha

Although this name is hardly known in this country other than from the singer Eartha Kitt, it is one of a group of names well-established among the Black population of the American South. Attempts have been made to link this name with an old Germanic earth goddess, but Eartha has a much more recent source. According to the 1953 edition of the journal *Names*, 'if a mother has lost two children in childbirth or shortly thereafter, she can be assured of the survival of her third child, according to popular belief, only if the second dead baby lies buried face down in its grave and the new baby is named for Mother Earth'. For boys, names such as **Clayton**, ASHLEY or Sandy would be chosen. For girls the name would be taken from the word 'earth', and included Eartha, **Ertha** and **Erthel**.

Ebenezer

This is another biblical name, but of a rather different kind from the majority. It is not a personal name in the Bible, but first appears as a place name (I Samuel iv.1.) and later as the name of a memorial stone erected to commemorate an Israelite victory (I

Samuel vii.12.). The word means 'stone of help', and Samuel sets it up as 'hitherto hath the Lord helped us'. The name was introduced by the Puritans, and it has been suggested that it was first adopted by the early American Puritan settlers with reference to Samuel's words. It is certainly more frequently used in the United States than in Great Britain, often in its short form, **Eben**.

Ebony
Ebony is a recently introduced girl's name, particularly popular among Black families seeking a name suggesting blackness, beauty and preciousness. **Sable** is sometimes used for the same reason, although it is as widely used by Whites.

Ebrilla, Ebrillwen: see APRIL

Eck, Ecky: see ALEXANDER

Ed, Eddie: see EDGAR, EDMUND, EDWARD, EDWIN

Edana: see AIDAN

Edgar
This comes from the common Old English name-element 'ead' ('happy, fortunate') plus the common 'gar' ('spear'). It remained in use after the Norman Conquest, but became obsolete in the Middle Ages. Shakespeare's use of it for the virtuous brother in *King Lear* reflects the play's early English setting. It shares the short forms common to all the Ed-names: **Ed, Eddy, Ned, Neddy**, and **Ted** and **Teddy**.

Edie: see ADAM, EDITH

Edith
Edith is the one surviving Old English feminine name that shows the common name-element 'ead' ('happy, fortunate') which is found in so many masculine names. It was the name of two English kings' daughters, one in the ninth century and one in the tenth, both of whom were canonized, and the name probably owes much of its early popularity to these two saints. The original form of the name was Eadgyth, the second element meaning 'battle'. Edith is sometimes shortened to **Edie**, and can be found in the Latinate form **Editha**.

Edmond, Edmund

This is an Old English name meaning 'happy or fortunate protection'. **Eamon** or **Eamonn** is the Irish form of the name, which shares the usual short forms with other Ed- names. King Edmund the Martyr was a ninth-century king of East Anglia who, according to his Old English biographer, was taken prisoner by the Vikings because he refused to fight, wishing to follow Christ's example, and was martyred by them in a way similar to St SEBASTIAN, being used as target practice for their spears until he was covered with their missiles 'just like a hedgehog's spines'. He was interred at Bury St Edmunds, where many miracles were ascribed to him.

Edna

A name of disputed origin, Edna occurs in the Apocrypha as the name of Enoch's wife and of Tobias's mother-in-law, in which case it probably comes from the Hebrew meaning 'pleasure'. However, it has also been described as a form of the name Edwina or of Edana, a form of Eithne (see AIDEN).

Edom: see ADAM

Edred

An Old English name meaning 'fortunate counsel', Edred was made more widely known at the beginning of this century by its use for the hero of E. Nesbit's *The House of Arden*.

Edward

This is the most popular of the Old English names beginning with the element Ed- ('prosperous, fortunate'), this time combined with the element meaning 'guard'. Its original popularity must owe much to its being the name of two canonized English kings. The first, Edward the Martyr (c.963–78) was a boy-king assassinated for what were probably political ends (see further under ELFRIDA). The second was King Edward the Confessor (c.1002–66), the last legitimate Saxon king of England. He had been brought up in Normandy, favoured the Normans at his court and had no children. William the Conqueror based his claim on the English throne on his having been made (so he said) Edward's heir, which would explain why this saint's name was one of the few Old English names to survive in common use after the Conquest. It shares the short forms **Ed, Eddy, Ned, Neddy, Ted** and **Teddy** with the other names in this group.

Edwin

This is an Old English name meaning 'fortunate friend' and was the name of a seventh-century king of Northumbria who was an early convert to Christianity. **Edwina**, a feminine form of the name, was coined in the nineteenth century. The names have the same short forms as EDWARD.

Effie, Effy: see EUPHEMIA

Egbert

Egbert was a common Old English name, its users including an archbishop of York, a hermit-saint, and a tenth-century king who became overlord of the whole country. It means 'edge-bright'.

Eibhlin, Eileen: see HELEN

Eiluned: see LYNETTE

Eilwyn: see ALVIN

Einion, Einiona: see EYNON

Eira [ierə]

A Welsh feminine name meaning 'snow', Eira is also found in the form **Eiry**. Other popular Welsh names from the same root are **Eirlys** ('snowdrop') and **Eirwen** ('snow-white'). **Eirian**, another Welsh feminine, looks as if it should belong with the same group, but is thought to come from the word *arian* ('silver').

Eirene: see IRENE

Eithne, Eithna: see AIDAN

Elaine

This is an Old French form of the name HELEN. However, since it is the name of a character in the Arthurian romances – she seduces Sir Lancelot and becomes the mother of Sir Galahad – it is possible the name comes from the Welsh **Elain** ('a fawn'), for many of the Arthurian names have a Welsh origin.

Eldon: see ELTON

Eldred

Eldred, with its variant **Aldred**, is an Old English name meaning 'old (thus mature) council'. It was the name of the last Anglo-Saxon bishop of York, who died in 1069. It was revived in the nineteenth century, but is now rarely used.

Elena: see HELEN

Eleanor

Despite the popularity of this name throughout Europe, its meaning is obscure. It may well come from the same root as HELEN, and mean 'bright, shining', but it has also been derived from the Greek for 'pity, mercy'; from the Arabic meaning 'god is my light'; and from a Germanic root connected with the word for 'foreign'. It first came into English from France in the form **Alienor**, and has developed spellings such as **Eleanore** and **Elinor**. Its short forms include **Ella, Ellen, Nell, Nellie, Nelly** and NORA. **Eleonora** is an Italian form of the name, which has a short form **Leonora** (sometimes **Leanora** or **Lenora**), made famous by Beethoven, while another form, **Lenore**, has been given fame by Edgar Allan Poe. **Annora** is said to be a northern English form of the name (see also HONORIA).

Eleri

This is a name of a fifth-century Welsh woman saint, as well as of a river and valley in Dyfed.

Elfrida

An Old English name meaning 'elf strength', it is usually found in the history books in its old form, Ælfthryth. It was the name of a very forceful tenth-century queen of England, who virtually ruled the country at one time. She has been held responsible for the murder of her stepson, EDWARD the Martyr, in order to secure the throne for her own son, Ethelred the Unready; but despite this unsavoury reputation her name was revived in the nineteenth century and became popular in the late nineteenth and early twentieth century, and some cases of **Freda** represent a short form. It is sometimes found in the form **Elfreda**. An allied name, revived at the same time but less popular, is **Elfgiva**, a Latinized form of Ælfgifu ('elf gift'), which was borne by a noblewoman whose family was persecuted by the same Ethelred. The family enmity led to her marriage to King Canute (c. 995–1035), who was fighting Ethelred for the English throne, and at one time she was his regent in Norway. She, too, had an unfortunate reputation, for she was deposed and 'Ælfgifu's days' became proverbial in Norway for bad times.

Eli

This was the name of the high priest in the Old Testament who was given the infant SAMUEL to bring up when he was dedicated at the temple. The name probably means 'high, elevated'.

Elias

Elias, as used in the New Testament, is the Greek form of the name of the Hebrew prophet **Elijah** ('Jehova is God'). The surname **Ellis**, now used as a first name, is derived from this name, and its pet form gives us **Elliot, Eliot** or **Eliott**.

Elinor: see ELEANOR

Elizabeth

This is the English spelling of the New Testament **Elisabeth**, cousin to the Virgin Mary and mother of John the Baptist, who was the first person to recognise the significance of the child that Mary was to bear (see Luke i. 40–45). Her role in the Bible made the name enormously popular throughout Christendom, where it took many forms, particularly in diminutives. English pet forms include **Eliza, Bess, Bessie, Bessy, Bet, Beth, Betsy, Betty** and **Bette; Libby, Lisa, Liza, Lisbeth, Lizbeth, Liz**, and **Lizzie**. In Scotland the name became **Elspeth**, with pet forms **Elspie, Elsie** and **Elsa**. French gives us **Babette** and **Lisette** as well as spawning a whole set of names from the form ISABEL and its diminutives. Italy gives us **Bettina**, which has developed **Bettyne**; and the Germanic languages give us **Elise, Ilse, Ilsa, Lise, Liesl** and **Liesel**. The modern names **Bethan** and **Bethany** may also come from Elizabeth, either directly or as compounds with ANN, although Bethany is also a biblical place name, and Bethan has been linked with the Celtic name **Bethia** ('life'), itself also a biblical place name.

Elke, Elkie: see ALICE

Ella

A Norman French name derived from the German word for 'all', Ella is also used as a pet form of ELEANOR and **Isabella** (see ISABEL).

Ellen: see HELEN, ELEANOR

Ellie: see ALICE

Elliot, Ellis: see ELIAS

Elma: see WILLIAM

Elmer

Elmer is a form of the Old English name Æthelmær ('noble and famous'), which also gives us **Aylmer**. It is principally an American name and probably best known in this country from Elmer Fudd the implacable enemy of Bugs Bunny. Its popularity in the United States is due mainly to the fame of the brothers Ebenezer and Jonathan Elmer who played an important part in the American Revolution. **Elma** looks like a feminine version of the name, but is a pet form of names such as Wilhelma (see WILLIAM).

Elmo: see ERASMUS

Eloisa, Eloise: see HELOISE

Elroy: see LEROY

Elsa, Elsie: see ALICE, ELIZABETH

Elshender: see ALEXANDER

Elspeth, Elspie: see ELIZABETH

Elton

Elton, best known through the stage name of the singer Elton John, is a surname coming from an Old English place name meaning 'Ella's settlement'. Similarly, **Eldon** means 'Ella's mound'. 'Ella' is a short form of an Old English name containing the same element, meaning 'elf', found in ALFRED and ELFRIDA.

Eluned: see LYNETTE

Elvira

This is a Spanish name of debated meaning, possibly meaning 'noble and true'. Its associations in this country are mainly with the arts: it is familiar through the character in Mozart's *Don Giovanni*

(1787) and other versions of the Don Juan story; as the ghost in Noël Coward's *Blithe Spirit* (1941); and through the film *Elvira Madigan*.

Elvis
Elvis Presley was lucky enough to be given a name so rare and striking that there was no need for him to use a stage name. Its origin has been much debated, but Dunkling is probably right in identifying it with the Irish saint's name **Ailbe** or **Ailbhe**, usually anglicized as **Alby, Elli** or **Elly**. However, the feminine form is usually anglicized as **Elva**, and there is a place called St Elvis in Dyfed. The name is not unique to the Presley family, but was rarely found before the singer made it famous.

Emanuel
Hebrew for 'God with us', Emanuel is the term used in the Old Testament for the Messiah. **Emmanuel** and **Immanuel** are variants and **Manny** the short form. The name is popular in Spain in the form **Manuel**. Feminine forms such as **Emanuela** or **Emmanuela** have been recorded, while **Emanuelle**, the French form, became notorious in a series of novels and films.

Emblem: see AMELIA

Emerald: see ESMERALDA

Emery, Emory
These are forms of the old Germanic **Almeric** ('labour + rule'). Modern uses come from the surname, which in turn derived in the past from the old first name.

Emily
Emily comes from the Roman family name of the Æmelii. The Renaissance Italian writer Giovanni Boccaccio named one of his heroines **Emilia** in the *Teseida* (*c.* 1339); and Chaucer, who based 'The Knight's Tale' on Boccaccio's work, introduced the name as Emily. **Emmy, Emmie** and **Em** are used as short forms. (See also EMMA and AMELIA.)

Emlyn
This is a Welsh man's name, traditionally said to derive from the Roman name Æmelius, the same source as EMILY; in fact, it is more likely to come from a place name in Dyfed.

Emma

Emma started life as a short form of names containing the Germanic element *'ermin'*, ('universal, entire'), such as **Ermyntrude** ('universal strength'). It was introduced in the eleventh century, has remained in use ever since, and in recent years has been one of the most popular girl's names. It shares the same short forms as EMILY, for which it is sometimes used as a pet form. The German names **Irma** and **Irm(e)gard** ('universal protection') come from the same root.

Emmeline: see AMELIA

Emrys: see AMBROSE

Emyr: see HONORIA

Ena

This is a name with a number of different sources. It can be a pet form of names ending -ena or -ina, such as Eugenia or Helena, and it can be a form of the name Eithna (see AIDAN). But its popularity in the past came from Queen Victoria's granddaughter, Princess Victoria Eugénie Julia Ena, always known as Ena, who became Queen of Spain. It is said that her last name was to have been Eva, but that at her christening the handwritten notice of her names was misread and she became Ena.

Eneas: see ANGUS

Enid

A Celtic name, Enid comes from the Welsh *enaid* ('soul'). In medieval literature it is the name of one of the outstanding heroines in the Arthurian stories, distinguished for her loyalty and patience, and it was brought back to the public's attention by Tennyson when he told her story in 'Geraint and Enid' (1859).

Enoch

This is a rare name, made widely known today by the politician Enoch Powell. It was adopted by the Puritans from the Bible, where Enoch is an early descendant of Adam who has a particularly close relationship with God. According to tradition he lived 365 years and was then translated to Heaven without experiencing death. The meaning of the name is disputed, and it is possible that the stories about the biblical Enoch may go back to a Babylonian sun-god.

Enola
A name from the French-speaking area of Louisiana, it gained notoriety when the United States bomber 'Enola Gay', named after the captain's mother, dropped the atom bomb on Hiroshima in 1945. It appears to be one of the many North American names coined by blending together sounds from other fashionable names.

Enya: see AIDEN

Eoghan: see EUGENE

Eoin: see JOHN

Ephraim
In the Bible Ephraim is a son of JOSEPH and founder of one of the 12 tribes of Israel. The name means 'fruitful'.

Eppie: see EUPHEMIA

Erasmus
This name comes from the Greek meaning 'desired, beloved' and was the name of an early Christian martyred in southern Italy. He became the patron saint of sailors in the area, his name changed to Ermo or **Elmo**, and it is after him that the strange phenomenon of St Elmo's fire is named. Gerhard Geerts (1466–1536) adopted the name Desiderius Erasmus in the mistaken belief that this was the Greek translation of his Dutch name, and the name Erasmus is now most closely associated with this great scholar. **Erastus** is a less common name from the same root and with the same meaning. **Rasmus** and **Rastus** are the short forms of these names.

Eric
Eric is a Viking name, the second element of which means 'power'. The first syllable probably means either 'eternal' or 'island'. It was little used until the middle of the nineteenth century when Dean Farrar wrote the improving book *Eric, or Little by Little,* a moral tale approved of by parents but the bane of generations of children. **Erica** is a feminine form, interpreted by some as a flower name as it is the Latin for 'heather'. **Rick** and **Ricky** are used as short forms for both sexes.

Erin

A poetic term for Ireland, Erin is used in many a sentimental poem on the country. It was turned into a first name in the United States, spread to Canada and Australia, and then to England; it has been particularly popular since the 1970s, but is rarely used in Ireland itself.

Erle: see EARL

Ermin, Ermine, Erminia: see HERMAN

Ermyntrude: see EMMA

Ernest

This German name was introduced into England by the followers of George I when he came over from Hanover to become king. It has the same root and meaning as the English adjective 'earnest' and the name is sometimes spelt with the extra 'a'. **Ern** or **Ernie** are short forms; **Ernestine** is a feminine form which was fashionable around the turn of the century but is little used now.

Errol

This name, made famous by the film star Errol Flynn and in steady use ever since, has been given a variety of origins. Some have linked it with a Scottish surname and place name; some have claimed that it is a variant of HAROLD or EARL; some have linked it with the Welsh name **Eryl**, used for both sexes, meaning 'a look-out post'. As many twentieth-century men's names come from surnames, this would seem to be the most probable source of the name, but that still leaves the source of the surname open to debate. In Frances Hodgson Burnett's *Little Lord Fauntleroy* (1886) the hero is called Cedric Errol, which may have some bearing on the use of the name.

Ertha, Erthel: see EARTHA

Erwin: see IRVING

Esmé

This name comes from the French word meaning 'esteemed', but at one time it was confused with the verb *aimer* ('to love'), whence the variants **Aimé** or **Aymé** (see also AMY). These were introduced as masculine names in the sixteenth century in Scotland, where they were used in the family of the dukes of Lennox, and spread from there. The name is now mainly feminine and has variants **Esme, Esmée, Esmee** and **Esma**. It was quite popular in the early part of the century, but is now rarely used. Its most distinguished literary bearer of recent times is the heroine-dedicatee of J.D. Salinger's 'For Esmé—With Love and Squalor' (1953).

Esmeralda
This is the Spanish for **Emerald**, which is also occasionally found as a first name. Use of this name owes much to the heroine of Victor Hugo's *The Hunchback of Notre-Dame* (1831).

Esmond
Starting off as an Anglo-Saxon name, probably a compound of 'grace + protection', Esmond became a surname in the Middle Ages. It was re-adopted as a first name in the middle of the last century, when so many Old English names were revived.

Estella, Estelle: see STELLA

Esther
Sometimes spelt **Ester**, Esther is said in the Old Testament to be a translation of a Hebrew name meaning 'myrtle', although it may actually be a Persian name meaning 'star'. The biblical Esther was a Jewish orphan of outstanding grace and beauty who replaced VASHTI as the queen of King Ahasuerus (Xerxes to the Greeks). When the jealous Haman plotted the death of all Jews, Esther was able to use her influence to save her people. **Hester**, an alternative form of the name, has been in use since the Middle Ages, and the names are shortened to **Ess, Essie** and **Hetty**.

Esyllt: see ISOLDA

Ethan
This is the name of several minor figures in the Old Testament, the most important of whom is cited for his wisdom. It is more common in the United States than Britain, probably after Ethan Allen (1738–89) who fought the British in the American Revolution. The name means 'firmness'.

Ethel
Ethel was originally a short form for a number of Old English

names starting with the common name element *æthel* ('noble'). It came into use as a name in its own right in the middle of the nineteenth century as a part of the revival of Old English names (see AUDREY and ALBERT).

Ethelbert: see ALBERT

Etheldred, Etheldreda, Ethelthryth: see AUDREY

Ethne, Ethna, Etney: see AIDAN

Etta: see HENRY

Eugene

Deriving from the Greek and meaning 'well born', Eugene was the name of a number of saints, the most prominent of whom was Eugenius, bishop of Carthage, who died an exile because of his faith in AD 505. The name is frequently shortened to **Gene**. The name has been popular in the Celtic areas of the British Isles, becoming **Eoghan** in Ireland, **Ewan** (sometimes **Euan** or **Ewen**) in Scotland, while in Wales it is **Owen** and **Owain**, a name found in a sixth-century poem by TALIESIN lamenting the death of its owner and praising his prowess against the invading English. The feminine form of the name, **Eugenia**, belongs to an early saint of whom little is known, but who has acquired a highly melodramatic legend in which she figures as a reformed fallen woman, who, disguised as a man, becomes abbot of a monastery, and when accused of breaking vows of chastity proves her innocence by revealing her true gender. The French form of the name, **Eugénie** (often spelt without the accent), became popular in this country out of admiration and sympathy for the French Empress Eugénie (1826–1920), who spent the last 50 years of her life in retirement in England. Queen Victoria was among the Empress's admirers, and the name was given to one of her grandchildren (see ENA). Thus it became one of the names used by descendants of the British Royal Family and has recently resurfaced as the name of the second daughter of the Duke of York. The pet form of Eugenia is one of the sources of the name ENA.

Eulalia [yooh'layleeə]

This is a Greek name meaning 'sweetly speaking', but the saint who spread the use of the name was Spanish. It is difficult to separate fact from fiction in her legend, but she seems to have been a 12-year-old girl who was martyred *c.* 304 AD after trying to stop the local magistrate persecuting Christians. It is said that after her death a dove appeared to fly from her mouth and a fall of snow covered her body. Her cult spread to England, where several Anglo-Saxon writers refer to her. Although it is a rare name, both Eulalia and the French form **Eulalie** can be found.

Eunice

This is a Greek name meaning 'good victory'. The Puritans borrowed it from the New Testament where it is the name of the mother of TIMOTHY, a Jew married to a Gentile, who had introduced him to Christianity and given him a careful religious training (2 Timothy i.5.and Acts xvi.1). The phonetic spelling **Unice** is also found.

Euphemia

This name means much the same as EULALIA. Euphemia was a saint martyred just a few years later, in *c.* 307 AD. Her legend, also highly fictionalized, tells of her survival through various attempts to put her to death, until she was thrown to the wild beasts. It was particularly popular as a name in Scotland, and was much used by the Victorians and at the beginning of this century, but is rarely found in its full form. **Effie** is by far the most common short form, possibly influenced by Effie Deans, the heroine of Scott's *Heart of Midlothian* (1818). **Eppie, Phemia, Phemie** are also used, and Euphemia is also one of the sources of the name PHOEBE. **Effy** and Effie were sometimes confused in Scotland with the Celtic name **Oighrig**, which developed into AFRIC.

Eurfron

A Welsh feminine name meaning 'gold breast', Eurfron is one of a large number of Welsh names beginning with the element 'eu' meaning 'gold', such as **Eurwen** ('gold + fair, white').

Eustace

This comes from the Greek meaning 'good harvest' and was the name of a saint who was popular in the Middle Ages but who is probably fictional. His legend has many connections with that of St HUBERT; it involves the loss of possessions, wife and children and their miraculous recovery, in a form found elsewhere in medieval romance. The name is not common now, but its pet form is one of the sources of the increasingly popular **Stacy**. **Eustacia** is a feminine form.

Evadne

Evadne is a Greek name of unknown meaning, born by two women in Greek legend. One of them features in the drama *The Seven Against Thebes*, as so devoted a wife that, when her husband is killed in battle, she throws herself onto his funeral pyre in order not to be parted from him. The name was obsolescent until brought back to public attention by the comedy couple Hinge and Bracket.

Evan: see JOHN

Evangeline

This name, which means 'good news', is from the same root as the word 'evangelist'. The Italian form of the name is **Evangelista**, and the poet Longfellow seems to have given this a French form for his poem of 1847 which introduced the name. The novelist Charlotte M. Yonge, writing in 1863, describes it as an American name, but it soon spread to Britain in both the basic form and as **Evangelina**.

Eve

Eve is the English, **Eva** the Latin form of the name given by ADAM to the 'Mother of Mankind', probably from the Hebrew for 'life'. This meaning led early Greek writers to translate the name as ZOE. In Ireland Eve has been used to translate the Celtic name AOIFE. **Evie** is used as a pet form, and **Evelina, Eveleen** and **Evaline** used as elaborations of both EVE and EVELYN.

Evelyn

The Norman conquerors brought over to England the name **Aveline** (obsolescent until revived by Carla Lane for the TV series *Bread*), which developed into the surname Evelyn. This was adopted first as a man's name in the seventeenth century, but has now become predominantly feminine, although the author Evelyn Waugh (1903–66) still keeps an awareness of the masculine use alive. The origin of Aveline is not clear; it could be from the Old French word for 'hazel nut', or it may come from the same obscure source as AVICE. **Evelina** is the Latinate form of the name and **Evilina, Eveline, Evaline** and **Eveleen** are variants.

Everard

This name comes from a Germanic root via Norman French and means 'brave as a wild boar'. The surname **Everett**, occasionally used as a first name, is a variant and **Ewart** is the Scottish form of the name. For female names from the same root, see APRIL.

Everild, Everilda: see APRIL

Evonne: see YVONNE

Ewan, Ewen: see EUGENE, JOHN

Eynon
A Welsh masculine name meaning 'anvil', Eynon is said to symbolize stability and endurance. **Einion** is a variant, and a feminine form, **Einiona**, has been recorded.

Ezekiel
Ezekiel was an Old Testament prophet whose name means 'God strengthens'. The name is rarely found in its full form, but the shortened **Zeke** is occasionally encountered.

Ezra
Another Old Testament prophet, Ezra means 'help'. Today it is chiefly associated with the poet Ezra Pound (1885–1975).

F

Fabian

The Roman patrician house of the Fabii, whose name comes from the Latin for 'bean' (presumably because some ancestor grew or sold them), gave Rome a number of eminent fighters and generals. Indeed, according to legend, at one point the family was all but wiped out fighting for their native city. The most famous of these was Quintus **Fabius** Maximus, nicknamed Cunctator ('the delayer'), who successfully wore down HANNIBAL and his invading forces in the Second Punic War by harrying them but refusing a direct engagement which he knew he would lose. It is after him that the Fabian Society (founded 1884) is named. A descendant of the family called Fabian was a martyred pope in the second century, thus giving the name Christian respectability. There are several feminine forms: a French direct femininzation, **Fabienne**; the Latin **Fabia** and **Fabiana**, and **Fabiola**. The last was the name of an energetic and enterprising member of the Roman family, active on behalf of the Church in the fourth century and later canonized; but it is better known today, as the name of Dona Fabiola de Mora y Aragon, the Spanish-born Queen of the Belgians.

Faith

As one of the three great Christian virtues, along with HOPE and CHARITY, Faith was popular with the Puritans. It seems probable that the twentieth-century name **Fay** or **Faye** comes from a short form of Faith, rather than from the synonym for 'fairy'. Although the French have a masculine name **Foy**, meaning 'faith', in most other languages the adjective rather than the noun is used, as it is with John Bunyan's character **Faithful**, which has been recorded as a real name. Thus we find Beethoven's *Fidelio* (1805), while **Fidel** Castro illustrates the Spanish form. The mainly Irish feminine

94

name **Fidelma** seems to be an elaboration of Fidel, possibly combined with MARY.(See also VERA).

Fanny: see FRANCIS

Fatima
While Fatima is primarily a Muslim name, popular because it was the name of the Prophet's daughter (its meaning is unknown), it is occasionally found used in honour of Our Lady of Fatima, a Portuguese village where visions of the Virgin Mary occurred.

Fausta, Faustina, Faustine, Faustus: see FELICITY

Fawn
The name of young of a deer is occasionally used as a girl's first name, presumably on account of its connotations of large-eyed innocence. **Bambi**, the name of a fawn in a book by Felix Salton published in 1921 and turned into a highly successful cartoon film in 1942, is also used, but probably only as a nickname.

Fay, Faye: see FAITH

Fearghas, Fearghus: see FERGUS

Fedor, Fedora: see THEODORE

Felicity
The Romans worshipped Felicitas, the embodiment of happiness or good fortune, as a goddess. Felicity comes from this and was also the name of several saints, an appropriate name as they were deemed to be happy in having found their martyr's crown. **Felice**, still to be found, was the medieval form of the name, and was used for the faithful and pious wife in the Guy of Warwick legends. **Felicia** is another form of the name.

The masculine form is **Felix**. Although now best known as the name of a cartoon cat, this was first adopted as a name by the Roman dictator Sulla (138–78 BC), who believed that he was especially blessed with luck by the gods: not only did he fight his way to wealth and power, but he was one of the few dictators fortunate enough to be able to divest himself of power in old age and die a private citizen. Sulla had twin children whom he named **Faustus** and **Fausta**, from an adjective with the same meaning as Felix, thus introducing another new name. **Faustina** was later also used by the Romans. The French form **Faustine** was given fame by the poet Algernon Swinburne (who also wrote a poem to **Félice**), although the notoriously 'decadent' and sensual poem of that name was written only to settle a bet as to who could find the most rhymes for the word. In Ireland Felix has been used as an English form for the name **Felim (Felimid, Felimy, Phelim)**, which means 'ever good'.

Fenella

This is the anglicized form of the Celtic name **Fionnuala** [fee-ə'noohl], also found as **Fionnghuala** and **Fionola**. This is shortened to **Finola**, and the two Celtic forms of the name produced further shortenings to **Nuala** and **Nola**, which are used as names in their own right. The form Fenella became well known in Britain as a result of Sir Walter Scott's use of it in *Peveril of the Peak*. **Fiona** comes from the same root, being the Celtic for 'white, fair' with a Latin ending. The name was invented by William Sharp (1855–1905), a Scottish poet who used it for his pen name of Fiona Macleod. It is, however possible that Sharp was influenced by early Celtic forms of the name CATHERINE. Early medieval Irish bards sometimes split names up into shorter units when writing them down, so that Catharina became in the peculiar Irish spelling Caitir Fhiona, which had the inflected form Caitreach Fiona.

Feodor: see THEODORE

Ferdinand

When the Visigoths invaded Spain in the sixth century they took with them a name based on the words *farth* ('a journey') and *nand* ('brave'); this developed into the Spanish name Fernando or Hernando, which in turn became Ferdinand in English. Short forms are **Ferd**, **Ferdie** and, rarely nowadays, **Nandy**.

Ferelith ['ferəlith]

This unusual Celtic name is said to mean 'perfect princess'. It is largely a literary name, but dog-lovers may be familiar with it from the work of Ferelith Hamilton.

Fergus

This Celtic name meaning 'man of vigour' is also spelt **Fearghus**, **Fearghas**. Traditionally it was brought from Ireland to Scotland in the fifth century by Fergus mac Erca, who led his people to settle in Scotland. Whatever the truth of that, it was certainly in use by the fifth century, for it is recorded as the name of St Columba's grandfather (see MALCOLM). From the same root comes the name **Fergal**, ('man of strength'), also an early Irish name, for it was the true name of the man known as St VIRGIL of Salzburg (d. 784), in his day a highly controversial academic as well as a missionary.

Fern
One of the newer plant names, Fern was introduced in this century. The variant **Ferne** is also found.

Ffion ['feeon]
This Welsh feminine name is a poetic word for the colour of a foxglove or peony. In medieval Welsh love-poetry it is typically used to describe the colour of a lovely girl's cheek. It has also been spelt **Fionn**, while the variant **Ffiona** presumably reflects the influence of the Scottish Fiona (see FENELLA).

Ffleur, Fflur: see FLORA

Fidel, Fidelma: see FAITH

Fifi: see JOSEPHINE

Finbar: see FINLAY

Fingal: see DOUGLAS, FINLAY, OSSIAN

Finlay
This comes from a Scottish surname meaning 'fair hero', traditionally given as the name of Macbeth's father, used as a first name. The variants **Findlay** and **Finley** are also found. It is one of a collection of masculine names based on the Celtic element *fionn* ('fair, white'). The simplest is **Finn** (sometimes **Fynn**), the name of one of the great heroes of Celtic legend. In folklore he is the giant Finn MacCool who builds the Giant's Causeway, but in mythology he is a hero fighting in Scotland where he was known as Finn na Gael, which became **Fingal**, a form of the name well-established by the fourteenth century, but made famous in the poems of James Macpherson (1736–96), purportedly by Finn's son OSSIAN. **Fintan** is a diminutive of Finn. Two Irish saints bear names from the same root: the fifth- to sixth-century St **Finbar** ('fair head (i.e. hair))' whose name is one source of BARRY, and the sixth-century St

97

Finian or **Finnian** ('the fair'). For feminine names from the same root, see under FENELLA.

Finola, Fiona, Fionola Fionnghuala, Finnuala: see FENELLA

Flann

This is an Irish name meaning 'blood red'. It is probably best known from Flann O'Brien, one of the pen names of Brian O'Nolan (1911–66).

Flavia

Flavia comes from an old Roman name, at one time the family name of the Roman emperors. The name would have started as a nickname, for it means 'golden yellow' or 'flaxen' and would have been used to describe someone of that colouring. Someone with tawny or dark yellow hair must have been the founder of the family which gave us the name **Fulvia**, the best known Roman holder of which was the wife of Mark Anthony, who fought actively on his behalf in the civil war, even though at the time he was neglecting his own interests in order to dally with Cleopatra. The masculine forms of these names, Flavian or Flavius and Fulvius, do not seem to be used.

Fleur: see FLORA

Flip: see PHILIP

Flora

The name of a Roman goddess of fertility and flowers, Flora was later seen as symbolic of spring. **Florrie** is used as a diminutive. The name has been popular throughout the British Isles in recent years, but in the past it was particularly associated with Scotland, no doubt in memory of Flora Macdonald (1722–90) who helped Bonny Prince Charlie escape. **Fleur**, the French word for 'flower', seems to have spread from its use by John Galsworthy in *The Forsyte Saga* series of novels, and it is said to have been more widely used after the successful TV version of the books, first shown in 1967. However, the similar Welsh form of the name, **Ffleur** or **Fflur**, has been in use since the mid-twelfth century. **Flower** and **Blossom**, the English translations of these names, are also found.

Florence

Florence Nightingale (1820–1910), who made Florence such a popular girl's name, was so named because she was born in the city of Florence. This city in its turn got its name from the Latin for 'to flower, flourish', so that the name really belongs with the FLORA group. In the Middle Ages Florence or **Florent** was quite a common name, but mainly a masculine one; as such it has long been obsolete except in Ireland, where it is said to be used to 'translate' FLANN. Florence is shortened to **Flo, Florrie, Flossie** and **Floy**.

Flower: see FLORA

Floyd: see LLOYD

Francis

In the fifth century a group of Germanic tribes who called themselves the Franks invaded and took over Romanized Gaul. From these rulers the country took its new name of France via the Latin Francia; and since only these people were fully free, the word **Frank** soon came to mean 'free', and in England **Franklin** was firstly a title given to a free landowner, then a surname which could also be used as a first name. In the twelfth century, when France already held an important cultural position, a young Italian called Giovanni Bernardone (*c.* 1181–1226) was considered by his contemporaries to be so Frenchified that he was given the nickname **Francesco** ('the little Frenchman'). It was in honour of this man, better known as St Francis of Assisi, that the name Francis became used in various forms throughout Europe. Frank is used as a short form of Francis as well as a name in its own right, as are **Fran, Francie** and **Frankie**. **Frances** is the feminine, which has **Fanny** as a pet form in addition to those used for Francis. The French **Francine** can also be found, while the Italian form **Francesca** [fran'cheskə] has now become quite popular.

Fraser, Frazer

These are variants of a Scottish surname of unknown meaning which are used as first names.

Fred, Freddy: see ALFRED, FREDERICK, WILFRED

Freda: see ALFRED, ELFRIDA, FREDERICK, WINIFRED

Frederick

This is a Germanic name meaning 'peaceful ruler'. Although it was used by the Normans, its modern use is due to its reintroduction by the Hanoverian rulers of Britain. It is sometimes spelt **Frederic** in the French fashion and is shortened to **Fred, Freddie** or **Freddy**, and more rarely to **Rick** and **Ricky**. **Frederica** is the usual feminine form of the name which shares the masculine short forms. In addition it has **Frieda**, a German spelling, and **Freda**, shared with ELFRIDA and WINIFRED, as short forms which are also used as independent names.

Freya

Freya was the name of the Norse goddess of fertility, so lovely that the Scandinavian myths are full of stories of plots made to win possession of her. She also had some of the attributes of the Valkyries, and fallen heroes were feasted in her palace in Asgard.

Frieda: see FREDERICK

Fulvia: see FLAVIA

G

Gabriel

In the Bible the archangel Gabriel ('strong man of God'), acts as God's messenger. It is he who announces to the Virgin Mary that she is to have a child. Although it is by no means common, it has a steady use as a man's name, but in recent years has been far more common in its feminine forms. **Gabrielle** is the French feminine, which has now been overtaken in popularity by the Italian **Gabriella**. Both sexes have **Gabi** and **Gabby** as short form, and the latter is sometimes further shortened to **Abby** (see ABIGAIL) for girls.

Gaenor: see JENNIFER

Gaia: see GEORGE

Gail, Gale, Gayle: see ABIGAIL

Gaius: see CAIUS

Galfrid: see GEOFREY

Gareth

The name of an Arthurian hero introduced by the fifteenth-century writer Sir Thomas Malory, Gareth is probably a corruption of the name of an earlier hero, but it has been linked with the Welsh word *gwared* ('gentle'), and is usually taken to mean that. **Gary** or **Garry** is often used as a pet form of this name, but Gary Cooper, the film star who made the name world-famous, took his stage name from his home town of Gary, Indiana. **Garth** is also sometimes thought of as a pet form of Gareth, but this too is an independent name, based on

101

a northern English word for an enclosure or small cultivated area.

Garfield

A surname used as a first name, Garfield probably came into use in honour of James Garfield (1831–81), the twentieth president of the United States. The surname is Old English and is usually interpreted as meaning 'field of spears', but the alternative of '(someone who lives by a) gore-shaped field' has been suggested. The cricketer Sir Garfield Sobers illustrates the use of **Garry** (see GARETH) as a pet form of Garfield.

Garmon: see GERMAINE

Garret, Garrett: see GERALD

Garry, Garth, Gary: see GARETH

Gaspar, Gaspard: see JASPER

Gavin

Gavin is the Scots form of the Arthurian hero Sir **Gawain**, which appears in early Welsh literature as Gwalchmai ('hawk of the plain'), a hawk being used as a symbol of a heroic warrior; but the name may come more directly from a form with *gwalch* ('hawk') + *(g)wyn* ('white'). This name became Gauvin in medieval French literature and was adopted as Gavin in Scotland, which in the Middle Ages had closer cultural ties with its ally France than with its enemy England. The use of the name was for a long time limited to those with Scottish connections, but the name has now spread throughout the English-speaking world.

Gay

With its alternative form **Gaye**, Gay is a modern name based on the vocabulary word. It has hardly been used since the general introduction of the word 'gay' as a synonym for 'homosexual' in the 1970s, and is unlikely to survive.

Gayle: see ABIGAIL

Gaynor: see JENNIFER

Gemma

This is an old Italian name, meaning 'gem'. The poet Dante's wife was Gemma Donati, but the most famous bearer of the name was St Gemma Galgani (1875–1903), a poor orphan who went into domestic service and suffered from ill-health all her short life, but who nevertheless experienced remarkable visions and showed on her body the marks of Christ's crucifixion. Her canonization in 1940 probably led to the steady rise in popularity of the name, either in its original form or in the spelling **Jemma**; it is now one of the most popular girl's names.

Gene: see EUGENE

Genevieve

Geneviève (*c.* 422–512) is the name of the patron saint of Paris. She was a young girl living with her grandmother in Paris, devoting her life to prayer and good works and vowed to eternal virginity, who nonetheless managed to play a prominent part in the affairs of the city. When it was threatened with attack by Attila the Hun she persuaded the citizens to stand fast, and when the expected attack failed to materialize this was put down to her prayers. When the city was later besieged by the Franks, it was Geneviève who led the convoy that broke the blockade and brought food to the starving citizens. **Ginette** and **Ginetta** are pet forms.

Geoffrey

This is a Germanic name which was very popular with the Normans. While the second half of the name is clearly from the word *frith* ('peace'), the meaning of the first half is not clear, and it seems likely that it represents the falling together of a number of different names. **Jeffrey** was an early variant. **Geoff** or **Jeff** are used as short forms. The name was sometimes written in the old Latin chronicles as Galfridus, and this led to a nineteenth-century pseudo-antique name **Galfrid**.

George

The name comes from the Greek word for a farmer, made up of the elements *ge* ('earth') from the same root as the name of the earth goddess **Gaia**, a name currently having a certain popularity with feminists, and *ergein* ('to work'). Despite St George's role as the patron saint of England from the fourteenth century onwards, the name was not in common use until the eighteenth century, with its four successive kings of that name. **Georgie** or **Georgy** is one short form; in the north we find **Geordie**, while the Scots are said to use **Dod** and **Doddy**. There are a number of feminine forms: **Georgia, Georgianna, Georgette** and **Georgina**, all of which use **Georgie** as a short form; Georgina is one source of **Gina**.

Geraint

Yet another name from Arthurian legend, Geraint was also in use in real life from a very early date, for a king of Cornwall of that name was killed in battle in AD 530. He may well be the original of the fictional character, for he was both noble and praised for his skill in battle. The name comes from the Latin (ultimately Greek) name **Gerontius** meaning 'old'.

Gerald

Gerald comes from a Germanic name made up of the elements 'spear + rule', by way of Norman French. It is shortened to **Gerry** or **Jerry** and **Ger**, and has the variants **Gerold, Gerrold** and **Geralt**. In the Middle Ages the name **Gerard** ('spear + brave'), was rather more popular than Gerald, and it is not always possible to distinguish the history of the two names. In Ireland the name Gerard developed into **Garret** or **Garrett** (see also JARED); these share the same short forms as Gerald. Ireland was also the source of the feminine form of Gerald, **Geraldine**. Prominent in the Norman invasion of Ireland was the FitzGerald ('sons of Gerald') family, also known collectively as the Geraldins, and it was a member of this family, Lady Elizabeth Fitzgerald, who was addressed in poetry by the sixteenth-century Earl of Surrey as 'The Fair Geraldine', thus creating a new name.

Gerda

Best known as the name of the girl in the fairytale 'The Snow Queen', Gerda was one of the Old Norse goddesses, the wife of Freyr the brother of FREYA, and like him a fertility deity.

Germaine

This name is probably best known from the Australian writer Germaine Greer, but it was in use particularly around the end of the last century. It was the name of the sixteenth-century St Germaine of Pibrac, a deformed child and a victim of what would now be called child abuse, who was nonetheless outstanding for her piety and about whom miracles were manifested both before and after her early death. Her canonization in 1867 gave a boost to the name. The masculine form, **German** or **Germain**, is rare in Great Britain, even though St Germanus of Auxerre (*c.* 378–448) is one of the few early saints associated with Britain. St Germanus was twice sent to Britain to counter the spread of the Pelagian heresy (see MORGAN), and is said to have won a notable victory on behalf of the British against the invading Picts and Scots. He arranged the troops in a strong and well-hidden position and on a given signal they all cried 'Alleluia!' The invaders are supposed to have been so taken by surprise that they fled without a blow being exchanged. 'The Alleluia victory', as it became known, was accounted a miracle. The name is found in Welsh in the form **Garmon**.

Geronimo: see JEROME

Gerontius: see GERAINT

Gerry: see GERALD

Gertrude
Gertrude is a Germanic name meaning 'strong spear'. It is thought that it was introduced from the Netherlands, where the seventh-century St Gertrude of Nivelles was widely venerated. She seems to have been remarkable more for being a capable and devout administrator of her abbey than anything else, but a large body of folklore grew up around her. Her emblem is a pastoral staff with a mouse running up it. The name's short forms are **Gert**, **Gertie** and **Trudy** or **Trudie**.

Gervase, Gervais
This was the name of a martyr of unknown date and history, whose remains were exhumed in Milan in 386 after a 'presentiment' by St Ambrose that they would be found. Despite his obscurity he was widely revered and his cult spread through western Europe. **Gervas**, **Jervis** and **Jarvis** are occasional variants and there is a feminine form **Gervaise**. The meaning of the name is obscure, but may come from the same root meaning 'spear' found in other 'Gar-' and 'Ger-' names.

Geunor: see JENNIFER

Ghislaine: see GISELLE

Gideon

A Hebrew name probably meaning 'having a stump for a hand', Gideon was the name of one of the great Old Testament leaders who liberated his people from the domination of their enemies. To help him the Lord manifested a number of signs, including a miracle when dew fell only on a fleece laid on the ground, and not on the earth, and vice versa. The fleece became the symbol of Gideon, which led in the Middle Ages to a curious association of Gideon and the classical hero JASON.

Gigi: see GILBERT

Gil: see GILBERT

Gilbert

Gilbert comes from Germanic words meaning 'pledge + bright'. **Gib**, at one time proverbial as the name for a cat, is probably now obsolete as a short form, but **Gil, Gillie** or **Gilly** (with a hard 'g') and **Bert** are still used. Gilbert is somewhat out of fashion at the moment, but it was a popular name in the Middle Ages, no doubt influenced by the fame of St Gilbert of Sempringham, the founder of the only specifically English religious order who died aged over one hundred in 1189. His order took a special interest in caring for orphans and lepers. There seems to be no English feminine of the name, but the French use Gilberte, which is the true name of the girl known as **Gigi** in Colette's novel. Gigi came into use as a first name after 1958, when a highly successful film was made of the musical based on the novel.

Giles

This name has come a long way from its original form of **Aegidius**, a Greek name derived from the word for the goat skin that this Athenian saint used to wear. He is said to have fled to France (where his name was shortened to Giles, now sometimes **Gyles**), in order to escape publicity, and to have become a hermit there. He became the patron saint of Edinburgh, and for a time **Aegidia** or **Egidia** was used as feminine form in Scotland.

Gill: see JULIA

Gilleasbuig, Gillespie: see ARCHIBALD

Gillian: see JULIA

Gina: see GEORGE, REX

Ginette, Ginetta: see GENEVIEVE

Ginny: see VIRGINIA

Giselle
This French form of a Germanic name, derived from a word for a hostage or pledge, can also be spelt **Gisèle**. The name **Ghislaine**, far more common in France than in England, seems to come from an Old French pet form of the name.

Gladys, Gwladys, Gwladus: see CLAUDIA

Glenn, Glen
This is the Celtic word for a valley; it is also spelt **Glynn** or **Glyn**, the first form being more obviously Scottish, the other Welsh. Glenn is predominantly a masculine name but is also used for women, along with the more obviously feminine **Glenna**. The feminine of Glynn is **Glynis** or **Glinys**.

Glenda
Glenda comes from the Welsh and is made up of words meaning 'holy, fair' and 'good'. **Glenys** comes from the same source, being *glan* ('holy, fair') plus a feminine ending. It is also spelt **Glenis** and **Glennis**. However, there is a rather grey area where the names listed under GLENN overlap with those coming from *glan*, and forms such as **Glinda** show how much the two groups of names have merged.

Glinys: see GLENN

Gloria
The Latin word for 'glory' used as a first name, Gloria seems, like CANDIDA, to have been introduced by Bernard Shaw, this time in his play *You Never Can Tell* (1898). However, **Gloriana** was well known as a poetic title given to Queen Elizabeth I, and this is occasionally used as a first name, sometimes transformed to look like a blend of Gloria and Anna in forms such as **Glorianna** and **Gloranna**.

Glyn, Glynn, Glynis: see GLENN

Godfrey

The Anglo-Saxons had a name **Godfrith** ('God + peace') but with the Norman Conquest this was more or less superseded by the Norman form of the same name, Godfrey. Nevertheless, some of the Old English names with 'God-' did survive, such as **Godric** ('God + rule'), the name of an Anglo-Saxon saint still used in his native East Anglia, and **Godwin** ('God + friend'), the name of the father of the last Saxon king of England, HAROLD.

Gordon

A Scottish surname, Gordon is derived from a place name possibly meaning 'spacious fort'. It seems to have become a first name only in the last century, used in honour of Gordon of Khartoum.

Goronwy

This Welsh name also occurs in such forms as **Gronwy**, **Gronw**, and **Grono**. The first part of the name means 'hero', but the second element is not understood.

Gotlieb: see THEODORE

Grace

Grace, one of the names introduced by the Puritans, is a word with strong Christian associations (see HOPE, FAITH, etc). It is very popular with parents at the moment, particularly as a second name. **Gracie**, made famous by the singer Gracie Fields, is a pet form.

Graham

This Scottish clan name used as a first name comes from Grantham in Lincolnshire, which is spelt 'Graham' in Domesday Book and probably means 'homestead on a gravel outcrop'. A William de Grantham was given lands in Scotland by King David I in the twelfth century, and thus the family name was transferred north of the Border. The name is also spelt **Grahame** and, increasingly, **Graeme**.

Grainne ['grahniə]

This is an Irish name which comes from the word for 'love'. In Irish legend Grainne eloped with DERMOT, one of the followers of her betrothed FINN MacCool. The English form is **Grania**.

108

Grant

Grant comes from a surname, in origin a nickname from the French *le grant*, given to a tall person. Its popularity in the United States may owe something to General Ulysses S. Grant (1822–85), eighteenth president of the country.

Granville

With its variants **Grenville** and **Greville**, this was originally a surname for someone coming from Granville ('large town') in Normandy.

Gregory

This is actually a Greek name meaning 'to be awake' or 'watchful', but since the Latin form of the name, Gregorius, was the more familiar, it was often interpreted as if from this language. Thus Caxton's translation (1483) of *The Golden Legend* tells us, in the life of Gregory the Pope – the man who made the name famous and was responsible for the conversion of the Anglo-Saxons – 'Gregory is of [the Latin] Grex, which is to say a flock; and of gore, which is to say a preacher. Then Gregory is to say as a preacher to an assembly or flock of people'. Its commonest short form is **Greg**. There is a Scots form **Gregor**.

Grenville, Greville: see GRANVILLE

Greta, Gretchen, Gretel, Grethel: see MARGARET

Griffith

Griffith, with its alternative forms **Gruffydd** and **Gruffudd** and derivative **Griffin** are all forms of an early Welsh name used by a number of the independent Welsh princes. Its meaning is uncertain, but it probably means 'lord' or 'strong warrior'. **Griff** is a common short form.

Griselda

A Germanic name, Griselda means 'grey battle-maiden', an inappropriate meaning for a name which has become inextricably associated with the word 'patient' after Chaucer's account of the long suffering wife in 'The Clerk's Tale'. In Scotland the name can take the form **Grizel** (or **Grizzel**, **Grissel**, **Grisell**), but much more fashionable is the short form **Zelda**, the name of the writer F. Scott Fitzgerald's wife.

Grono, Gronw, Gronwy: see GORONWY

Gruffydd, Gruffudd: see GRIFFITH

Gudrun

Gudrun is a common name in Norse saga and German epic. One character of that name is very important in the stories that Wagner used in the *Ring Cycle*, and another Gudrun is central to the thirteenth-century *Laxdale Saga*, one of the best of the Icelandic sagas. In England the name is probably best known from Gudrun Brangwen, one of the main characters in D.H. Lawrence's *Women in Love* (1920). The name is made up of elements meaning 'God' or 'good' + 'rune, wisdom'.

Guenevere, Guinevere: see JENNIFER

Gus, Gussie: see AUGUSTINE

Guy

The old Germanic form of Guy is Wido, a name of uncertain origin, possibly meaning either 'wide' or 'wood'. There was a tenth-century Belgian saint of this name about whom very little is known, but who appears to have taken to the life of a wandering pilgrim after becoming a bankrupt. The name became all but impossible to use after the capture of Guy Fawkes, but was revived again in the nineteenth century. It continued to be popular well into this century, but does not seem to be much used at the moment.

Gwen

Gwen is a Welsh feminine name element, a form of the word *gwyn* meaning 'white, fair, blessed'. It has been used as a name in its own right since the fifth century, is either the first element or the final one in many Welsh names, and a short form of many such names. The most common of the compound names is **Gwendolen** (also spelt **Gwendolyn, Gwendolyne, Gwendoline, Guendolen**), the second element of which means 'bow' and 'ring'. The name may have been that of an ancient moon-goddess, and is traditionally the name of Merlin's mother. (See also SABRINA.) **Gwenda** is a combination of 'gwen' and the word for 'good', although it is also used as a short form of Gwendolen. **Gwenfrewi** ('gwen' + 'reconciliation') was the name of the seventh-century saint known in English as WINIFRED. **Gwenfron** ('white breast') is the reversed form of the name BRONWEN; **Gwenhwyfar** is the Welsh source for JENNIFER; while **Gwenllian** (rarely, **Gwenlian**) means 'fair and flaxen' and was in use in twelfth-century princely houses. **Gweno** is the Welsh form of JUNO and with **Gwennie** is used as a pet form of all these names. **Gwyn** is the masculine form of the name, which is anglicized to **Wyn** or **Wynn**. It also has many compounds, the best known of which is **Gwynfor** ('gwyn' + 'great'), anglicized as **Wynford**.

Gwil, Gwillym, Gwilym: see WILLIAM

Gwl-: see GL-

Gwyn: see GWEN

Gwyneth
Although often associated with the names in the GWEN group, Gwyneth probably comes from the Welsh for 'bliss, happiness'.

Gwynfor: see GWEN

Gwythyr: see VICTORIA

Gyles: see GILES

Hadrian: see ADRIAN

Haidee: see HEIDI

Hailey: see HAYLEY

Hal: see HAROLD, HENRY

Hamish: see JAMES

Hank: see HENRY

Hannah: see ANN

Hannibal

This is a Phoenician man's name, meaning 'mercy of Baal'. It is said to have been particularly used in Cornwall, which has traditional, but unproved, links with Phoenician traders. The historical Hannibal was a third-century BC Carthaginian whose father brought him up from childhood to hate Rome. As an adult Hannibal invaded Italy via the Alps, and for many years ravaged the country and almost brought about the destruction of Rome, but was finally defeated more by force of circumstances than by superior skill. (See also FABIAN.)

Harold

Harold is the name of the last king of England before the Norman invasion; he was part Danish, and bore a Scandinavian-influenced name. Harold is a typical Germanic compound made up of elements meaning 'army' and 'power'. It died out after the Norman Conquest, but was revived along with other Old English names in the nineteenth century. **Hal** is sometimes used as a short form.

Harriet, Harrison, Harry: see HENRY

Harvey
This is a form of the French name Hervé, a Breton saint. Little is known about the saint's life, although according to the somewhat fantastical legends about him, he was a wandering monk and minstrel. Until the French Revolution a Breton church kept his supposed cradle as an object of veneration. The Normans brought the name over to this country.

Hatty: see HENRY

Havelock: see OLIVER

Hayden, Haydn: see AIDAN

Hayley, Hailey
Hayley is a surname meaning 'hay field' and is used as a first name. It owes its currency to the film actress Hayley Mills, who was named after her mother, Mary Hayley Bell. The name caught the public's attention and has been popular throughout the English-speaking world.

Hazel
Hazel seems to have been little used as a first name before the end of the last century, when plant names in general became very popular.

Heather
Like HAZEL, Heather seems to have come into fashion in the late nineteenth century along with a number of other plant names.

Hebe ['heebee]
In Classical Greek mythology Hebe was the goddess of youth, which is the meaning of her name, and cupbearer to the gods. Fairly popular in the last century, the name is rarely used now. As it is the name of a genus of plants, it may sometimes be thought of as one of the flower names.

Hector

Hector was the great warrior of Troy who, until he was killed in battle by the Greek hero **Achilles**, was the chief defender of the city in the Trojan war. It is therefore appropriate that his name means 'holding fast', which should probably be understood as 'defender, support'. It can be shortened to **Heck**. The name has been particularly popular in Scotland, where it was used as an anglicization of the Gaelic name **Eachann**, which means 'lord of horses'. Since the Trojan Hector is depicted by HOMER as fighting from a horse-drawn chariot, this, as much as similarity of sounds, may lie behind the association of the two names.

Hedda, Hedy, Hedewig, Hedwige: see AVICE

Hedley

A man's name, Hedley comes from a place and surname meaning 'a clearing where HEATHER grows'. It was popular around the turn of the century, but is now little used.

Heidi, Haidee

These are two distinct girl's names, although they may sometimes be used as variants. The first is Austrian, the second Greek: both owe their use to literary sources. Heidi, the more common of the two names, owes its introduction to the popularity of Johanna Spyri's book *Heidi*. It is a pet form of the name, **Adelheid**, the German form of Adelaide (see ADELA). **Haidee** is probably a form of the Greek name Haido ('to caress') and came into fashion after its introduction by Lord Byron in *Don Juan* (1819). In this poem the adolescent Juan and Haidee fall deeply in love, and the depiction of combined innocence and passion forms some of Byron's most memorable writing.

Helen

Like HECTOR, Helen is a name from Homer's *Iliad*. Helen, the wife of the Greek king Menelaus, was the most beautiful woman alive, and her abduction by the Trojan prince **Paris**, led to the long siege of Troy described in Homer's epic. The name means 'the light, the bright'. However, the popularity of the name throughout Europe probably owes more to St Helen or **Helena**, empress and supposed finder of the True Cross. Tradition makes her a British princess, but in fact she was born in Asia Minor of humble parents. There are many variants and short forms. **Ellen**, sometimes ELAINE, and **Elena** are early forms of the name, the last giving **Lena**. These are now used

114

independently. **Nell, Nellie, Nelly** are pet forms. In Ireland **Eileen** or **Aileen** is considered a form of the name, although it may come from EVELYN. (The Irish spelling is **Eibhlin**, and this is generally pronounced [ie'leen], but in some parts of the country [ev'leen]). **Ilona**, sometimes found in this country, is a Hungarian form of the name, as is **Ilana**. See further under ELEANOR.

Helga: see OLGA

Heloise

Abelard and Heloise were two twelfth-century lovers whose real-life story, preserved in the letters they wrote to each other after they were parted, rivals anything to be met with in fiction. Despite the fact that Abelard had secretly married Heloise, he was castrated by her guardian for having seduced her, and they each ended their lives as the heads of learned religious institutions, only to be reunited in death, when Heloise's body was buried next to Abelard's grave. Heloise is also spelt **Héloïse**, and is often found in the form **Eloise** or **Eloïse**, or more rarely **Eloïsa**. The origin of the name is disputed. Some derive it from an old German name, **Helewise**, used in England until at least the thirteenth century; others argue that it is a form of the name Louise (see LEWIS), via the Provençal form **Aloys, Aloyse**, which may also have been an influence on LOIS.

Henry, Henrietta

Henry comes from an old Germanic name meaning 'home-rule'. It was brought to England by the Normans in the French form Henri, and the French pronunciation is reflected in **Harry**, which was the normal English form of the name until the seventeenth century. This use, and the pet-form **Hal**, are well illustrated in Shakespeare's *Henry V*. **Hank** is a pet form more often met with in North America. **Harrison**, the surname meaning 'son of Harry', has shown a recent increase in popularity as a first name.

The feminine forms of the name do not see to have been used until after the marriage in 1625 of Charles I to the French princess **Henriette** Marie, who became known in this country as **Henrietta** Maria. These names were soon anglicized to **Harriet**, and developed the short forms **Hatty, Hattie, Hetty** and **Etta**.

Hephzibah

This is a Hebrew name meaning 'my delight is in her'. In the Bible it is mentioned as the name of the mother of one of the kings of Judah, but more importantly is used by the prophet Isaiah as a symbol of Jerusalem. The name is more often found in the United States than in Britain, as is the name **Beulah** ('married'), which occurs in the same verse of Isaiah. The name is usually pronounced, and sometimes spelt **Hepzibah**, and has a short form **Hepsie**. It is probably best known in this country through the pianist Hephzibah Menuhin.

Herbert

A Germanic name meaning 'army-bright', Herbert is found very early in the form of Charibert, who was King of the Franks from 561–67. His daughter BERTHA married the pagan king of Kent, and it was she who welcomed St Augustine of Canterbury to convert the English (see AUGUSTUS). The name more or less died out in the Middle Ages, but was revived again in the nineteenth century, possibly in connection with the aristocratic surname of Herbert. It shares **Bert** and **Bertie** as short forms with other names ending -bert, and **Herb** and **Herbie** are also used.

Herman

This is a Germanic name meaning 'army man', and is sometimes spelt in the German manner, **Hermann**. The French form of the name is **Armand**, and from this come the unusual feminine names **Armine** and **Arminel**, the latter regarded as a local name in Devon. **Hermine**, another unusual feminine name, also found as **Ermin, Ermine** or **Erminia**, comes from the same Indo-European root, but via the Latin family name of Herminius, although it has no doubt been influenced by the Germanic forms.

Hermione [her'mieonee]

Hermione is a Greek name, meaning 'dedicated to the god Hermes'. The best-known Hermione in Greek legend was the daughter of HELEN; she was first unhappily married to Achilles' son Neoptolemus, and then to her cousin Orestes. The Athenian tragedian Euripides wrote a play on the subject, and the name probably became more widely known in the seventeenth-century through the French playwright Racine's *Andromaque* (1667), which adapted Euripides' work. In the twentieth century the name has been given publicity by two comic actresses Hermione Baddeley and Hermione Gingold. Shakespeare used Hermione in *A Winter's Tale* and he introduced another form of the name, **Hermia**, in *A Midsummer Night's Dream*, but this name has found little favour.

Hester: see ESTHER

Hetty: see ESTHER, HENRY

Hew: see HUGH

Hieronymus: see JEROME

Hilary

Hilary means cheerful and was the name of St Hilary of Poitiers, a theologian and writer of the fourth century. Since his feast day falls in mid-January, his name was given to the 'Hilary Term' of the Law Courts and some universities, which begins at about that time. The name is used for both sexes, although there is also an uncommon feminine form, **Hilaria**. The author **Hilaire** Belloc (1870–1953) shows the French masculine form of the name.

Hilda

An Old English name meaning 'battle', Hilda was the name of a Northumbrian princess who founded the monastery at Whitby where the seventh-century cowherd **Caedmon** is supposed to have written the first religious poetry in English. Hilda was a much respected woman who acted as an adviser to kings and bishops. The name died out after the Conquest along with other Anglo-Saxon names, but was revived in the nineteenth century. It is occasionally spelt **Hylda**. From the same root comes the German saint's name **Hildegard**. There has recently been a revival of interest in the work of St Hildegard of Bingen (1098–1179), who was a visionary, theologian, writer on science, poet and very fine composer, and took an active part in the controversies of her day. This name has always been more common in the United States, particularly among those of German descent, than in Great Britain.

Hiram

Hiram is a Hebrew name meaning 'brother of the exalted one'. It was the name of a king of Tyre who was an ally of King DAVID and his son SOLOMON, and who sent building materials for the Temple at Jerusalem. It was one of the biblical names which became popular in the seventeenth century, was taken over by early settlers to America, and also had a certain popularity in the nineteenth century.

Hodge: see ROGER

Holly

This is a plant name which has been in use only since the beginning of this century.

Homer

This is the name of the great Greek poet used as a first name. It is rarely found in this country, but is well-used in the United States, where there is a long tradition of naming after heroes of the past. The British have not been reluctant to name their children after classical writers such as HORACE and TERENCE, but for some reason Homer has never caught on.

Honoria

This name means 'honour, honourable'. Honorius was a title given to the Emperor Theodosius the Great, and his niece was named Honoria. The name is also found in the forms **Honor** and **Honora**. In England a form **Anora, Annora** or **Anorah** developed, while in Ireland, where the name was particularly popular, it became NORAH. In Welsh the masculine form of the name developed into **Emyr** and **Ynyr**.

Hope

One of the abstract nouns that were introduced as names by the Puritans, Hope was originally used for both sexes but is now confined to women. NADIA has the same meaning.

Horace

Horace is the name of the first century BC Latin poet, used as a first name. It was introduced during the Renaissance revival of interest in all things classical. In the form **Horatio** it was the name of Admiral Nelson but, surprisingly, even his fame did not make this form widely used. However, **Horatia**, the name given to his daughter by Lady Hamilton, and also used for his god-daughters, did have a certain vogue.

Hortensia

This is the feminine form of a Latin family name meaning 'gardener'. **Hortense** is widely used in France, and the name has sometimes been used in Britain in this form.

Howard

The aristocratic surname Howard was one of many adopted by parents as a first name in the nineteenth century. The origin of the surname is confused. In some cases it may be a form of the occupational term 'hayward', a man whose job it was to make sure that the hedges were kept cattle-proof; in others it may be an old Germanic name meaning 'heart-protector'.

Howel, Howell: see HYWEL

Hubert

Hubert comes from a Germanic root and means 'bright-mind'. It is the name of an eighth-century saint who is the patron of hunters, having, according to his legend, been converted to the devout life as a young man by a vision of a stag with a crucifix between its antlers. The stag is his emblem in art. (See also EUSTACE.)

Hugh

Hugh comes from the Germanic world for 'mind' or 'thought' and was introduced by the Normans. The city of Lincoln can boast two St Hughs. One (c. 1135–1200) was a remarkable bishop of Lincoln, famous as much for his bold fights for justice for the common man as for his pet swan, which was reputed to be so fierce that no one else could come near him, but which was so affectionate towards Hugh that it would nestle with its head up his sleeve. The other, 'Little St Hugh', is probably apocryphal, and the sensational story of his 'martyrdom' at the hands of the local Jews was used as an excuse for much anti-Semitism. **Hew** and **Huw** are Welsh forms of the name, and the Latin form **Hugo** is not uncommon. Pet forms are **Hughie, Huey** and **Hughy**. The Irish name **Ulick** may well come from the same source – from the Viking name Hugleik ('mind + reward'), although it has also been explained as a pet form of Uilliam, the Irish form of WILLIAM. In Ireland Ulick is sometimes anglicized as ULYSSES.

Humphrey

This is another Germanic name popularized by the Normans. The meaning of the first element of the name is uncertain, but the second element means 'peace'. **Humph** and **Hump** are used as short forms. **Humbert** is thought to come from the same unknown root as Humphrey, its second element meaning 'bright'.

Hunter

An occupational surname used as a first name, Hunter seems to have come into use first in Scotland.

Huw: see HUGH

Hyacinth: see IRIS

Hylda: see HILDA

Hywel [howəl]

This name is Welsh and means 'conspicuous, eminent'. It is also spelt **Howel** or **Howell**. Its pet form is **Hywyn** and there is a feminine **Hywela**. It is found as early as the ninth century, and King **Hoel** of Brittany, King Arthur's relative and ally in the legends, is probably the same name. It has become well-known to the general public through the actor Hywel Bennett.

I

Iago: see JAMES

Iain, Ian: see JOHN

Ianthe: see VIOLET

Ianto: see JAMES

Ib, Ibby: see ISABEL

Ida

Ida is a girl's name which was very popular in the nineteenth century and the first half of this one, as part of the revival of medieval names. Tennyson used it as the name of the heroine of his poem mocking female pretensions to education, 'The Princess' (1847), and the name was given further currency by the adaptation of this work by Gilbert and Sullivan as *Princess Ida* (1870). It is a Germanic name, but its meaning is obscure. It probably has some connection with a word meaning 'work'. In Ireland, in the forms Ida, **Ita** or **Ide**, it comes from the Erse word for 'thirst', the name of a sixth-century Irish saint renowned for her austerity.

Idonea [ie'dohneeə]

This unusual name is associated with the north of England. It has been suggested that it comes from a Latin adjective meaning 'fit, suitable' but, since the name is not used in countries where the language is descended from Latin, this seems unlikely. A much more attractive idea is that it is a form of the name of the Norse goddess Iduna, the guardian of the Apples of Youth, the eating of which kept the gods young. When she was abducted by the giants, the gods experienced the effects of age for the first time,

121

although their youth was restored when they won her and the apples back.

Idris ['idris]

This is one of the more popular Welsh names, with a long history. The name, meaning 'ardent or impulsive lord', was held by Idris the Giant who was killed in 632. He has entered Welsh legend as an astronomer and magician, and one of the highest mountains in Wales, Cader Idris ('Idris's Chair'), was supposed to have been his observatory. From the same root comes **Idwal** [idwəl] ('lord + rampart') probably signifying 'defender', another ancient name, having been held by two tenth-century kings of Gwynedd.

Iestin, Iestyn: see JUSTIN

Ieuan, Ifan: see JOHN

Ifor: see IVO

Ignatius

This old Latin name means 'fiery', but its use is almost entirely in association with the Spanish saint Ignatius Loyola, who founded the Jesuit order in the sixteenth century. The Spanish form of the name is Inigo, and this was the form given to the Catholic architect **Inigo** Jones (1573–1652). Jones' associations with Wales has led to Inigo being claimed and used as a Welsh name.

Ike: see ISAAC

Ilana: see HELEN

Illtyd, Illtud [ihltid]

St Illtyd was an outstanding Welsh saint of the fifth to sixth centuries, famous as a scholar and teacher, the founder of a school where numerous other Welsh saints studied. Legend credits him with introducing the plough to the Welsh, who hitherto had only used spades to turn the soil.

Ilona: see HELEN

Ilsa, Ilse: see ELIZABETH

Imelda

The name of a medieval saint, Imelda is the Italian form of the Germanic name **Irmhild** meaning 'universal battle'. It has never been a common name, and has no doubt suffered recently from the notoriety of Imelda Marcos.

Immanuel: see EMMANUEL

Imogen

The heroine of Shakespeare's *Cymbeline* owes her name to a misprint. The name first seems to appear in the eleventh-century *History of the Kings of Britain* by Geoffrey of Monmouth as Ignoge, wife of Brutus, the mythical first king of Britain. She re-appears in Spenser's *Faerie Queene* as 'fayre Inogene of Italy'. Shakespeare seems to have used the 'n' spelling, for in a contemporary description of the play the name is spelt Innogen, but the form Imogen is found in the First Folio, the earliest printed text of the play. Despite the fact that Imogen is one of the most attractive of Shakespeare's heroines, the name has not been particularly popular, although recently there have been signs of an increased interest in it. The form **Imogene** is occasionally found.

Ina [eenə, inə]

This was originally a pet form of various names ending in -ina, such as Georgina, Edwina, etc., which has since come to be used as a name in its own right. In Ireland it is the name of two saints, and probably represents a local form of the name AGNES.

India

This is simply the name of the country used as a girl's name. It has been quite popular in the United States in recent years, and is now coming into use in this country. It may owe its use to the appearance of a character of that name in Margaret Mitchell's *Gone With the Wind* (1936), but its spread may also be connected with the interest in India and its culture of the hippy generation of the 1970s. **China** is similarly recorded as a girl's name.

Ines, Inez: see AGNES

Ingrid

Ingrid is a Scandinavian name with connections with the pagan past. Ing was a Scandinavian god of peace and plenty, known also to the Anglo-Saxons. Ingrid has been explained in two ways: either it means 'Ing's ride or steed', probably a reference to the sacred golden boar associated with the god, or else it means 'beautiful under the protection of Ing'. The fame of the actress Ingrid Bergman undoubtedly played a large part in turning this into an international name. **Ingeborg** and its diminutives **Inge** and **Inga** (also used for Ingrid) come for the same root and mean 'Ing's protection'.

Inigo: see IGNATIUS

Innes: see ANGUS

Ioan: see JOHN

Iolanthe: see VIOLET

Iolo ['yohloh]
This is the more widely used pet form of the Welsh name **Iorwerth**, formed from elements meaning 'lord' and 'value, worth'. For some reason it has been used in the past as the Welsh equivalent of Edward, although there is no known connection between the names. There is a less common feminine form **Iola**.

Iona

The Hebridean island of Iona was already an ancient religious site when St Columba (see under MALCOLM) settled there in 563 and founded its monastery, which formed a base for the spread of Christianity through Scotland and the north of England. The island is still an important religious centre as well as a popular place to visit for its beauty and ancient ruins, so it is not surprising that a place name with so many associations, and with a form that fits in so well with other female names, should have come into use. It is first found in Scotland, and its spread south over the past 30 years may have been helped by Iona Opie, the expert on children's games and literature. Attempts have been made to link the name with other names beginning 'Ion-' from the Greek root meaning VIOLET; but, although these may have helped in the acceptance of the name, the island seems a much more likely source. Its name, despite its romantic history, is merely a Latinate form of the Irish word for 'island'.

Ione: see VIOLET

Iorwerth: see IOLO

Ira

A Hebrew name meaning 'watchful', Ira is found in the Bible as the name of one of King David's priests. It is little used in this country, possibly because it is so easily mistaken for a feminine name, but is a part of the Puritan heritage of biblical names in the United States. The best-known modern holder is probably Ira Gershwin, lyricist to so many of his brother George's best tunes.

Irene [ie'reenee, ie'reen]

The three-syllable pronunciation of this name comes from the original Greek, where the word means 'peace'; the shorter form is a modern pronunciation based on the spelling. Irene was the name of an early fourth-century martyr, whose legend, probably embroidered, tells of her being confined, but unmolested, in a brothel before being burnt. It was also the name of a number of Byzantine empresses, one of which in the eighth century managed to reign in her own right, even though holding on to the throne meant putting out the eyes of her son. The name is also spelt **Eirene**, while **Irena** reflects the Slavic form. **Renie** is a pet form.

Iris

In Greek mythology Iris is a goddess who acts as messenger for the gods. She uses the rainbow as her bridge between the heavens and earth. It is from the colours of this rainbow that the flower gets its name. The Romans used the name **Hyacinth** for what we would call an iris. In myth Hyacinth was the name of a particularly beautiful boy, accidentally killed by the god Apollo, and then transformed into a flower. It has been used as a boy's name in the past, but very rarely nowadays. It is, however, sometimes used as one of the flower names for girls. In France and Spain Hyacinth became **Jacinthe** and **Jacintha** (with **Jacinth** and **Jacinta** as variants); these too, were originally boy's names, but are now mainly feminine. These names are rare in England, but are sometimes found in Ireland.

Irma, Irm(e)gard: see EMMA

Irving

This Scottish surname comes from the place and river name meaning 'west river'. It is also found in the forms **Irvin** and **Irvine**. The very similar-sounding **Irwin** or **Erwin** technically come from a different root, an Anglo-Saxon name meaning 'boar-friend' (and hence are possibly linked to the sacred role of the boar mentioned under INGRID), but in practice the two names are often treated as variants of each other.

Isa: see ISABELLA

Isaac, Izaac

We are told in the Old Testament that when Abraham was 100 years old, and his wife Sarah was ninety, God told him that they would have a son. Abraham's reaction to the idea of having a child at their age was to laugh, and when a son was born he was named Isaac, which is Hebrew for 'he laughed'. In Britain the name has tended to be associated with the Jewish community, but in the United States it has been more widely used, and there has been something of a revival of the name in its pet form, **Zac**. **Ike** is another pet form, but the use of Ike as a nickname for President Eisenhower is unconnected with the name Isaac. The seventeenth-century fishing enthusiast, **Izaak** Walton, author of *The Compleat Angler* (1653), illustrates the other spelling of the name.

Isabel, Isobel

This name properly belongs with ELIZABETH, with which it was interchangeable from the twelfth until at least the sixteenth centuries. Short forms are **Bel, Bell, Belle, Ella** and **Izzy**. In France the name, often in the forms **Isabelle** or **Isabeau**, all but replaced Elizabeth, while **Isabella** was the form adopted in Spain. The Old Alliance of France and Scotland against the English may have helped Isabel become particularly popular in Scotland, where it developed a wide variety of pet forms including **Ib, Ibby, Isa, Belag, Tib, Tibbie** and **Tibby**. In Gaelic the name became **Iseabel**, from which comes the form **Ishbel**, and which led to such wild variations as Easabell, Easybell and Eysie.

Isadora, Isadore: see ISIDORE

Isaiah

This is a Hebrew name meaning 'salvation of the Lord', and the name of one of the great prophets of the Old Testament. Although it is not frequently used, it is kept before the public by such holders as Sir Isaiah Berlin.

Iseabel: see ISABEL

Iseult: see ISOLDA

Ishbel: see ISABEL

Isidore, Isidora

This ancient Greek name has been variously interpreted as meaning 'gift of Isis' or, more convincingly 'gift of strength'. It is a name particularly associated with Spain, where one of its early holders, St Isidore of Seville (*c.* 560–636), wrote one of the first ever encyclopaedias – a fascinating combination of knowledge from the classical world, some of which would otherwise have been lost, and arrant nonsense – which formed the basis of much medieval learning. **Isodor** and **Isadore** are variants of the masculine form of the name, and it is shortened to **Izzy**. **Isadora** Duncan made the alternative spelling of the female form widely known through her innovative dancing and scandalous personal life.

Isla ['ielə]

Isla is a Scottish river name that means 'swiftly flowing'. Originally confined to Scotland, it has become more widely known through the television appearances of Isla St Clair.

Isleen: see ASHLING

Isobel: see ISABEL

Isodor: see ISIDORE

Isolda

This name occurs in numerous different spellings and forms, including **Iseult, Isold, Isolde, Isolt, Ysold, Ysolda, Ysolde, Yseult, Yseut** with **Esyllt** as the Welsh form; the variety reflecting the fame of the name through Europe. Its exact meaning has been much debated without any convincing result. In the medieval love-tragedy of *Tristan and Isolda* she is the heroine torn between her duties as a wife and queen and her unquenchable love for TRISTAN brought about by the accidental drinking of a love potion. Thus she becomes a symbol of undying and unhappy love. The name was popular until the sixteenth century, then went into a decline until a mild revival from the end of the nineteenth, due in part to Celtic nationalism and in part to the success of Wagner's opera. (See also BRONWEN.)

Ivan, Iwan: see JOHN

Ivor, Ivo, Ifor

This is a confused and confusing group of names. Strictly speaking Ivor is interpreted as a Teutonic name probably connected with the god Ing (see under INGRID), Ivo is the Latinate form of Yves (see under YVONNE) and Ifor is the Welsh for 'lord'. However, these three names have become inextricably tangled, each influencing the other from an early date, and it is not possible to draw any hard lines between them.

Ivy

Ivy is one of the plant names introduced in the nineteenth century, but not much used today. Its introduction may have been helped by a feeling that there was a gap left by there being no female equivalent of the Ivor group of names, although there is a rarely found **Iva**, which may be a feminine of IVOR or of Ivan (see JOHN).

Izaac: see ISAAC

Izzy: see ISABEL, ISIDORE

J

Jabez

According to the Old Testament Jabez was so called by his mother 'because I bare him with sorrow'. He is a minor character in the Bible, with a reputation for being an honourable man.

Jacalyn: see JAMES

Jacinta, Jacinth, Jacintha, Jacinthe: see IRIS

Jack: see JOHN

Jackeline, Jackelyn: see JAMES

Jackie, Jacky: see JAMES, JOHN

Jacquetta, Jacqui: see JAMES

Jacob

This may go back to an ancient Babylonian name meaning 'God rewards'; but it is understood in the Bible to mean 'supplanter', from the story that Jacob got his elder twin brother Esau to sell him his birthright for 'a mess of pottage'. **Jake**, which has recently become more popular than its original, is a pet form, which is found as **Jaikie** in Scotland. There is a rare feminine **Jacoba**; and the form **Jacobina** was in the past a popular name for the daughters of Scottish Jacobites. JAMES is a form of the same name.

Jacqueline, Jacques: see JAMES

Jade

Although there is a long tradition of using jewels as girls' names in this country, this one seems to have been in use only in the last 30 or so years. It may have been popularized by its use by the singer Mick Jagger for his first daughter. (See further under JEWELL.)

Jago: see JAMES

Jaikie: see JACOB

Jake: see JACOB, JESSE

James

In Latin the name JACOB occurs in two forms: *Jacobus*, from which we get Jacob, and *Jacomus*, from which we get James. The two forms have proved useful for distinguishing the Old Testament patriach Jacob from the New Testament saints St James the Less, the brother of Jesus, and St James the Great, the son of ZEBEDEE. The shrine of St James the Great at Santiago de Compostella in Spain was one of the most popular places of pilgrimage throughout the Middle Ages, and this has resulted in James, in its various forms, being one of the most widely-spread names in western Europe. In the British Isles it occurs as **Hamish** in Scotland; **Shamus** or **Seamus** in Ireland, with the form **Seumus**, or less commonly **Seumas**, popular with Scots Gaelic speakers; as **Iago** with its pet form **Ianto**, ['yahgoh, 'yantoh] in Wales; and **Jago** in Cornwall. **Jim, (Jimmie, Jimmy)** and **Jamie** are the commonest pet forms of James, while **Jem** and **Jemmie** were common in the past.

The name has also been productive of feminine forms, although these are mostly derived from the French form of James, **Jacques**. **Jacqueline** is the most usual one; it is found in a very wide variety of spellings including **Jackeline, Jackelyn, Jacalyn, Jaqueline**, and shortened to **Jackie, Jacky, Jacqui**, etc. **Jacquetta** is another form of the name, known in this country since at least the fifteenth century when Jacquetta of Luxemburg was bigamously married to Humphrey, Duke of Gloucester, then *de facto* ruler of England, as part of her long, brave, but ultimately unsuccessful attempt to inherit her duchy in her own right rather than have it pass to a distant male relative. By yet another marriage she was grandmother to the princes in the Tower. Shakespeare uses a further form of the name, **Jacquenetta**, in *Love's Labour's Lost*, but this has never really caught on. From the male form of the name comes the Scottish **Jamesina**, while since the 1960s **Jamie** has been popular as a girl's name, particularly in the United States.

Jamilla
This is an Arabic woman's name which is sometimes used by American Muslims. The form **Djamila** is more usual on the continent. It means 'beautiful'.

Jan: see JOHN, JANE

Jane, Jean, Joan
This large group of names represents feminine forms of the name JOHN, the first two coming from the early French form 'Jehane', the third from the Latin 'Johanna'. All three have developed a large number of variants and pet forms. **Joan** seems to have been the earliest form of the name. It gives us the forms nearer to its Latin root, such as **Johanna** and **Joanna**; it is sometimes spelt **Joanne** and has the pet form **Joanie**. **Jane** seems to have come into use in the fifteenth century and developed into **Janet, Janette, Janetta**, with pet forms **Netta** and **Nettie**. In this century many variants have become popular, such as **Janine** and **Janina, Janice** and **Janis, Jana** (particularly in Ireland), **Jan, Janelle**, and **Jancis**, which was made better known through its use for a character in Mary Webb's highly successful novel *Precious Bane* (1924). Pet forms include **Janie, Janey, Jen** and **Jenny** (see also JENNIFER), and the name is also spelt **Jayne**. **Jean** started life as the Scottish form of Jane or Joan, and has given rise under French influence to **Jeanette** or **Jeanet** and **Janetta**. **Jeannie** is the usual pet form, but in Scotland **Jess, Jessie, Jessy** (see also JESSICA) are used, as well as **Jinty, Janny, Jancey** and **Jinsie**. The Spanish form of the name **Juanita** [hwa'neetə], its pet form **Nita** and **Juana** are occasionally found in England, but are more common in the United States.

The Celtic languages have also adopted this group of names, giving us **Sian (Sîan, Siwan)** [shahn] in Welsh, with pet forms **Siani** or **Shani; Sheena** (also spelt **Sine**) with its variant **Shona**, in Gaelic for Jane; and **Sinead** [shi'nayəd] as the Irish, **Seonaid** as the Scottish Gaelic forms of Janet, and **Siobhan** [shi'vawn] for Joan.

Jared
In the book of Genesis Jared is the father of ENOCH, but the only information we are given about him is that he lived for 962 years. The name probably means 'a rose' and is therefore unusual in being a masculine flower name. It was used by the Puritans, but then went into decline and was only occasionally used until a revival in the 1960s. In recent years it has become very popular in the United States and Australia. **Jarrad, Jareth, Jarrath, Jered** are

variants, with the forms **Jarett** and **Jarrod** also being used, although technically these come from surnames derived from Garret (see GERALD).

Jarvis: see GERVASE

Jasmine

One of the flower names, also spelt **Jasmin**; the eastern forms **Yasmin** and **Yasmine** are also sometimes used. **Jessamy** is an old form of the word, which was once synonymous with a fop; and **Jessamine**, with a pet form **Jess**, were also found.

Jason

Jason is the Greek form given to the Hebrew JOSHUA. There are at least four Jasons in the Bible, it is also the name of the reputed author of the Old Testament book of *Ecclesiasticus*, so that when it was adopted in the seventeenth century it was thought of as a biblical name. However, it is highly unlikely that when the name came back into fashion in the 1960s, parents associated the name with anyone from the past other than the hero of Greek myth, leader of the Argonauts and winner of the Golden Fleece. The name means 'healer'.

Jasper

This is the English form of the traditional name of one of the three Magi (the others being **Balthazar**, which is very occasionally found, and **Melchior**), and as such appropriately comes from the Persian meaning 'master of the treasure'. **Caspar** or **Kaspar** are the German forms of the name, and **Gaspar** and **Gaspard** the French.

Javonne: see YVONNE

Jay, Jaye

Often this is just a pet form of any name beginning with J, but it can also derive from the surname, which in its turn was originally a nickname implying that the person so called was a chatterer, from the noise made by the bird. It is used for both sexes.

Jayne: see JANE

Jean, Jeanet, Jeanette, Jeanie: see JANE

132

Jedidiah

An Old Testament masculine name adopted by the Puritans and more commonly used in the United States, Jedidiah means 'beloved of the Lord'. **Jedediah** is an alternative spelling, while the short form **Jed** seems to have become a stock name for minor characters in Westerns.

Jeff, Jeffrey: see GEOFFREY

Jem: see JAMES

Jemima

The biblical Jemima was the eldest daughter of JOB. She was born after her father's return to prosperity, so escaped the calamities which befell him. We are told that 'in all the land were no women found so fair as the daughters of Job', which would support those who want to interpret the name as meaning 'fair as the day' rather than the more usual 'dove'. **Mima** is an occasional short form. (See further under KEZIAH.)

Jemma: see GEMMA

Jemmie: see JAMES

Jen, Jennie: see JANE, JENNIFER

Jennifer

This is the Cornish form of **Guenevere** or **Guinevere**. The Welsh form is **Gwenhwyfar**, meaning 'fair' or 'white' and 'smooth, yielding'. This was shortened in Wales to forms such as **Gaenor**, **Gaynor** and **Geunor**, which were also used in England. In Scotland it became **Vanora**, and in Cornwall Jennifer or **Jenifer**. Although it is possible to find examples of the name being used, for example, at the end of the last century, it was for a long time a rare name, regarded as strictly local, until it became fashionable in the 1930s, possibly as a result of its use for characters in plays by Shaw and Coward. It has remained popular ever since. Short forms are **Jen**, **Jennie** and **Jenny**, which was earlier used as a pet form of JANE and Janet. The recent popularity of **Jenna**, another Cornish form of the name, can no doubt be attributed to the exposure given to it on the TV 'soap' *Dallas*.

Jenny: see JANE, JENNIFER

Jered: see JARED

Jeremy

Jeremy is the English form of **Jeremiah**, the Old Testament prophet whose warnings and reproofs to the people of his day gave rise to the term 'jeremiad'. **Jeremias**, the Greek form of the name, is occasionally found. The pet form **Jerry** is shared with a number of other names.

Jerome

This comes from an pre-Christian Greek name meaning 'sacred name', which was adopted by Christians in honour of St Jerome (c. 342–420), the hermit and biblical scholar whose translation of the Bible into Latin was used by the Catholic church until recently. The Latin form of St Jerome's name was **Hieronymus**, as in the painter Hieronymus Bosch, while the Indian chief **Geronimo** shows another form of the name. **Jerry** is used as a short form of Jerome.

Jerry: see GERALD, JEREMY, JEROME

Jervis: see GERVASE

Jess: see JANE, JASMINE, JESSE, JESSICA

Jessamine, Jessamy: see JASMINE

Jesse ['jesee]

In the Bible Jesse, whose name means 'God is', is the father of DAVID. He is regarded as the founder of the family which culminated in Jesus Christ, and 'Jesse windows' can sometimes be found in medieval churches showing this descent. The name is also spelt **Jessie**, and **Jess** (and occasionally **Jake**, although this is more usual for JACOB) are used as pet forms.

Jessica

Jessica is a difficult name. There have been at least half a dozen different attempts to derive it from Hebrew words, of which the most convincing is that it means 'God is looking'. A recent researcher has suggested that it is in fact a name invented by Shakespeare for the character in The Merchant of Venice, based on a name such as JESSE; and that, while the first part of her name is

Jewish, the ending is Venetian, a transition which reflects her role in the play. **Jess** and **Jessie** are used as pet forms.

Jessie, Jessy: see JANE, JESSE, JESSICA

Jesus: see JOSHUA

Jet: see JEWELL

Jethro

This is another biblical name, that of the father-in-law of Moses, meaning 'pre-eminence, excellence'. It belongs with the other Old Testament names introduced in the sixteenth century. Its most outstanding holder was Jethro Tull, the eighteenth-century agricultural reformer, whose name was adopted by a 1970s pop group; but the name is probably most widely known as that of a character in *The Archers*.

Jewell

Also spelt **Jewel** and **Jewelle**, this name came into use in the 1920s when exotic precious stones for women's names came into fashion; some women, such as **Emerald** Cunard, even went so far as to change their names to suit the fashion. Jewell is now rarely used, but there has been a revival of certain precious names, such as AMBER, particularly in fiction. A number of stone names will be found under their own entries, but unusual ones that have been recorded include **Diamond, Opal, Amethyst, Jet, Onyx** and **Topaz**.

Jill, Jillian, Jilly: see JULIA

Jim, Jimmie, Jimmy: see JAMES

Jinny: see VIRGINIA

Jinsie, Jinty: see JANE

Jo, Joe

As a masculine name this is a pet form of JOSEPH; for women it is a form of names such as Joanna (see JANE) and Josephine (see JOSEPH). It is also used in blends and compound such as **Billy-Joe** (for both sexes) and **Jolene** or **Joleen**.

Joan, Joanna, Joanne: see JANE

Job

This is interpreted as the Hebrew for 'persecuted', reflecting the afflictions, ranging from the deaths of his family to a plague of boils, sent by God in the Old Testament *Book of Job* to test this 'perfect and upright' man. He is eventually restored to greater prosperity than ever. The name is better known in its pet forms **Joby, Jobie, Joabee, Jobey**, thanks in part to the appearance in *The Archers* of a character of that name.

Jocelyn, Joscelin

Experts try to distinguish between the two forms of this name, deriving Jocelyn from the Latin for 'sportive' and Joscelin from the Latin for 'just', the same root as for JUSTIN. The name has also been derived from the word for 'a Goth'. In practice the two forms are so confused that it is pointless to distinguish them. Jocelyn or **Jocelin** was a common name for men in the Middle Ages, as in the chronicler Jocelin de Brakelond, but the name is now uncommon for men. The form **Joycelin** is also found, possibly through combination with the name JOYCE.

Jock, Jockie: see JOHN

Jodi(e), Jody: see JUDITH

Joe, Joey: see JO, JOSEPH

Joel

The name of one of the Old Testament prophets, Joel means 'Jehovah is God'. Introduced in England by the Puritans and taken by them to North America, where it has been more used than in this country, a recent increase of interest in the name may owe something to the success of the actor Joel Grey. In France a feminine form **Joelle** is also used.

Johanna: see JANE

John

Derived from the Hebrew meaning 'the Lord is gracious', John has remained one of the most popular names for boys since the early Middle Ages. It is the name of numerous saints, notably John the Baptist and John the Divine. As in the case of the feminine form JANE, the name has developed a wide variety of forms in the British Isles, the number being multiplied by duplicate forms derived from both the Latin form of the name 'Johannes' found in the Bible, and the Norman-French form 'Jehan' (modern French Jean) adopted from the Norman conquerors.

In Wales the name is found as **Ieuan** ['yieən], **Ioan**, **Ifan** and **Iwan**, the latter two being Anglicized to **Evan** and **Ewen**, and there is also a form which reflects the Welsh pronunciation of the English name, **Sion**. The Scots form of the name is **Ian** or **Iain**, as well as the archetypal **Jock** and **Jockie**. Ireland gives us **Sean**, with its various phonetic spellings **Shaun**, **Shawn** and **Shane** (which in turn have spawned rare feminine forms **Shauna** and **Shawndelle**), as well as the less frequent **Eoin** which comes directly from the Latin. From further afield the Russian **Ivan** is sometimes used (although this can also represent a spelling of the Welsh Ifan); **Jan** is a Germanic form of the name as well as being the traditional West Country pronunciation; and **Juan** [hwahn], the Spanish form, is increasingly popular in the United States.

Jack (derived via the old pet form **Jankin**) is a common pet form, along with **Johnnie** and **Jackie**. The spelling **Jon** is also used, although this properly belongs to the related JONATHAN. Sometimes a child is named directly after one of the saints and called **St John**, in which case the name is pronounced ['sinjn].

Joi, Joie: see JOY

Joleen, Jolene: see JO

Jolly, Jolyon: see JULIA

Jon: see JOHN, JONATHAN

Jonah, Jonas
The Old Testament Jonah, meaning 'dove, pigeon', has become such a byword for bad luck that only the most dismal of Puritans would want to saddle their child with such a burden. Consequently the New Testament Greek form of the name, Jonas (the father of Simon Peter) has always been much the commoner.

Jonathan
This name means 'gift of God'. In the Bible Jonathan is the son of King Saul and loyal friend of David, whose lament on the death of Jonathan is justly famous. In the eighteenth century 'Brother

Jonathan' was as widely recognized a reference to Americans as 'Uncle Sam' is today. The short form is **Jon**. The name seems never to have developed a feminine form, but DOROTHY and THEODORA have the same meaning.

Jonquil

One of the flower names introduced this century, Jonquil was briefly popular in the 1940s and 1950s, but is little used for children today.

Jordan

It is hardly surprising that the name of the river Jordan (which means 'flowing down'), with its strong associations with baptism, became a Christian name. It is recorded as a man's name from the thirteenth century onwards, but is now more usual as a woman's name. It can also be spelt **Jourdan**, and the French use a feminine form **Jourdana**.

Joscelin: see JOCELYN

Joseph

Joseph is a Hebrew name meaning 'increase, addition (to the family)'. In the Old Testament Joseph is the best-beloved of the twelve sons of the patriach JACOB, by whom he is given the coat of many colours. In the New Testament Joseph is the husband of the Virgin Mary. The feminine form of the name **Josephine**, owes its popularity to Napoleon's wife, the Empress Josephine. Other feminine forms are **Josepha** and **Josephina** or **Josefina**. The pet forms **Jo** or **Joe**, **Josie** or **Josey** are used for both sexes, but **Joey** is usually restricted to the masculine. **Fifi** is a French pet form of Josephine.

Joshua

A Hebrew name meaning 'the Lord is my Salvation', Joshua was the name of the commander who led the Israelites in the conquest of the Promised Land. **Josh** is used as a pet form. **Jesus** is an alternative form of the same name, which, while it is felt to be blasphemous if used in Britain, is not at all uncommon as a first name in Spanish-speaking countries.

Josiah

This was the name of one of the Kings of Israel, and means 'may the Lord heal'. Its most famous British holder was probably Josiah

Wedgewood, (1730–95), the founder of the china firm. The Greek form of the name **Josias** is also found, and pet forms are **Josh** and **Jos**.

Josie: see JOSEPH

Josse: see JOYCE

Jourdan, Jourdana: see JORDAN

Joy
An abstract noun used as a first name, Joy therefore has connections with the name JOCELYN. It is found as early as the twelfth century, but did not come into its own until the nineteenth. The French spelling **Joie** as well as **Joi** are sometimes found.

Joyce
This name is of disputed, or perhaps mixed, origin and is used for both sexes. Some derive it from a Breton Saint **Jodocus** (giving the French name **Josse**), others from the same root as JOY. It has been in and out of fashion over the centuries, and is now very rare as a man's name, although the author Joyce Cary (1888–1959) shows its survival into the twentieth century.

Joycelin: see JOCELYN

Juan: see JOHN

Juana, Juanita: see JANE

Jude
Jude has never been a particularly popular name, although its use was given a boost by the Beatles' song *Hey Jude*, and it is known in literature through Thomas Hardy's *Jude the Obscure* (1896). **Yehudi** Menuhin shows the Hebrew form of the name, which means 'praise'. It is found in the Bible as **Judah**, and the Hellenized form of the name is found in Judas Iscariot. Jude was the form of the name used for the apostle who was elected to replace Judas, but neither this nor the attractive fact that St Jude is the patron saint of lost causes, has been enough to displace the taint to the name of the treacherous Judas.

Judith

This name means 'a Jewess' and the Biblical Judith is one of the great heroines of the Bible. When the Israelites are under attack she gets herself invited to spend the night with the enemy general **Holofernes**, and cuts his head off with his own sword. Inspired by her return to her native city with the head, the Israelites fall upon the enemy and are victorious. Pet forms of the name, often used as names in their own right, are **Judy** or **Judie, Jodi, Jodie** or **Jody**.

Julia, Julian

The ancient Roman clan of the Julii claimed direct descent from **Venus** or **Aphrodite**, the goddess of love and generation, through her son Aeneas (see under ANGUS). We are told by the poet VIRGIL that Aeneas' son **Ascanius** had his name changed to Iulus, meaning 'the first down on the chin', because he had not yet reached the age of a full beard when he killed his first man. From him the Julii derived their name. Modern scholars have doubted this story, and have suggested that the name might be from the Latin *deus* ('god'). Julia is the feminine form of the name, and **Julie** is both its pet and the French form of the name, now as much used in its own right. **Juliet** and **Juliette** reflect the Italian form of the name, and their use derives from Shakespeare's heroine.

Julius, the masculine form of the name is rarely found, but **Julian**, from the Latin adjective meaning 'connected with the Julii' is now quite common, sometimes shortened to **Jule** or **Jools** (influenced by the French form **Jules**). **Jolyon** is a form of the name from the north of England, given publicity by John Galsworthy's use of it in his *Forsyte Saga* novels along with its pet form **Jolly**. **Juliana** is the feminine form of Julian, and this was corrupted in the Middle Ages to **Gillian** or **Jillian**, which later developed into **Jill** or **Gill** and its pet form **Jilly**. In the nineteenth century Juliana or **Julianne** developed in France into **Lianne** with its many variants such as **Leanne, Lian, Leana** and **Lianna**, although some parents prefer to interpret this as a blend of the names LEE and ANNE.

June

June is the name of the month used as a first name. It has been used as a name only in this century, but the name for the month is very old, going back to the Latin meaning 'month sacred to JUNO'.

Juno

Juno was the Roman queen of the gods and a goddess with special responsibility for the lives of women. There is disagreement over the meaning of her name, which may mean simply 'goddess or divine one' or may signify 'young woman'. It is not in common use as a first name, but can be found in Ireland, as in Sean O'Casey's play *Juno and the Paycock* (1924), where it is used as an English equivalent of the Irish UNA. The Welsh form is Gweno (see GWEN).

Justin

Derived from the Latin word meaning 'just', Justin was the name of a Christian martyr and theologian who died *c.* 165. **Justus** and **Justinian** are rare forms of the name. In the form **Iestyn** or **Iestin** ['yestin] it has been used in Wales since at least the sixth century. **Justina** is the older feminine form, but since the success of Lawrence Durrell's novel *Justine* (1957) and of the film made from it, this has been the more frequently used form. Occasionally the masculine form of the name is used for a woman.

K

Kai: see CAIUS

Kane
Popular in Australia since the Sixties, Kane is a surname used as a masculine first name. The surname can have several origins, the two most common being from Irish, meaning 'son of a warrior'; and from the French place-name Caen.

Karel: see CHARLES

Karen, Karin, Karina: see CATHERINE

Karenza: see KERENZA

Karl, Karla: see CHARLES

Kate, Katerina, Katharine, Katherine, Kathleen, Kathryn, Kathy, Katrina, Katrine: see CATHERINE

Karol, Karoline: see CHARLES

Kasia: see KEZIAH

Kasimir: see CASIMIR

Kaspar: see JASPER

Katia, Katie, Katja, Katy: see CATHERINE

Kay: see CATHERINE, CAIUS

Kayleigh

This girl's name, which is currently enjoying enormous popularity, is probably best analysed as a blend of Kay and Leigh rather than a phonetic rendering of the Gaelic *ceilidh* ('party'). As with so many recently fashionable names, the sound is probably more important than the sense, for the name completes a set with other recently fashionable names, KELLY and KYLIE.

Keelan: see KILLIAN

Keeley: see KELLY

Keir

A Scottish surname and place-name meaning 'a fort', Keir is occasionally used in honour of (James) Keir Hardy (1856–1915), one of the founders of the Labour Party.

Keira, Keiron: see KIERAN

Keith

Keith is another Scottish place and surname, meaning 'a wood'. It was not adopted as a first name until this century.

Kelly

This is an Irish surname, which probably means something like 'war, strife,' used as a first name for both sexes. In the form **Kelley** it was well-established in the American Bible Belt by the 1950s, but the form Kelly seems to have come into use rather later in this country. It is now rarely given to boys. The name **Keeley** is a variant that lies somewhere between Kelly and the fashionable KAYLEIGH and KYLIE.

Kelvin

Attempts have been made to link this name with the old English name **Kelwin**, meaning 'keel-friend', but it is far more likely that a bearer of this Scottish first name has connections with Glasgow, through which the river Kelvin flows, and which has a Kelvingrove Park, a Kelvin Hall and a benefactor in the scientist Lord Kelvin (1824–1907), who chose the river name as his title. The exact meaning of the river name is debated but probably means either 'wooded river' or 'narrow river'. The name is sometimes shortened to **Kel**.

Kenelm

An Old English name meaning 'brave-helmet', Kenelm was the name of an Anglo-Saxon saint. It is not a common name, but had a famous bearer in Sir Kenelm Digby (1603–65) who in his varied life was a diplomat, privateer, writer and a scholar who left behind a magnificent collection of important manuscripts, as well as being the husband of VENETIA Stanley. The name is said to have remained traditional in his family.

Kenneth

The Gaelic name **Cinaed**, meaning 'come from fire', was a common one in the MacAlpine family and when one of their clan became the first king of Scotland in the ninth century the name was anglicized to Kenneth. There was another Gaelic name, **Coinneach**, meaning 'fair-haired', from which the MacKenzies get their surname, which was also anglicized as Kenneth. Short forms are **Ken, Kennie** and **Kenny. Cenydd** is the Welsh form of the name.

Kent

This masculine name, popular in North America, comes from the surname; this in turn is derived from the county name, which means 'coastal district'.

Keren

Keren is the short form of **Kerenhappuch**, one of the three daughters of JOB (see also JEMIMA and KEZIAH). The name means 'horn [i.e. container] of antimony', which refers to the kohl used even then to enhance the eyes. Although not a common name, it has been used quietly but steadily since at least the seventeenth century, and there are even recorded cases of three daughters being given the names of Job's three. Keren may sometimes be used as an alternative form of **Karen** (see CATHERINE), although the names are unrelated.

Kerensa

A traditional Cornish girl's name meaning 'affection, love', Kerensa is also found in the forms **Kerenza** and **Karenza**.

Keri: see CERI

Kermit: see DERMOT

Kerry

The Irish county name is the obvious source of this name, but its popularity may have been helped by the existence of the Welsh name CERI (pronounced in the same way) and by the fact that Kerry has been used, particularly among the Boston Irish, as a pet form of CATHERINE. The name first became popular in Australia in the 1940s, when it was primarily thought of as a masculine name, as in the case of the businessman Kerry Packer, but it is now used mainly as a feminine name.

Keshia: see KEZIAH

Kester: see CHRISTOPHER

Keturah

This is the name of the second wife of Abraham which was adopted by the Puritans. It has been used regularly since then, although more frequently in America than Britain, but it has declined in popularity in this century. The name means 'fragrance' or 'incense'.

Kevin

Kevin is the name of a seventh-century Irish saint, who founded an important school at Glendalough, which became equally famous for its learning and the beauty of its situation. The name was restricted to Ireland until the 1920s, but in recent years has been enormously popular throughout the English-speaking world, and is now even conquering France. Kevin means 'comely birth'. The spelling **Kevan** is often treated as a variant, but strictly speaking is a separate name meaning 'little handsome one'.

Keziah, Kezia

This is the Hebrew word for cassia, a type of shrub much admired for its fragrance. It was the name of the middle of Job's three beautiful daughters, the others being JEMIMA and Kerenhappuch (see KEREN). The fame of these three must have been great, for, unusually for the Bible, we are given his daughters' names, but not his sons'. It was the name of one of John Wesley's sisters, who was known by the pet-form **Kissy**. She took it to America, where, along with WESLEY it became a popular black name. It is also found as **Keshia** and **Kasia** (although this is also a Polish form of the name CATHERINE) and has the further pet forms **Kizzie**, **Kissie** and **Kezie**.

145

Kieran

Derived from the Irish word *ciar* ('black'), Kieran means 'little dark one'. There are as many as 15 Irish saints of this name, one of whom, St Kieran of Saighir, is said to have been a missionary in Ireland even before St Patrick got there. Another, St Kieran of Clonmacnoise, is said to have used parchment made from the skin of his favourite cow to write down the great Irish national epic of *The Tain*. A twelfth-century copy of this sixth-century manuscript has come down to us as *The Book of the Dun Cow*. The Irish form of the name is **Ciaran**, although the K- form is commoner in England as it makes the pronunciation clearer. The name can also be spelt as **Kieron** or **Keiron** and the feminine forms includes **Ciara, Kiera** and **Keira**.

Killian, Kilian

This is the name of an Irish saint who went as a missionary to Germany in the late seventh century and was martyred at Würzburg, where a cathedral was later built in his honour. The survival of the name into modern times may owe something to its use by Sir Walter Scott in *Anne of Geirstein* (1829). The name is a diminutive of the Irish word meaning 'strife' and is spelt **Cillian** in Irish. **Keelan** is another variant, and **Killie** is used as a short form.

Kim, Kimberly

The name Kim comes primarily from Rudyard Kipling's novel of that name, published in 1901. His child hero, the 'little friend of all the world', is known as Kim in the Indian bazaars, but his full name is **Kimball** O'Hara. The success of the book led to Kim being used occasionally as a boy's name, and more often as a pet name, but Kimball does not seem to have been used. Within a few years Kim was being used for girls, and has remained predominantly a female name. The spy 'Kim' Philby (real name Harold) is an example of its use as a masculine nickname. When he got to Moscow, Philby would have found that the name is also in use there as a quite common masculine name, created from the initial letters (in Russian) for 'Communist Youth International'.

Kim is also used as a short form of **Kimberly**, the commoner spelling as a first name for **Kimberley**, the South African diamond town. This came into use at about the same time as Kipling's book was published. Soldiers used to have a custom of naming their children after the garrison in which they were born, or after battles, and at the turn of the century there were many British soldiers around Kimberley, fighting in the Boer War. (This custom is well illustrated in Kipling's short story 'Daughter of the Regiment', where Colour-Sergeant McKenna's children are called Colaba, Muttra and after the cantonments where they were born). Kimberly was at first mainly masculine, and is still used occasionally as a man's name, but it is now predominantly female. It was well-established in America by the 1950s and is still very popular there as well as in Britain.

Kirk

This comes from the Old Norse word for 'church'; it was brought to public notice as a name by the film star Kirk Douglas.

Kirsta, Kirstie, Kirsty, Kirsten, Kirsteen, Kirstine: see CHRISTINE

Kissie: see KEZIAH

Kit: see CHRISTOPHER, CATHERINE

Kittie, Kitty: see CATHERINE

Konrad: see CONRAD

Kristel: see CRYSTAL

Kristin, Kristina: see CHRISTINE

Krystal: see CRYSTAL

Kurt: see CONRAD

Kyle

Kyle is the name of a district in Scotland, used first as a surname, then as a first name, mainly for men but occasionally for women. It has become particularly popular in the United States. Tradition links the district of Kyle with the name of Old King Cole, but less romantic place-name experts derive it from the river Coyl, which means 'narrow'.

Kylie

This name has been popular in Australia for a number of years, but it burst upon the rest of the world with the success of the Australian actress and singer Kylie Minogue. It already shows signs of gaining wider popularity. According to Leslie Dunkling it is a Western Australian Aboriginal word meaning 'curl' or 'boomerang', but it probably owes its success to being thought of as a feminine version of KYLE, or as a variant of KELLY.

Kyra, Kyrie: see CYRIL

L

Lachlan ['loklən]
This Highland name comes from the Gaelic name for Norway, Lochlann. It is the origin of the surname MacLachlan. It can also be spelt **Lachlann** and **Lachunn**, and has pet forms **Lachie, Lachy** and **Lauchie**. Its recent popularity in Australia may perhaps owe something to a memory of General Lachlan Macquarie, who was an exceptionally liberal governor of New South Wales in 1809–21, and whose encouragement of building projects led to the local late-Georgian style of architecture being called Macquarie style.

Ladonna: see DONNA

Laetitia, Letitia
The Latin world for 'joy, delight', it has been used as a girl's name in England since the twelfth century, and was early on anglicized to **Lettice**. It is shortened to **Lettie** or **Letty**, and **Laeta** is an alternative form of the name.

Laila, Lailah: see LEILA

Lalage ['laləgee]
This name comes from the Greek word for 'to babble, prattle'. The name was used in the first century AD by the Latin poet Horace for the woman addressed in his love poems, and has been similarly used by a number of English poets since then. **Lallie** or **Lally** are short forms.

Lambert
Lambert is an old Germanic name meaning 'land-bright', which should perhaps be interpreted as 'pride of the nation'. It was the name of a seventh-century saint and was popular in the past, but

it is rarely used today, although a knowledge of the name is kept alive by the fame of Lambert Simnel, the pretender to Henry VII's throne.

Lana: see ALAN

Lance, Launce
These are the commonly used short forms of **Lancelot** or **Launcelot**, the great knight of King Arthur's court. Despite his fame, we do not really know where the name comes from. Lancelot first appears in French Arthurian literature, and the name may have originated in the word *ancel*, diminutive, *ancelot*, meaning a servant (perhaps a reference to his humility or to his time spent learning from the Lady of the Lake), the French article in front giving 'L'ancelot'.

Lara
Lara is the pet form of the Russian **Larissa**. Lara is the tragic heroine of Boris Pasternak's *Doctor Zhivago* (1957), and the name became widely known as a result of the success of the 1965 film of the novel. Some parents may use it as a variant of LAURA.

Lariane, Larraine: see LORRAINE

Larry: see LAWRENCE

Launce, Launcelot: see LANCE

Laura
The Latin equivalent of DAPHNE, Laura comes from the word for a laurel tree. To be crowned with a wreath of laurels was an honour given in the ancient world to those triumphant in war, sport and the arts; a vestige of it survives in our term 'poet laureate'. Although the name comes from Latin, the Romans did not use it; but it was in use in the Middle Ages, probably with the idea that the bearer was of such excellent qualities or beauty that she deserved the laurel crown. In the fourteenth century the Italian poet Petrarch gave the name fame celebrating his love for Laura (perhaps Laure de Noves) in his great *Canzoniere*. The name is also spelt **Lora**, and has pet forms **Lori** and **Lolly**. It has a number of derivative forms, the most widely used of which at the moment is **Lauren**, a name that seems to have been coined for the film actress Lauren

Bacall. The alternative form **Loren** is also used for boys (see LAURENCE). The plant name **Laurel** is also used, along with diminutives **Lauretta** or **Loretta**, as well as such elaborations as **Lorana** and **Lorinda**. **Lowri** is the Welsh form of the name. These names may sometimes be used as feminine forms of LAURENCE.

Lauraine: see LORRAINE

Laurence, Lawrence

This name shares with LAURA a derivation from the word for a laurel, probably via the name of the Roman town of Laurentium. It came into use owing to the popularity of the third-century saint who was martyred by being roasted on a grid-iron because he would not hand over money which had been entrusted to him to distribute to the poor. The pet form **Larry** is sometimes used as a name in its own right. Other short forms are **Laurie** and **Lawrie**, and in Scotland **Lowrie**. **Laurent** is the form of the name used in France and sometimes found here (confusingly, Laurence is the French feminine form), and **Lorenzo**, the Italian and Spanish form of the name, is sometimes used in the United States. This gives a short form **Loren**, which is not uncommon in this country. In Ireland Lawrence became popular due to St Lawrence O'Toole, bishop of Dublin and a man deeply involved in caring for his people at the time of the twelfth-century Norman invasion of Ireland. In his case Lawrence was used as a substitute for the native Gaelic name **Lorcan** ('little fierce one') and, although the native form is now not uncommon, Lawrence is still used in this way.

Lavinia

In Roman mythology Lavinia was the daughter of the King of Latium, and wife of Aeneas (see ANGUS), the Trojan who became the founder of the Roman people. It was not used by the Romans as a name, but was taken up in the fifteenth-century with the Renaissance revival of interest in things classical. It was particularly popular in the eighteenth century after the success of a poem by James Thomson called 'Lavinia and Palemon' (basically a retelling of the biblical story of RUTH and Boaz), but is now only quietly used. **Vina** is a short form of the name, and there is a variant, **Lavina**.

Lea: see LEE

Leah
This is the name of one of the more hard-done-by women in the Bible. According to the story (Genesis xxix) Jacob fell in love with his cousin RACHEL and served her father Laban for seven years to win her, but her elder sister Leah was secretly substituted on the wedding night. Although Jacob was later given Rachel to be Leah's co-wife, he hated Leah, but God compensated her with numerous sons. **Lia**, the Italian form of the name, and **Léa**, the French, are sometimes used as variants.

Leana, Leanne: see JULIA

Leanora: see ELEANOR

Lee, Leigh, Lea
This comes from the common surname, which means 'a meadow'. Its popularity in the southern United States probably stems from the once common practice of naming children after people admired by the parents, in this case after the Confederate general Robert E. Lee (1807–70). From there it spread, developing variant forms, throughout the United States and then to this country, where it has been particularly popular in the 1980s. Use seems to be equally divided between the sexes.

Leila
Leila is an Persian name meaning 'darkness' or 'night' and thus a type of dark beauty. She is the heroine of a popular romance called *Leila and Majnun*. The name was made widely known in England by Lord Byron who used it both for the Turkish child brought to England in *Don Juan* and, earlier, for the tragic heroine of *The Giaour* (1813). It was subsequently used by other writers as a name for Eastern beauties. Variant forms are **Laila, Lailah, Leilah, Leyla, Lila** and **Lilah**.

Lena: see HELEN, MAGDALEN

Len, Lennie, Lenny, Lennard: see LEO

Lenore, Lenora: see ELEANOR

Leo, Leonard, Leonie

There is a large group of names containing the element 'Leo' meaning 'lion'. **Leo** was the name of thirteen popes, and was popular in the Middle Ages; but, although still used, it is now more common as a short form of various Leo-names. It took the form **Leon** in France and from there it spread to this country. **Leonard**, sometimes spelt **Lennard**, is an old Germanic name meaning 'brave as a lion', and is shortened to **Len, Lennie** or **Lenny**. **Lionel**, the name of one of King Arthur's knights, also belongs in this group since it means 'little lion'. **Leopold** looks as if it also belongs with the lion names; in fact, it comes from the Old German name Leutpold, formed from words meaning 'people' and 'bold', but it changed its form under the influence of Leo-names. (See also LLEWELLYN.)

The feminine forms of the name mostly come from the French Leon. They include **Leonie, Leontia, Leontine, Leola** and **Leona**. **Leonora** is not a lion name, but a form of ELEANOR.

Leroy

The old French for 'the king', Leroy may have been used originally to describe those who were servants to the king of France. It is a name particularly associated with the United States, and is sometimes found in the form **Elroy**.

Leslie, Lesley

This name comes from the Scottish place and surname, which probably means 'garden of hollies'. From the evidence of Robert Burns' poem to 'Bonnie Lesley', it seems to have come into use as a girl's name before being used as a boy's in the second third of the nineteenth-century. This is a reversal of the usual pattern of boys' names becoming girls'. There used to be a careful distinction made between Lesley as a feminine form, and Leslie as the masculine, but the distinction is no longer made, at least for girls.

Lester

Lester is a modified spelling of the place name Leicester, meaning 'dwellings on the River Legra'. It has been used for the past 100 or so years, wellknown holders being the Canadian statesman Lester Pearson, the jockey Lester Piggott and the tenor sax player Lester Young.

Letitia, Lettice, Letty: see LAETICIA

Lewis, Louis, Louise

When the barbarian Franks invaded France in the Dark Ages, they brought with them a name meaning 'famous battle' that was written down by the literate, but conquered, Gauls as Hludowig or Chlodowig. This name developed into **Clovis**, the name of the first Merovingian king (481–511), and later lost its first sound to become **Louis**, a name almost synonymous with French kingship. **Ludovic** comes from the Latin form of the name, and **Aloys** and **Aloysius** – the name of a Spanish Jesuit saint, but probably best known as the name of Sebastian Flyte's teddy-bear in Evelyn Waugh's *Brideshead Revisited* (1945) – was a form which developed in Provence, and spread to Spain and Italy. The English form of the name is **Lewis**. Pet forms of the name include **Lou, Louie, Lew** and **Lewie**.

The feminine forms of the name, **Louise** and **Louisa** and occasionally the Spanish form **Luisa**, with their pet forms **Lou, Louie** and **Lulu**, are at the moment more popular than the masculine counterparts. Clovis has recently developed the feminine form **Clova**, although this may owe something to the flower name **Clover**, found in Susan Coolidge's 'Katy' books.

Lex: see ALEXANDER

Lia: see LEAH

Liam: see WILLIAM

Lian, Lianna, Lianne: see JULIA

Libby, Liesl, Liesel: see ELIZABETH

Lila, Lilah: see LEILA

Lilith

A name from Jewish mythology, Lilith has been variously interpreted as 'a serpent', 'a screech-owl' or 'a vampire'. According to tradition she was the first wife of Adam, before the creation of Eve, but refused to submit to him, and as a result was expelled from the Garden of Eden. She became an evil spirit particularly dangerous to new-born children, and one tradition says she took her revenge by becoming the serpent of the Tree of Knowledge. The name is very rarely given to children, but in recent years Lilith has been used as a symbol by some sections of the feminist movement.

Lily

Lily is a once-popular flower name, now somewhat in decline. Its use may owe something to Christian symbolism, both to the association of the Madonna lily with the Virgin Mary as a symbol of purity, and to the recommendation of the Sermon on the Mount to 'consider the lilies of the field'. Historically, it has been used as a pet-form of ELIZABETH (German **Lili** is still used in this way), and it is impossible to distinguish between these two uses. The name is also spelt **Lilly. Lilian** (or **Lillian**) comes from the Spanish form of the name, **Liliana,** and in Scotland this was transformed into **Lilias, Lillias** or **Lillas**. Lilian may have influenced the development of the name Lianne (see JULIAN). SUSAN is the Hebrew equivalent of Lily.

Lina

This is a short form of a number of names ending in -lina, such as Angelina and Selina, which has come to be used as a name in its own right.

Linda

Linda started life as a short form of names ending -linda, such as BELINDA. These were old Germanic names where the -linda means 'serpent'. However, a much more obvious meaning for 'linda' is the Spanish adjective meaning 'pretty', and most users of the name probably think of it in this sense. It is also found in the forms **Lynda** and **Lindy**. The shortenings **Lyn** and **Lin** are shared with a number of other names.

Lindsay

An aristocratic Scottish surname used as a first name, Lindsay probably comes from family connections with the district in Lincolnshire. When used for men it is usually in the form Lindsay, but for girls, now the more frequent use, it also occurs as **Lindsey, Linsey, Linsay** and various other spellings.

Linette, Linnette: see LYNETTE

Linus ['lienəs]

A Greek name meaning 'flax', Linus is found in the New Testament (II Timothy iv.21), where St Paul sends greetings from Linus and CLAUDIA. There is an unsubstantiated tradition that these two were brother and sister, and British, and invited some of the first missionaries to Britain. There is, coincidentally, a Welsh feminine name **Llian** ['hleeən], which also means 'flax'. Linus is probably best known today as the name of a character in the *Peanuts* cartoon, but the name is used in real life, as in the double Nobel Prize-winning chemist Linus Pauling and the actor Linus Roach.

Lionel: see LEO

Lisa, Lisbeth, Lise, Lisette: see ELIZABETH

Livia, Livy: see OLIVER

Liz, Lizzie, Liza, Lizbeth: see ELIZABETH

Llewellyn
This is a Welsh man's name, traditionally interpreted as meaning 'lion-like', but which probably derives from the word for a leader. It is also spelt **Llywelyn**, and is shortened to **Llew, Llelo** and **Lyn**, which last is often used as a name in its own right. It has been anglicized to **Leoline** or LEWIS.

Llian: see LINUS

Llinos, Llio: see LYNETTE

Lloyd
Lloyd is a Welsh name usually described as meaning 'grey', but in fact the word covers a range of colours including browns and greys. The correct Welsh spelling of the name is **Llwyd**, and it is also found as **Lhuyd, Loyd** and, particularly in America – as in the case of the boxer Floyd Patterson – as **Floyd**.

Llywelyn: see LLEWELLYN

Lodowick: see LEWIS

Lois ['lohis]
This is another New Testament name: she was the grandmother of TIMOTHY, and is praised in St Paul's second Epistle to Timothy for her great faith. The name came into fashion, along with other biblical names, among the Puritans, and they took it to America, where it is still more common than in this country. The name is thought to be Greek, but its meaning is not known. The use of the name has been reinforced by Lois also being a form of HELOISE,

155

via a contraction of the Provençal form **Aloisa** or **Aloys**. Lois is probably best known in this country as the name of Superman's girlfriend, Lois Lane.

Lola, Lolita: see CHARLES, DOLORES

Lolly: see LAURA

Lora, Lorana: see LAURA

Lorcan: see LAURENCE

Loren: see LAURA, LAURENCE

Lorenzo: see LAURENCE

Loretta, Lori, Lorinda: see LAURA

Lorna

Lorna was invented by R.D. Blackmore for the heroine of his novel *Lorna Doone* (1869). He probably based it on the Scottish place and family name of Lorn or Lorne, but the name also has associations with the old English word 'lorn' as in 'forlorn', meaning 'lost, forsaken', which would be appropriate for the state of his kidnapped and isolated heroine. The form **Lorne** has been used as a feminine name, but is more frequently found as the male equivalent of Lorna, as in the case of the actor Lorne Green. The surname Lorn is said to come from Loarn, a king of the Dalriada Scots *c.* 500 AD, his name possibly coming from a Celtic root meaning 'a fox'.

Lorraine

Lorraine comes from the district of France of this name, its use possibly influenced by Joan of Arc who was known as the Maid of Lorraine as well as the Maid of Orleans. The name is not used in France, but has been used in England and America since the last century. There are numerous variants, of which the most common are **Loraine, Laraine, Larraine** and **Lauraine**.

Lothair: see LUTHER

Lottie: see CHARLES

Lou: see LEWIS

Louanne, Louella: see LUELLA

Louis, Louisa, Louise: see LEWIS

Lowrie: see LAURA

Lowrie: see LAURENCE

Loyd: see LLOYD

Lucas: see LUKE

Lucasta
This name was coined by the seventeenth-century poet Richard Lovelace, for his poems addressed to LUCY Sacheverell. It is said to have been formed from the Latin *lux casta* 'chaste light'. His poem 'To Lucasta, Going to the Wars', contains the famous lines:

> I could not love thee, Dear, so much,
> Lov'd I not honour more.

(See also ALTHEA.)

Lucretia [looh 'kreeshə]
In Roman traditional history Lucretia is a model of feminine virtue and modesty. According to the story Lucretia is raped by Sextus, the son of TARQUIN, the despotic king of Rome. Unable to live with the shame, she summons her husband and her father, and, begging them to take vengeance, commits suicide in front of them. The outrage of her family and all who heard of what happened is said to have led to the overthrow of the kings and the foundation of the Roman Republic. Shakespeare tells the story in his poem *The Rape of Lucrece* (1594). **Lucretius**, the male form of the name, was occasionally used in the past in honour of the great first-century BC poet and philosopher of that name.

Lucy
Lucy comes from the Latin word *lux, lucis* 'light'. It is owing to this association with light that St Lucy, the fourth-century virgin martyr, is invoked against blindness and eye trouble. (St CLARE, whose name means 'bright, clear', is invoked against eye trouble for the same reason). **Lucia** is the Latin and Italian form of the name, and **Lucilla** and **Lucille** Latin and French diminutives. **Lucinda** is another diminutive, particularly popular for fictional

characters in the seventeenth and eighteenth centuries. Its pet form **Cindy** or **Sindy** is now a name in its own right.

The masculine name **Lucius** comes from the same root. **Lucian** or **Lucien** are often used as variants, but come from a Greek name of unknown meaning, made famous by the first-century AD satirist.

Ludovic: see LEWIS

Luella

A blended name, Luella is formed from LOUISE and ELLA, and is also spelt **Louella**. Similarly **Louanne, Luanne, Luana** are formed from LOUISE and ANNE.

Luisa: see LEWIS

Luke

The fame of St Luke the Evangelist has made this a steadily popular name since the Middle Ages. St Luke was a physician and was also traditionally supposed to have been a painter and to have made portraits of the Virgin Mary, and he is the patron saint of both professions. He was a Greek, and his name means 'man from the district of Luciana'. The Greek form of his name, **Lucas**, is occasionally used.

Lulu: see LEWIS

Luned: see LYNETTE

Luther

The use of Luther as a first name is entirely due to the fame of the sixteenth-century religious reformer Martin Luther, although its use in recent decades has been given a boost in honour of the civil rights campaigner named after him, Martin Luther King (1929–68). The name is a form of the German first name **Lothair**, meaning 'famous army' or 'warrior'.

Lydia

This name simply means 'woman of Lydia' (now western Turkey). It has strong literary associations. There is an anonymous Latin poem, once thought to be by VIRGIL, lamenting a lost love, addressed to a Lydia, and the name is given respectability by a brief mention in the Acts of the Apostles. Greater fame was given to it by its use by Ariosto in *Orlando Furioso* (1532) for a beautiful but cruel daughter of the King of Lydia, and it was a popular literary name in the eighteenth century, as in the case of Lydia Languish in Sheridan's *The Rivals* (1775).

Lyn, Lynn, Lynne: see LINDA, LYNETTE, LLEWELLYN

Lynda: see LINDA

Lyndon

A place and surname meaning 'hill with lime trees', used as a first name. The former president of the United States, Lyndon Johnson (1908–73), illustrates the commonest form of the name, while the president of the Bahamas, **Lynden** Pindling, illustrates an alternative form.

Lynette

This name comes from the Welsh name **Eluned** or **Eiluned** [e'lined], which means 'idol, icon', so the name probably has some connection with ancient religion. **Luned** is the short form of Eluned, and this became **Linet** or **Linette** in the medieval French Arthurian romances in which she features as a heroine. The name was given what is now its commonest form, Lynette, by Tennyson in his story of 'Gareth and Lynette' in the *Idylls of the King*. **Lyn, Lynn, Lynne** are used as short forms. The name is only coincidentally like that of a bird, the linnet, although some parents may have used it for that association, and there is a Welsh name **Llinos** or **Llio** [hlio], which means 'linnet', the bird being used as the symbol of a pretty woman.

M

Mabel

This name started life as a pet form of **Amabel** 'loveable' (see AMY), but has all but replaced its original. In its turn it developed into such forms as **Maybelle** and **Maybelline**, although these can also be thought of as developments of MAY; in turn, MAY, along with **Mab** and **Mabs**, is sometimes a pet form of Mabel. There is a Welsh form, **Mabli**, and Mabel can also be spelt **Mable**.

Madeline

Madeline with its various spellings, such as **Madeleine, Madaline, Madaliene, Madaleine** and **Madalain**, comes from St Mary Magdalen, the reformed sinner who anointed Christ with costly perfume and washed his feet with her tears and hair. Her second name means 'woman of Magdala', a village on the Sea of Galilee. Other forms of the name include **Magdalen(e)**, shortened to **Magda**, and **Madelena** or **Madalena**, shortened to **Lena**. From the old pronunciation of the name, **Maudlin** (which also gives us the adjective, from her tears of repentance), come the occasional short form **Maude** or **Maud**, which properly belongs to MATILDA. **Madge**, properly belonging to MARGARET, can also be found as a pet form. **Maddie** or **Maddy** is, however, the usual short form.

Madge: see MARGARET, MADELINE

Madoc, Madog

This Welsh masculine name means 'fortunate, good'. A certain Madog ap Owain Gwynedd is supposed to have discovered America ahead of everyone else in about 1150, and from this story come legends of blue-eyed, Welsh-speaking Red Indians. The name **Marmaduke**, with its short form **Duke**, is said to derive from the Irish Maelmaedoc ('servant of Madoc'). Marmaduke has strong associations with Yorkshire, where the name has always been more common than in the rest of the country. The name is often described as obsolescent, but Marmaduke Hussey, chairman of the BBC, has shown this judgment to be hasty.

Madonna: see DONNA

Mae: see MAY

Maelmore: see MILES

Maeve

Maeve, also spelt **Meave** and **Maev**, comes from Irish mythology, where she appears in two forms; one as the powerful and forceful queen of Connacht; the other as the queen of the fairies, the origin of Shakespeare's Queen Mab. The name probably means 'joy'. **Meaveen** is a diminutive form.

Magda, Magdalen, Magdalene: see MADELINE

Maggie, Mags: see MARGARET

Magnus

Stories of Charlemagne, whose name means 'Charles the Great', the king of the Franks and defender of the Christian faith against the heathen, were popular throughout Europe in the Middle Ages. The name translates into Latin as Carolus Magnus, and the second half of the name was given to the son of St Olaf, king of Norway (995–1030), a convert from paganism. This Magnus was later king of Norway and Denmark. Magnus became a traditional royal name, whence it spread to the general population. Among the Viking settlers of Ireland the name was softened to **Manus**. Although the television appearances of Magnus Magnusson and Magnus Pyke have made the name better known, it is still rare outside Scotland and Ireland.

Mahalia

This name, best known from the gospel singer Mahalia Jackson, is a form of the Hebrew name **Mahala** 'tenderness'.

Mai, Maia: see MAY

Mair, Maire: see MARY

Maisie: see MARGARET

Malachy

An Irish name, Malachy was used by two high kings of Ireland and by a popular saint, and early on it became identified with the Old Testament prophet **Malachi** ('messenger'). The name is not usually found outside Ireland.

Malcolm

Malcolm is a Scottish name, from the Gaelic name Mael-Colum, 'follower of St **Columba**' also known as **Colmcille**. St Columba, whose name means 'dove', was an Irish noble who founded the monastery on IONA in 563 which became the centre of Celtic Christianity and the base for the conversion of Scotland. The Gaelic form of his name gives us **Calum, Callum, Colm**.

Malvina

In the mid-eighteenth century Europe was swept by an enthusiasm for the poems of OSSIAN. Supposedly ancient Gaelic epics, they were in fact largely the work of James MacPherson (1736–96). MacPherson seems to have invented the name Malvina (which may be meant to represent the Gaelic for 'smooth brow') for the name of the betrothed of the hero OSCAR. Many of the poems are dedicated to her. The enthusiasm for things Ossianic was particularly strong in Scandinavia, and it may be immigration from this area that led to the name being more common in the United States. The name has nothing to do with Islas Malvinas, the Spanish name for the Falkland Islands. Variants are **Melvina** and **Malvena**. (See also MELVIN.)

Mamie: see MARY

Mandy: see AMANDA

Manny, Manuel: see EMMANUEL

Manon: see MARIAN

Manus: see MAGNUS

Marc, Marcel, Marcelin, Marcella, Marcelle, Marcelline, Marcia, Marcine, Marcus, Marcy: see MARK

Maredudd: see MEREDITH

Margaret

This name comes from the Latin Word for PEARL. However, the French form **Marguerite** is also French for 'a daisy', and our name **Daisy** started life as a pet form of Margaret. It owes its early popularity throughout Europe to the fame of Saint Margaret of Antioch, a legendary early martyr who was swallowed alive by Satan in the form of a dragon, but on making the sign of the cross, she burst through the monster's side, thereby saving her life and killing the dragon. In Scotland this popularity was reinforced by another saint who was queen of Scotland 1070–93, and it took on a number of different forms: **Margery** (**Marjory, Marjorie**, pet forms **Marge, Margie, Madge**), **Maisie, Mysie** and MAY. Pet forms of Margaret include **Maggie, Mags, Meg** and **Meggie**, and by alteration of the first letter **Peg, Peggie** or **Peggy. Megan** is the Welsh form of the name. From the Continent we get **Margarita, Marghanita, Margaretta, Margoletta**, and pet forms **Greta, Gretchen, Grethel** or **Gretel, Meta** and **Rita. Margot** is the French pet form; the variant **Margaux** has recently become popular; but the model and actress Margaux Hemingway, who probably started the fashion, was named after the wine.

Mari, Maria, Mariam, Mariamne: see MARY

Marian

Originally a pet form of Mary, Marian came to be analysed as a combination of MARY and ANN, hence the variants **Marianne** and **Mary-Ann. Manon** is a French pet form of the name. The form **Marion** is also used in the United States as a man's name (it was, for example, the true first name of the actor John Wayne). In this case it comes from the surname with the same etymology as the first name, and probably owes its use to Francis Marion (d. 1795), who won fame fighting in the American War of Independence.

Marie, Mariel, Mariella, Marietta, Mariette: see MARY

Marigold

Marigold was the symbol of the Virgin Mary, the name coming from Mary + gold, the name given to the flower from its colour.

Because of its healing properties the flower was also chosen as the symbol of the apothecaries and can still be seen in use as a symbol by many herbalists. It was particularly popular as a girl's name at the turn of the century.

Marilyn: see MARY

Marina

This is the name by which St MARGARET of Antioch is known in the eastern Mediterranean. Although it may not be the true derivation, Marina is usually taken to come from the Latin meaning 'of the sea'; and in this sense was used by Shakespeare for the sea-born heroine of *Pericles*. The name became established in England after 1934, when Princess Marina of Greece became the Duchess of Kent, and attained such popularity that her favourite shade of blue-green became known as 'Marina blue'.

Marion: see MARIAN

Marisa, Marissa: see MARY

Marjerie, Marjory: see MARGARET

Mark

Mark is the English form of **Marcus**, a Latin name probably derived from the Roman god of war, Mars. **Marc**, the French spelling of the name, has become popular in recent years. The Latin pet form **Marcellus** became the French **Marcel**. The feminine forms of the name do not come directly from Marcus, but from this French form or from the related Latin name Marcius. From the latter we get **Marcia** ['mahseeə or 'mahshə], the second pronunciation giving the spelling **Marsha**. From the French come a number of forms: **Marcelline, Marceline** and their short form **Marcine, Marcella** and **Marcelle**. **Marcy** is used as a short form of these names. (See also MARTIN.)

Marlene

A German pet form of Mary Magdalen (see MADELINE), Marlene was introduced into this country by the film star Marlene Dietrich and by the popularity with the troops on both sides of the German song 'Lili Marlene' in the last war. The variant form

Marlena reflects the German pronunciation, but Marlene is now often pronounced ['marleen] by British users.

Marlon
Something of a mystery, this name has not been found before its use by the actor Marlon Brando, and its spread is due entirely to him. It is assumed to be a surname used as a first name.

Marmaduke: see MADOC

Marsha: see MARK

Marshall
This comes from the surname, which derives from German via French and originally meant a farrier or one who looked after horses. Its use as a first name may have been helped by the fact that the name of the Latin poet Martial (c. 40–104 AD) has the same sound in standard English pronunciation.

Martha
Martha is the name of the biblical woman who worked so hard to cater for Jesus and his disciples, only to be told that her sister had chosen the better course by sitting at His feet. Hence the name became popular from the sixteenth century onwards with those who wanted their daughters to grow up to be diligent housewives. Short forms shared with MATILDA are **Mat**, **Mattie** or **Matty**, and by a change in first letter (also found in other pet forms in 'm') **Pattie** or **Patty**, although this is also used for Patricia (see PATRICK). The name is Aramaic for 'lady'.

Martin
An old Roman name, Martin comes from Mars, the Roman god of fertility and war (see also MARK). Nowadays it is also spelt **Martyn** and has the short form **Marty**. It became part of the basic stock of European names because of the popularity of St Martin of Tours, (c. 316–97), the Roman soldier who cut his military cloak in half in order to share it with a beggar, turned pacifist and left the army, and eventually became a missionary and bishop of Tours. Feminine forms include **Martina** or **Martine**, and more rarely **Martitia**, **Martita** and even **Martinella**.

Marvin: see MERVIN

Mary

A name of disputed meaning, Mary has long been one of the most popular of girl's names, used in honour of the Virgin Mary and the numerous other saints who bear the name. The Hebrew form of the name is **Miriam**, also found in the forms **Mariam, Maryam** and **Mariamne**. **Maria** is the Latin form of the name, and **Marie** the French. These names have innumerable pet forms, including MAY, **Moll, Molly, Mally, Mamie, Minnie, Poll, Polly** and **Ria**. Diminutives from the Continent include **Mariel** and **Mariella, Mariette** and **Marietta, Marisa** or **Marissa** as well as MARIAN. **Marilyn** or **Marylyn** is a derivative. In Welsh the name appears as **Mair** [mier] or **Mari**, while in Ireland it is **Mhairi** ['mahree] or **Maire** ['mahryə], which has developed into **Moira, Maura** or **Moyra** and **Maureen** or **Moreen**.

Maryanne: see MARIAN

Mat, Mattie, Matty: see MARTHA, MATILDA, MATTHEW

Matilda

This is a Germanic name, from *maht* 'might' and *hild* 'battle', the same element as in the name HILDA. It is puzzling to be told that **Maud** or **Maude** is a variant form of the name, but the transformation comes through the French, where the Germanic Mahthilda became something like Maheud, anglicized as Maud. Matilda would then be the Latin form of the name, the form written down by the chroniclers, while Maud would be the way ordinary people pronounced the name. Just as Mary became Molly which changed to Polly, so the short form **Mat** or **Matty** had its first sound changed to **Patty**, a short form shared with Patricia (see PATRICK), PATIENCE and MARTHA. **Tilly** and **Tilda** are also used as short forms.

Matthew

This is the commonest form of the name of the first Evangelist; **Matthias**, the Greek form of the name, is the alternative. Both forms are also spelt with a single 't', and they are shortened to **Mat** or **Matt** and **Matty**. The name means 'gift of God'.

Maud, Maude: see MATILDA, MADELINE

Maura, Maureen: see MARY

Maurice

Maurice is the French form of the Latin *Maurus* ('a Moor'), which was used not only for those from North Africa, but of anyone with a dark complexion. The name gave us the surnames **Morris** and **Morse**, which have come in their turn to be used as first names. The Welsh form of the name, **Meurig**, gives us the surname **Merrick**, which is also found as a first name. (See also SEYMOUR.)

Mavis

An old dialect word for a song thrush, Mavis does not seem to have been used as a girl's name before the end of the nineteenth century. In this century a similar name, **Merle**, the French for blackbird, has come into use. It has been used in the American Bible Belt as a male name, but thanks to the actress Merle Oberon is now primarily a female name. **Merlene** is an elaboration of the name, probably influenced by MARLENE.

Maximilian

This is one of the best-known 'invented' names, having been made up by the Emperor Frederick III (1415–93), for his son. Maximilian is a blend of the names of two admired Romans whose qualities Frederick hoped his son would inherit, Fabius Maximus and Scipio Aemilianus. However, it is worth noting that Maximilianus already existed as a Roman name, based on the word for 'great'. The short form of the name, **Max**, is shared with the unrelated **Maxwell**, which comes from a Scots place name ('Mack's well'); but the French name **Maxime**, used for either sex, does come from the word meaning 'great'. English speakers have used **Maxim** for the masculine, uncomfortable with the feminine feel of the final 'e' in the French form. **Maxine** seems to be a modern coinage, a female version of Max. There is also a feminine form of Maximilian, **Maximilienne** or **Maxilmilianne**.

May

As well as being a pet form of MARGARET and MARY, May is used as an independent name, associated either with the other month names or the other flower names. **Mai** is the Welsh form of the name, while **Mae** is a common form in the United States. **Maia** and **Maya**, which have appeared in recent years, seem to be variants, rather than deriving from the name of the Central American people, or a use of the obscure Roman earth-goddess or the legendary Greek mother of Hermes.

Maybelle, Maybelline: see MABEL

Meave, Meaveen: see MAEVE

Meg, Megan, Meggie: see MARGARET

Mel: see MELVIN

Melanie

Melanie comes from the Greek word for 'black'. Melaina was one of the titles of the goddess Demeter (see DEMETRIUS) in her winter aspect, mourning for the loss of her ravished daughter **Persephone**. **Melany** is a variant, and **Melony** is said to be an old Cornish form. (See also CHLOE.)

Melchior: see JASPER

Melicent, Melisande, Melisenda: see MILLICENT

Melissa

The Greek for 'honey bee', Melissa was the name of a nymph who is said to have introduced the use of honey to mankind. She is probably the remnant of an earlier earth or fertility goddess, for there is evidence of an important goddess associated with bees in Minoan Crete and in even earlier cultures. Associated names which comes from the word for honey are **Melinda, Melita** (the Latin name for the island of Malta) and **Melina**.

Melody

This is simply the word for a tune used as a first name. It is a twentieth-century innovation.

Melony: see MELANIE

Melvin

With its variant **Melvyn**, this comes from a Scottish surname with various sources, the most important of which is a form of **Melville**, derived from a noble family taking its name from a place in Normandy, meaning 'poor settlement'. It has also been explained as a masculine form of MALVINA via the variant Melvina. **Mel** is the short form.

Mercy
The Christian virtue used as a first name, Mercy was popular with the Puritans. **Mercedes** (see DOLORES) is the Spanish equivalent. **Merry** is said to be a pet form of Mercy, but nowadays is probably more often used as an independent name or as a short form of MEREDITH. **Mercia**, the name of an Anglo-Saxon kingdom which came unto use at the beginning of this century when Old English names were popular, can also be used as a Latinate version of Mercy.

Meredith
This Welsh masculine name, also found as **Meredydd** and **Maredudd**, has been in use since the sixth century and means 'magnificent chief'. Its use as a girl's name, which probably started in the United States, is a twentieth-century development. **Merry** is used as a short form.

Merfin: see MERVYN

Merial, Meriel, Merille: see MURIEL

Merle, Merlene: see MAVIS

Merlin, Merlyn: see MERVIN

Merna: see MYRNA

Merrick: see MAURICE

Merry: see MERCY, MEREDITH

Mervyn
The Welsh name **Myrddin** or **Merfin** has been anglicized as both Mervyn and **Merlin**, the wizard from Arthurian legend. Although the town of Carmarthen is traditionally said to take its name from Merlin, it seem probable that it was the other way round, and that the Welsh name for the wizard, Myrddin Emrys, means 'EMRYS from Carmarthen'. The town's name means 'fort by the sea'. There is a variant spelling, **Merlyn**, as in the politician Merlyn Rees, which is sometimes used for girls (and then perhaps thought of

as an elaboration of MERLE). **Marvin** is an old variant of **Mervin**.

Meryl: see MURIEL

Meta: see MARGARET

Meurig: see MAURICE

Mhairi: see MARY

Mia
The source of this name is not clear. It is the Italian and Spanish word for 'my', and so may come from an endearment in one of these languages. On the other hand this may be coincidental, and the name be a pet form of some name such as Maria. Less doubtful is the role that the success of the actress Mia Farrow has had in spreading the name.

Michael
This name comes from Hebrew and means 'who is like God?'. It also appears in the Old Testament in the form of the name of the prophet **Micah**. The popularity of the Archangel Michael, the defeater of Satan and weigher of souls, guaranteed the early spread of the name throughout Europe in various forms. It also became a surname and, as **Mitchel**, is occasionally re-used as a first name. Pet forms are **Mick, Micky** and **Mike**. **Misha** or **Mischa** is a Russian masculine pet form, which, because of its apparently feminine ending, is sometimes used in this country as a girl's name (see also Sasha under ALEXANDER). The French feminine forms **Michelle** or **Michèle** have recently been popular and have developed two pronunciations ['meeshel] and [mi'shel], but there is now some evidence that the German **Michaela** [mi'kaylə] may be starting to replace it in popularity. The name SHELLEY seems to have started life as a pet form of Michelle.

Mildred
Mildred is a form of the Anglo-Saxon name Mildthryth ('gentle strength'). St Mildred was a seventh-century abbess who seems to have been well named, for she had a reputation for kindness and as a great comforter of the afflicted. The short forms **Millie** or **Milly** are shared with MILLICENT and AMELIA.

Miles

Miles is an old name of disputed meaning, although it is generally agreed that the name being the same as the Latin word for 'soldier' is pure chance. In Ireland the name is used as an English version of **Maelmor** ('servant of the Virgin Mary'). **Myles** and **Milo** are variants.

Millicent

This is the English form of the French **Melisande**, itself from a German name meaning something like 'strong in battle'. **Melicent** and **Melisenda** are variants. The short form **Millie** or **Milly** is shared with AMELIA and MILDRED.

Millie, Milly: see AMELIA, MILDRED, MILLICENT

Milo: see MILES

Milton

This English surname is made up of the elements 'mill' and the old word for 'an enclosure'. It is used as a first name in honour of the Puritan poet John Milton (1608–74), and is more common in the United States, where there is a stronger tradition of using surnames of the famous as first names.

Mima: see JEMIMA

Mina, Minella: see WILLIAM

Minerva: see ATHENE

Minna, Minnie: see MARY, MAY, WILLIAM

Minta, Minty: see ARAMINTA

Mira: see MYRA

Miranda

The Latin for 'worthy to be admired, deserving admiration', Miranda was coined by Shakespeare for the heroine of *The Tempest*. **Mirabel** or **Mirabelle** is an older name from the same root, meaning 'admirable, lovely'. The French name **Mireille** [mi'ray] and its Provençal form **Mirèio** also come from the same root. The story runs that the Provençal poet and champion of

Provençal culture, Frédérique Mistral (1830–1914) found the name in local legend, and used it as the title for a verse epic. He wanted to use the name for his god-daughter, but the priest refused to use a non-liturgical name, upon which Mistral emphatically stated that the name was a Provençal form of Miriam. As he was an expert in such things the priest could hardly demur, and so the name came to be officially accepted in France, despite the fact that the name actually comes from the Provençal *mirar* ('to admire').

Miriam: see MARY

Mischa, Misha: see MICHAEL

Mitchel: see MICHAEL

Moira: see MARY

Moll, Molly: see MARY

Mona

An Irish name, Mona comes from a word meaning 'noble'. However, in Wales it is sometimes used as the Welsh name for Anglesea, Môn, with a feminine ending.

Monica

St Monica was the mother of St AUGUSTINE. We learn a lot about her in his autobiographical writings. She must have been a rather overwhelming, as well as loving mother, combining ambition for her favourite son with a determination to save his soul. Because she was instrumental in his conversion to Christianity, her name was at first derived from the Latin *monire* ('to warn'), but the true source of her name is unknown, and may be Phoenician, as she was a native of Carthage. **Monique**, the French form of the name, is also used.

Montague, Montgomery

These two, which share the short form **Monty**, are both French baronial names brought over by the Normans. Montague ('pointed hill') is a common place name in France, but the surname comes from the place in the district of La Manche in Normandy. Montgomery is a more complicated place name, being 'mount' plus the name of an earlier German invader made up of the elements *guma* ('man') and *ric* ('power'), and is a place in Calvados, a region of Normandy.

Montserrat: see DOLORES

Morag
A Scots name, Morag is probably made up of the Gaelic element *mor* 'great' with a feminine ending indicating a pet form. However, it has been suggested that it shares with MURIEL a derivation from the word for 'sea'.

Morcant: see MORGAN

Mordecai
A Biblical name ultimately of Persian origin, Mordecai means 'a follower of the god Marduk'. It is now very rare, but kept before the public by the Canadian novelist Mordecai Richler.

Moreen: see MARY

Morfydd, Morfudd: see MORWENNA

Morgan
This is a Welsh name of disputed meaning. It seems likely that it is a conflation of several names, made up of the Welsh *môr* ('sea') or *mawr* ('great'), coupled with *can*, ('bright'), or *gen* ('born'). The sense 'sea-born' is supported by the Latin name **Pelagius**, also meaning 'sea-born', which probably translates Morgan, and was the name of the only notable early British heretic (born *c.* 370). On the other hand, another early form of the name, **Morcant**, would support a sense 'great and bright'. It is primarily a masculine name, but the appearance of Morgan or **Morgana** Le Fey in Arthurian legend as Arthur's magic-working half-sister and implacable enemy has led to its occasional use as a feminine name.

Morna: see MYRNA

Morris, Morse: see MAURICE

Mortimer
Another Norman baronial name, Mortimer derives from a French place name which comes from *mort mer* ('dead sea or pond'). There are traditions associating the adoption of the name with

Crusaders and the Dead Sea in the Holy Land. It came into fashion with other aristocratic names in the nineteenth century, but to some extent its use as a first name is influenced by the Gaelic name **Murtagh** ('sea man') being transliterated as Mortimer.

Morwenna

This name comes from the Welsh word *morwyn* ('a maiden'). **Morwena** is a variant spelling, and there are the names **Morwyn** and **Morwen** as variants. **Morfydd** or **Morfudd**, the name given to his beloved by the medieval Welsh poet Davydd ap Gwilym, probably comes from the same root.

Moses

Moses is a biblical name of disputed meaning. It is possible that, since the original Moses was born and brought up in Egypt, the name may be of Egyptian origin. It was regularly used until the eighteenth century, but is now rare. **Moss**, as both a first and a surname, started as a diminutive of Moses.

Mostyn

This is a Welsh place name meaning 'field-fortress' which was adopted as a surname in the sixteenth century, and then became a masculine first name.

Moyra: see MARY

Muirne: see MYRNA

Murdo, Murdoch ['muhdoh]

A Scottish masculine name, this is the English equivalent of the Gaelic **Murchadh** ('seaman'). It is thus also the equivalent of the Irish Murtagh (see MORTIMER), as well as being the source of the common surname. There is a rare feminine, **Murdina**.

Muriel

Muriel is an ancient Celtic name meaning 'sea-bright' which came back into use in the nineteenth century. It was revived in two main forms, Muriel and **Meriel**, and has since developed a large number of variants including **Merial, Meryl, Merille, Merrill, Merril** and **Muryell**.

Murray

A surname now used as a first name, Murray comes from Moray in north-east Scotland. This got its name from the old Celtic, meaning 'settlement by the sea'. **Murry** is the Irish spelling.

Murtagh: see MORTIMER

Muryell: see MURIEL

Myfanwy

This is a medieval Welsh name meaning 'my rare or fine one', which was revived in Wales in the nineteenth century. **Myf**, **Myfi** and **Myfina** are used as short forms.

Myles: see MILES

Myra

This is a poetic name invented in the seventeenth century by Fulke Greville, Lord Brooke (1554–1628), and remained a purely literary name until the nineteenth. Its intended meaning is not clear, but if it meant to include the sense of the Latin *mirare* ('to admire') as seems likely, then the name would be similar to MIRANDA. In the United States it has been used as the female equivalent of MYRON. The notoriety of the moors murderer Myra Hindley has not helped the popularity of the name. **Mira** is a variant.

Myrna, Morna

These two names are both forms of the Irish **Muirne**, meaning 'beloved'. **Merna** is a rare, further variant. Myrna was popularized by the American film actress Myrna Loy.

Myrddin: see MERVYN

Myron

Although this name is hardly used in this country, it is not uncommon in the United States, where it belongs to the group of first names adopted from the names of the famous, in this case the fifth-century BC Athenian sculptor of the 'Discus Thrower'. In Greek the name meant 'fragrant'.

Myrtle

This plant was probably adopted as a girl's first name because it has been used to symbolize love and fidelity. Until quite recently it was worn or carried by brides at weddings in the same way as orange blossom is today, and women would try to grow the plant from cuttings taken from their wreath or bouquet.

Mysie: see MARGARET

N

Nadia
Nadia is the pet form of the Russian name **Nadezhda** ('HOPE'), although only pet forms of the name seem to be much used outside Russia. **Nadine** is a popular French variant, and in the past the form **Nadège** was also used in France.

Nahum
A prophet in the Old Testament, Nahum wrote in the seventh century BC. As well as the usual oracles about the rewards of respecting God and the vengeance that awaits those who do not, his book gives a vivid description of the fall of Nineveh. The name means 'full of comfort', and is probably a short form of a name describing God as comforter. It is rarely used, but an awareness of it is kept alive by the hymn writer Nahum Tate.

Nan, Nana, Nanette, Nanna, Nannie, Nanny: see ANN

Nance, Nancy, Nansi: see ANN, AGNES

Nandy: see FERDINAND

Nanty: see ANTONY

Naomi
Naomi is the model mother-in-law of the Old Testament. When she and her daughter-in-law RUTH were left widows, Naomi wanted to travel back to her own land. Such was the love Ruth had for Naomi that she refused to be separated from her, even though it meant leaving her own people. Naomi means 'pleasant'.

Nat: see NATHANIEL

Natalia, Natalie, Natalya, Natasha, Natasja, Nathalie: see NOEL

Nathaniel

A Hebrew name meaning 'gift of God', Nathaniel was the name of one the apostles, probably the same as BARTHOLOMEW. **Nathan** ('gift') was the name of a character in the Old Testament who was a prophet, and counsellor and critic of kings David and Solomon. Nathan is sometimes used as a short form of Nathaniel, and they share the short form **Nat** and more rarely **Nath** and **Nate**. There has recently been an increase in the popularity of these names.

Neal, Neale: see NEIL

Ned, Neddie, Neddy: see EDGAR, EDMUND, EDWARD, EDWIN

Neil

This name comes from the Irish word for 'champion'. The Irish form of the name is **Niall**, correctly pronounced the same way as the English form, but often given a spelling pronunciation ['niəl]. **Neal** or **Neale** is a common alternative form. The name is also the source of **Nigel**, which comes from Nigellus, the form given to the name in written Latin. This was not at first a spoken form, but the Latin was later misunderstood, and the name Nigel became linked with the Latin word *niger* ('black'). Admiral **Nelson** probably inherited his surname from a 'Neil son', and this is now used as a first name in memory of him. There have been attempts to form feminine forms of the name: **Nelda** from Neil and **Nigella** and **Nigelia** from Nigel, but none of them is very common.

Neirin: see ANEURIN

Nell, Nellie, Nelly: see ELEANOR, HELEN

Nelson: see NEAL

Nerissa

Nerissa is the name of the delightful and witty maid and companion to PORTIA in Shakespeare's *Merchant of Venice*. Not as common as other Shakespearean girls' names, it is nevertheless steadily if quietly used. The name comes from the Greek sea nymphs, the Nereides, daughters of Nereus, the sea god, who also give us the rarer **Nerida** and **Nerina**.

Nerys
This comes from the Welsh word *ner* ('lord'), plus a feminine ending. It is a recent Welsh name, given fame by the actress Nerys Hughes.

Nessa, Nessie, Nest, Nesta: see AGNES

Net, Netta, Nettie, Netty: see AGNES, ANTHONY, JANE

Neville, Nevil
This is a noble surname used as a first name. The fifteenth-century Earl of Warwick, known as 'Warwick the Kingmaker', was the first Neville Earl of Warwick. Three of his five paternal uncles were earls, and all four of his aunts married dukes, so the family name spread through the aristocracy. The name, which means 'new town', came into use as a first name in the seventeenth century, but became popular only in the nineteenth.

Nial, Niall: see NEIL

Niamh ['neev]
This is an Irish girl's name meaning 'bright'. The anglicized form is **Niav**. In Irish mythology she takes the poet OSSIAN to the otherworld Land of Promise, where she is a princess.

Nicholas
Nicholas comes from a Greek name meaning 'victory of the people'. **Nicolas** was the original form of the name, the insertion of the 'h' being a hypercorrect form, like the 'h' in Anthony. **Nicol** or **Nichol** is an old pet form, **Nick**, with **Nicky** and **Nicco** being more common today. The old form was shortened to **Col**, given a further diminutive ending, and thus gave rise to the now separate name COLIN. St Nicholas was a fourth-century bishop in Asia Minor, who, according to legend, secretly supplied three destitute girls with dowries by leaving the money at their windows. As his feast day is 6 December, this deed became associated with Christmas. The feast day of St Nicholas – or Santa **Claus**, as he is known in Dutch – is still celebrated in many parts of Europe as the beginning of the Christmas season, or as a time for giving presents. Dutch settlers took the tradition to the United States, where it became

more firmly associated with 25 December, and from there it spread to other parts of the world. **Nichola** is the commonest feminine form of the name along with the French **Nicole**; the latter has the diminutive **Nicolette**, which in turn leads to Colette (see COLIN). The short form of the name is spelt variously **Nicky, Nickie, Nikki** or **Nicci**.

Nigel, Nigelia, Nigella: see NEIL

Nina, Ninette, Ninon: see ANN

Ninian

St Ninian was a fifth-century Briton who became a missionary to the Picts in Scotland. This led to the name being a popular one in Scotland in earlier times. There has recently been something of a revival of interest in this as well as other local names, possibly helped by the name being kept alive by its appearance in Scott's *The Antiquary*. **Ringan** is a dialect form of the name.

Nita: see ANN, JANE

Noah

This is a Hebrew name meaning 'repose'. The story of Noah and his ark must be one of the best known Bible stories, but despite this the name is not much used now. One bearer of the name, Noah Webster (1758–1843) had a considerable impact on the cultural history of the United States, being not only the creator of Webster's *Dictionary* but also introducing the spelling reforms that distinguish American English from that of Great Britain.

Noel, Noël

This, the French word for **Christmas** (itself occasionally used as a first name), was originally given to children born on or about the 25 December. **Noelle** or **Noëlle** is the French feminine form of the name, with **Noella** a variant. In English-speaking countries **Noele, Noleen, Noelena** and **Noeline** are also found. **Natalie** is a name with the same meaning, since it comes from the Latin *dies natalis* ('the birthday (of Christ)'), which is the root of the French *noël*. **Nathalie** is the French spelling. The Russian version of the name, **Natalia** (occasionally found as **Natalya** and shortened to **Talia**) has a pet form **Natasha** (sometimes spelled **Natasja**) which had a spurt of popularity in the 1960s after a television adaptation of Tolstoy's *War and Peace* (1863–9), which has a Natasha as the heroine.

Nola: see FENELLA

Noll, Nolly: see OLIVER

Nora, Norah
This started life as pet form of names such as HONORIA, LEONORA and ELEANOR, but it has long been used as an independent name. Honoria was a particularly popular name in Ireland, and was frequently reduced to Nora. It then acquired a diminutive suffix, and **Noreen** was formed. This name has been further elaborated to **Norlene** and **Noreena**. **Nonie** is a pet form of Nora.

Norman
This name means 'man from the north' and was in use in England for Scandinavian settlers even before the country was invaded by the Normans – themselves Scandinavian settlers in France. **Norma**, which is used as the feminine form of the name, seems to have been invented by Felice Romani, the librettist of Bellini's opera of that name, which was first performed in 1832. Some would derive it from the Latin *norma* meaning 'rule, standard, measure'.

Nuala: see FENELLA

Nye: see ANEURIN

Oberon: see AUBREY

Octavia
The Latin feminine for 'eighth', Octavia was originally a Roman name given to an eighth child, but later it was associated with the imperial family, the first Emperor, AUGUSTUS, being called **Octavius** or **Octavian** before he took his title. Octavia is shortened to **Tavy**, **Tave** or **Tavia**.

Odette, Odile, Odo: see OTTO

Odysseus: see ULYSSES

Oighrig: see AFRIC, EUPHEMIA

Olaf: see OLIVER

Olga
This is the Russian version of the Scandinavian name **Helga**, meaning 'holy, blessed'. Although Helga was found in pre-Conquest England, its use today is a modern re-introduction. The predominance of Olga over Helga probably reflects the popularity of Russian literature.

Oliver
ROLAND and Oliver were inseparable companions and the two greatest of Charlemagne's peers in the old French stories. The followers of Charlemagne in both fact and fiction were Franks, a Germanic people, and their names reflect this. Thus, although Oliver looks as if it is based on the olive, symbol of peace, and the French form of the name, **Olivier**, is identical with the French for

an olive tree, the name most probably is a form of the name **Olaf**, ('remains + ancestors'), which in its old form Olafr would have a very similar pronunciation to the modern name. Oliver was long out of fashion after the fall of Oliver Cromwell (whose nicknames illustrate the old pet forms **Noll** and **Nolly**), but time has reduced the close association of the Protector and the name, and Oliver is now firmly back in fashion. **Ol** and **Ollie** are now the more common short forms. The name **Havelock** is said to be the Welsh form of the name.

Feminine forms of the name are even more closely associated with the plant, being **Olive** and **Olivia**. Olivia is another Shakespearean introduction, used for the noble lady beloved by the duke in *Twelfth Night*. The name is sometimes shortened to **Livia** or **Livy**, although Livia is a name in its own right, being an Roman family name made famous by the wife of the emperor AUGUSTUS.

Olwen

Olwen is a character from the medieval Welsh story of *Culhwch and Olwen* in which her advice enables her lover to win her from her ogre father. She was of outstanding beauty, and four white trefoils sprang up in her footprints wherever she trod, hence her name, which means 'white footprint'. **Olwyn** is a common variant of the name, and it is not surprising that this charming legend has made the name popular with Welsh parents.

Olympia

Mount Olympus was the home of the gods in Greek mythology. From this mountain the Greek name **Olympias** was coined. It was the name of the ruthless but admired mother of ALEXANDER the Great, and from there spread through the lands he conquered. It was given to a fourth-century AD Byzantine woman of equally strong but rather more attractive character who was later canonized, and as St Olympia the name spread through Europe. Both forms of the name occur early in England, but now the name is rare, and more often found in France as **Olympe**.

Onyx: see JEWELL

Oona, Oonagh: see UNA

Opal: see JEWELL

Ophelia

Another Shakespearean introduction, Ophelia is the young girl rejected by the prince in *Hamlet*. Parents do not seem to have been put off by the story of her madness and suicide, and the name has a steady use. It probably comes from a Greek root meaning 'help'.

Oriel, Oriole: see AURELIUS

Orla ['awlə]

An Irish name meaning 'golden lady', Orla thus has the same meaning as the AURELIUS group of names. In Irish it is spelt **Orfhlaith**, and it can also be found in the form **Orlagh**. **Aurnia** is a variant. There is also a masculine Orla who occurs in the poems of OSSIAN, but while this was used at the height of the European Ossianic craze in the nineteenth century, it is probably now obsolete.

Orlando: see ROLAND

Orson

This name means 'bear cub'. In medieval legend Valentine (see VALERY) and Orson were twins born to an exiled Byzantine princess. The new-born Orson is stolen by a bear, who brings him up. Despite his rough behaviour and ursine appearance, his noble nature shows through in his fighting skills, and after many adventures he is finally re-united with his family and regains his rightful place in society. By no means a common name, it has become well known this century through the fame of the actor-director Orson Welles. URSULA is the feminine equivalent of the name.

Orville: see WILBUR

Osbert

Osbert is one of a group of Old English names containing the first element *os*, meaning 'god', combined with other common name elements. Thus we have **Osric** ('god + rule'), **Oswald** ('god + power'), **Oswin** ('god + friend'), as well as Osbert ('god + bright'). They all share **Os**, **Oz**, **Ozzie** and **Ossy** as short forms. There was a revival of these names in the nineteenth century, but they are not popular at the moment.

Oscar

Although some authorities give this name a German source meaning 'divine spear', it is much more likely to be an Irish name meaning 'champion warrior'. It has strong associations with Scandinavia, but despite its being a Swedish royal name, this is not evidence for a Germanic inheritance, for it comes from Napoleon Bonaparte's passion for the poems of OSSIAN. In 1799 Napoleon was godfather to the first son of his Marshal Jean-Baptiste Bernadotte, who became king of Sweden as Karl XIV Johan. Napoleon chose to name his godson Oscar after the hero of Macpherson's poems, and this child became Oscar I of Sweden in 1844. From him the name spread to the general population, along with a number of other Ossianic names. King Oscar had as his court physician a certain Sir William Wilde, and it is probably this connection, rather than the Irish one, that led to his son being christened with two Ossianic names, Oscar FINGAL O'Flahertie Wilde. Oscar had been a popular name in the nineteenth century, but the scandalous trial of Oscar Wilde in 1895 led to a distinct fall in its popularity and it became rare, although there are now slight signs of its returning to favour.

Osric: see OSBERT

Ossian

Ossian means 'fawn' and is the name of the legendary son of Finn (see FINLAY). The name is also found as **Ossin** and **Oisin**. According to legend Ossian was the leader of the Irish Fenians who were defeated at the battle of Fabhra by King Carbery in 283. Ossian was left as the last survivor of the Fenians and after spending some years in fairyland (see NIAMH) he was converted to Christianity by St Patrick. In the eighteenth century James Macpherson created a great stir by publishing a series of poems associated with Ossian, supposedly ancient but in fact mainly his own work, and this led to a number of names which occurred in these poems, such as OSCAR, FINGAL, SELMA and MALVINA, coming into use. A feminine form, **Ossia**, is also found.

Ossy, Oswald, Oswin: see OSBERT

Otis: see OTTO

Otto

The Germanic name element *ot* or *od*, meaning 'riches, prosperity', has developed into a number of names. Otto is the German form which has not been used very long in this country, but the name came over with the Normans in the form of **Odo**, William the Conqueror's avaricious half-brother. The French feminine forms of the name, **Odile** and **Odette**, reflect this form in 'd', but the 't' forms are also to be found in **Ottilie**, **Ottoline** and **Ottilia**. The name **Otis** comes from a surname which developed from the same root.

Owain, Owen: see EUGENE

Oz, Ozzie: see OSBERT

P

Paddy, Padraic, Pádraig, Padrig: see PATRICK

Paloma
The Spanish for 'dove', Paloma was used by Picasso for his daughter's name, and is occasionally found in this country, probably as a direct result of Paloma Picasso's fame. For masculine names meaning 'dove' see MALCOLM.

Pamela
This name was invented by Sir Philip Sydney (1554–86) for use in his pastoral *Arcadia*. He seems to have intended the word to be pronounced [pa'mela] and may have intended it to be understood as from the Greek, meaning 'all honey'. When it became a famous name with the success in 1740 of Samuel Richardson's long novel *Pamela: or, Virtue Rewarded*, the name was still not pronounced ['pamelǝ] as today, for Pope in one of his *Epistles* refers to the novel, and prints the name Pamēla. **Pamella** is a variant and **Pam** the short form.

Pandora
In Greek mythology Pandora plays the same role as EVE in the Bible, bringing misfortune upon mankind. She was created by the gods on the orders of Zeus, to take vengeance for the stealing of fire for mankind's use. Each god gave her a gift of some desirable quality (the name means 'all gifts'), but she was also made inquisitive. Her husband had a sealed box which she had been forbidden to open, but she did so, and out flew all the ills which afflict mankind. Hope had also been sealed in the box, and that alone made the afflictions bearable. Pandora is now quite regularly used, and can be shortened to **Panda**.

Pansy

One of the less common flower names, Pansy has been in use since the end of the nineteenth century. The name of the flower comes from the French word *pensée* ('a thought').

Paris: see ALEXANDER, HELEN

Parnel: see PETER

Parthalon, Partholon: see BARTHOLOMEW

Pascal

The name means 'Easter' and was originally given to those born at that time of year, just as NOEL was given to those born at Christmas. The surname **Pascoe** comes from the Cornish form of the name. **Pascale, Pascalle** or, rarely, **Pascaline** are its feminines.

Pat: see PATRICK, MARTHA

Patience

This is one of the Christian virtues, and as such came into use in the seventeenth century by the Puritans. It has recently been out of favour, but now shows slight signs of coming back into fashion.

Patrick

Patrick comes from the Latin *patricius* ('a nobleman'). The Irish form of their patron saint's name is **Pádraig**, with **Padraic** and **Phadrig** as variants, but the name was not used in Ireland in early times, possibly out of reverence for the great saint. St Patrick was not a native Irishman, but a Briton, and his name has survived in Welsh as **Padrig**. **Pat** and **Paddy** are the commonest short forms of Patrick, with **Patsy**, once common, now more generally female. **Patricia**, the feminine, comes from the Latin form of the name, and has a number of short forms such as **Pat, Patty, Patsy, Tricia** and **Tisha**.

Pattie, Patty: see MARTHA, MATILDA, PATRICK

Paul

This name comes from the Latin *paulus* ('small'), and was a suitably humble name for SAUL of Tarsus to adopt after his conversion from persecutor of Christians to Apostle. **Paula** is the direct Latin feminine of the name, with **Pauline** a diminutive derived from **Paulina**. **Polly** is occasionally a pet form of Pauline.

Pearce: see PETER

Pearl
Although it is one of the jewel names, Pearl has the same meaning as MARGARET, so is also found as a pet form of that name.

Pedran, Pedr: see PETER

Peg, Peggie, Peggy: see MARGARET

Pelagius: see MORGAN

Penelope
In Homer's *Odyssey*, Penelope is the faithful wife of Odysseus (see ULYSSES), who successfully resists the wooing of the 50 suitors who wish to win the kingdom by marrying her, for the 10 years it takes for her husband to reach home after the fall of Troy. Her main ploy is to say that she will not choose a new husband until she has woven a shroud for her father-in-law. Although she diligently weaves all day, at night she unpicks her work. The meaning of the name is something of a problem. It appears to come from the word for a duck, but it is very difficult to see why the ancient Penelope should have been named after this bird. **Pen** and **Penny** are its short forms.

Percy
The first of the Percys came over with the Conqueror and founded the great Northumbrian family of that name. The surname comes from the common French place name, Percé, in his case probably from the village near St Lô. The village name, in its turn, comes from the Gallo-Roman name Persius (see DANÄE). The surname came into use as a first name in the eighteenth century. Percy is also used as a short form of **Percival**, which comes from the Arthurian romance. It was invented in the twelfth century by the French poet Chrétien de Troyes for his perfect knight. It seems to be made up of the elements *perce-val* ('pierce-valley'), but the reason for this is not clear, and it may be that the name is a corruption of the Welsh name for a hero who shares some of the same adventures, **Peredur**,

whose name means 'hard spears'. Percival is sometimes shortened to **Val**.

Perdita

This name means 'the lost one' and was created by Shakespeare for the heroine of *The Winter's Tale*, who is abandoned as an infant. Despite the charming personality of the original, and the happy outcome of the play, this is not one of the commoner Shakespearean names, although it was certainly in use among the ruling classes in the early part of this century, for the name was given to the granddaughter of the prime minister, H.H. Asquith, in 1910.

Peregrine

Peregrine comes from the Latin for 'a pilgrim, traveller', and was a common early Christian name, emphasising the transitory nature of life on Earth against the eternity of Heaven. Its only connection with the peregrine falcon is that they share a common root. Most birds used for falconry were taken from the nest, but the peregrine was captured while travelling to its breeding ground; hence its name. **Perry** can be used as a short form of Peregrine, but is also used as an independent name in the United States in honour of two Admiral Perrys, one of whom, Oliver Hazard Perry, defeated the British fleet on Lake Erie in 1812, while Matthew Galbraith Perry opened up Japan to foreign interests.

Perkin, Pernel: see PETER

Persephone: see CORINNA, DEMETRIUS, MELANIE

Perry: see PEREGRINE

Perseus: see DANÄE

Persis

This name means 'Persian woman'. It is now rare, but was not uncommon in the seventeenth century, when obscure names from the Bible were in fashion. The biblical Persis is mentioned in the Epistle of St Paul to the Romans (xvi.12), when he writes 'Salute the beloved Persis, which laboured much in the Lord'. Nothing else is known of her.

Peter

Peter means 'stone', and started life as a nickname, given to the Apostle SIMON by Christ, who, punning on the word, says 'Thou art Peter, and upon this rock I will build my church' (Matthew xvi.18). Peter is formed directly from the Latin *petrus*; but **Piers**, the alternative form of the name, comes via the French **Pierre**. Piers was the common vernacular form of the name in the Middle Ages, and gives us the surnames **Pearce** and **Pierce**, sometimes used as first names. **Pete** is now the common pet form, but in the past **Peterkin** and **Perkin** were used. In Welsh the name became **Pedr**, with the pet forms **Pedran** and **Petran**.

There are a large number of feminine versions of the name. According to legend St **Petronilla** or **Petronella** was the daughter of St Peter (the name is actually a form of the Roman family name of the Petronii), and this was used as a feminine equivalent. It was very common in medieval England, when it was shortened to **Petronel**, **Pernel** or **Parnel**. **Peta**, **Petra** and **Petrina** are based more closely on the masculine.

Phebe: see PHOEBE

Phelim: see FELICITY

Phemia, Phemie: see EUPHEMIA

Philip

A traditional name in the ancient Macedonian royal family, Philip means 'loving horses'. It was spread by the Macedonian conquests (see further under ALEXANDER), became common throughout the Middle East, and was the name of one of the Apostles and a number of saints, which guaranteed the spread of the name through Europe. It is sometimes spelt **Phillip**, as in the surname, and shortened to **Phil** and **Pip**. **Flip** is a contracted form of the name. **Philippa** (sometimes **Phillipa**, **Phillippa** or **Philipa**) is the usual feminine and this is shortened to **Pippa**, which is originally an Italian form. The French feminine **Philippine** is occasionally found.

Phillida, Phillis: see PHYLLIS

Philomena

This name means 'beloved'. In 1802 an inscription and some bones were discovered in the Catacombs at Rome, and interpreted as being the bones of a St Philomena. In 1863 Charlotte M. Yonge could write 'So many wonders are said to have been worked by this phantom saint, the mere produce of a blundered inscription, that . . . she is by far the most fashionable patroness in the Romish Church'. The name was particularly popular in Ireland, but has lost favour there since the saint was declared spurious. However the name is still regularly used, with the French form **Philomène** occasionally found.

Phineas

Phineas is the name of two minor characters in the Old Testament, where the name appears as **Phinehas**. Its meaning is obscure, but it may mean 'oracle'. Little used now, the name is kept alive by the stories about the American showman Phineas T. Barnum (1810–91) and in literature by Trollope's novel *Phineas Finn* (1869).

Phoebe ['feebee]

The name means 'the shining one' and was an epithet of the goddess Artemis, sister of Phoebus Apollo, in her aspect of moon goddess (see also DIANA, CYNTHIA). It is found in the Bible in the same chapter of Romans as PERSIS, in the form **Phebe**, and this justified it being adopted as a Christian name. It has been rather out of favour since the early part of this century, but is now showing distinct signs of coming back into fashion. Phoebe is also used as a short form of EUPHEMIA.

Phyllis

Phyllis is a Greek name meaning 'leafy'. In mythology Phyllis is a Thracian maiden who hangs herself when her lover does not return from his own country, where he has gone to settle his affairs, within the promised time, and is transmogrified into an almond tree. When her lover finally returns he embraces the almond tree, and the plant, hitherto barren, puts forth green leaves. **Phyllida** is a literary elaboration of the name. They are also found as **Phillis** and **Phillida**.

Pia ['peeə]

The Latin feminine for 'pious', Pia is an Italian name which has only recently come into use in this country, although the masculine, Pius, has long been familiar as the name of numerous popes.

Pierce, Pierre, Piers: see PETER

Pip, Pippa: see PHILIP

Pollux: see COSMO

Polly: see MARY, PAULINE

Poppy

Poppy is another flower name which became particularly popular at the end of the last century and the beginning of this. Out of favour for a number of years, it is once more coming back into use.

Portia ['pawshə]

A Roman family name, coming from the word for 'pig', Portia has become dissociated from its roots thanks to Shakespeare. He has two Portias in his plays. One, Cato's daughter and Brutus' faithful and stoical wife in *Julius Caesar*, is a Roman matron who really existed. The other, the heroine of *The Merchant of Venice*, combines charm with wit and wisdom, and it is after her that most Portias are named.

Primrose

Like POPPY, Primrose was a very popular name at the turn of the century, but there does not seem to have been quite the same return of interest in it. **Primula**, the Latin name for the plant, has also been used.

Priscilla

This is a biblical name. Priscilla was very active in the early church, being both a supporter and follower of St Paul. She is mentioned in various books in the New Testament, including the chapter of Romans that gives us PHOEBE and PERSIS. Priscilla comes from an old Roman family name meaning 'ancient'. **Prissy** and **Cilla** are the short forms.

Prudence

Like other virtue names, Prudence was much loved by the Puritans, but before that had been found in the form **Prudentia** as a saint's name; this in turn was probably modelled on **Prudentius**, a much admired early Christian Latin poet of the fourth century. **Prue** is its short form.

Prunella

Prunella may be a diminutive of the Latin *prunus* both the word for 'plum tree' and the botanical name for a large group of flowering trees that brighten gardens in winter and spring. Prunella is also the name for a kind of silk and the Latin name for both the wild flower self-heal and the hedge sparrow, but this is probably coincidental.

Pythias: see DAMIAN

Queenie: see REX

Quentin

This name comes from the Latin name *quintus* ('fifth'), traditionally given to a fifth son. St Quentin was a third-century missionary and martyr who met his death in the French city now named after him. **Quintin** is a common variant, and **Quinton** is also found on occasion.

Quincy

An aristocratic surname, Quincy comes from the French place-name of Cuinchy (north of Arras). This in its turn comes from a Roman personal name Quintus, so the name has the same root as QUENTIN. Quincy (sometimes **Quincey**) is used more frequently in the United States, where it came into use in honour of John Quincy Adams (1767–1848), the sixth president of that country.

R

Rab, Rabbie: see ROBERT

Rachel
A Hebrew name meaning 'ewe', Rachel was a suitable name for a girl who kept her father's sheep (Genesis xxix.9). The biblical Rachel was 'beautiful and well favoured' and dearly loved by her husband JACOB, although she did not get on with her sister and co-wife LEAH. The name is often spelt **Rachael** and has developed in a number of different directions. The variant **Rachelle** [ra'shel] has in turn developed the form **Rochelle**. This is a more likely source than the name of the Breton port, which means 'little rock'; although it is worth noting that it is an American name, and Rochelle is also a transatlantic place name – for example, Rochelle Park in New Jersey. Rachelle and Rochelle use SHELLEY as a short form. Rachel can be shortened to **Rae** or **Ray**, and this has been elaborated into **Raelene**. **Raquel**, the Spanish form of the name, has come into use since it was made famous by the actress Raquel Welch.

Rae: see RACHEL, RAYMOND

Rafael, Rafaela: see RAPHAEL

Rafe: see RALPH

Raine: see REX

Raisa
After the success of Mrs Gorbachev's visit to this country, a few instances of babies being given this name were recorded. The name is an unusual one in Russia. It comes from Greek, and means 'to lighten, alleviate'.

196

Ralph

This comes from an old Germanic name Rad(w)ulf made up of the elements 'counsel + wolf'. The spelling **Ralf** is closer to the original, the -ph form being an eighteenth-century 'improvement'. The variant **Rafe**, found since the Middle Ages, reflects the pronunciation ['rayf] which was the norm until this century. **Raoul** (usually [rowl] in this country) is the French form of the word. **Rolf**, from Hrodulf ('fame + wolf') is a closely allied name, which was absorbed by Ralph in the Middle Ages, and obsolete until revived as a separate name in the nineteenth century. **Rollo** was the medieval Latin form of Rolf, while in Germany the name became **Rudolph** or **Rudolf**, with a short form **Rudy** or **Rudi**. This was introduced into the English-speaking world in the last century, but, despite the enormous popularity of Rudolph Valentino in the 1920s, the name has never been very common. Its more recent association with red-nosed reindeer cannot have helped!

Ramon, Ramona: see RAYMOND

Ranald: see REGINALD

Randolph, Randolf

An Old English name, Randolph means 'shield wolf'. It has two major variants, **Ranulf** (very occasionally **Renouf**) and **Randal** or **Randall**, which at the moment is probably more frequently given than the original form. The short form **Randy** is now treated as an independent name, especially in the United States, but the alternative **Dolph** is rarely heard now.

Raoul: see RALPH

Raphael

The archangel Raphael's name means 'God heals', reflecting his role in the Apocryphal *Book of Tobit*, where he restores Tobit's sight. The name has been less popular than the other archangels MICHAEL and GABRIEL, despite his being the patron of doctors and travellers, and for a long time it was regarded as a particularly Jewish name. Nowadays it is probably most closely associated with the Italian Renaissance painter. **Rafael** is a variant, and the Italian feminine **Raphaela** or **Rafaela** is sometimes found.

Raquel: see RACHEL

Rasmus, Rastus: see ERASMUS

Ray: see RACHEL, RAYMOND

Raymond

The old Germanic name Raginmund ('counsel + protection') became Raimund in Old French and was brought over to this country by the Normans, where it became Raymond or **Raymund**, with the short form **Ray** or **Rae**. When the Normans later conquered Ireland they took the name with them, and there it became **Redmond** or **Redmund**, an increasingly popular name. In Spanish it became **Ramon**, sometimes used in the United States, but rare compared with the feminine **Ramona**, made famous as the title of a popular song. The French feminine **Raymonde** is also occasionally found.

Rebecca

The meaning of the name Rebecca is not clear, although it may mean either 'cow' or 'noose'. She appears as **Rebekah**, a form that is occasionally used, in the Old Testament, Rebecca being the spelling used in the New. She was the mother of Esau and JACOB, the founder of the house of Israel. Jacob was her favourite son, and it was Rebecca who planned the scheme by which Jacob deprived his brother of his birthright (Genesis xxvii). Rebecca comes across as a strong-minded woman, used to giving orders and with no patience if contradicted; but also as a woman capable of great love. **Becky**, the usual short form, is familiar from Becky Sharp, the heroine of Thackeray's *Vanity Fair* (1847–8).

Redmond, Redmund: see RAYMOND

Redvers

General Sir Redvers Buller (1836–1908) played a prominent part in the Boer War. He was greatly criticised for his conduct of the war, and later was dismissed from his post after coming into conflict with the government of the day, but his actions were often prompted by a care for his troops, and he was popular with the men under his command, which is no doubt the reason for the brief popularity of this name at the turn of the century. It comes from an aristocratic surname which derives from the French place name Reviers in Normandy. The name is very rarely used today.

Reece, Rees: see RHYS

Regina, Regine: see REX

Reginald
Reginald, with its short forms Reg, Reggie and occasionally REX, comes from the Latin form of the name Reynold, the Norman version of an old Germanic name Reginwald ('might + rule'). Ronald, with its short forms Ron and Ronnie, is from the Old Norse form of the same name. In Scotland Ranald is an occasional variant.

Reine: see REX

Rena: see ANDREW

Renée, Renee
This is the French form of the Latin name Renata ('reborn'), referring to Christian baptism. It can also be spelt Rennie or Renie (see also IRENE), Rene and Renny. The masculine form René, from Renatus, is very common in France, but little used here.

Renouf: see RANDOLPH

Reuben
The name given to the eldest son of JACOB, Reuben was interpreted in the Bible (Genesis xxix.32) as meaning 'behold a son'. It is also spelt Ruben.

Rex
Rex, the Latin word for 'king', came into use as a first name in the nineteenth century (see also REGINALD). The French equivalent of Rex is Regis, the inflected form of the Latin, although this was adopted as a first name in honour of Saint Jean François Regis, the apostle of the Vivarais region. There is a wide range of feminine equivalents. Regina (sometimes shortened to Gina) is the Latin for 'queen' and Queenie started life as a pet form of this name. In French the name becomes Regine. Raine and Reine are based on the French word for 'queen', while the Irish name Riona had the same meaning and ultimately the same root.

Reynold: see REGINALD

Rhiannon

An important figure in early Welsh literature, Rhiannon's antecedents go back even before the earliest surviving legends, for she seems to be a survival of an ancient Celtic goddess, possibly having some connection with horses. Her name means 'nymph, goddess'. It is also spelt **Rhianon**, and is beginning to spread to non-Welsh areas. There are a number of other Welsh girls' names which come from the same root. **Rhian** or **Rhiain** means 'maiden', and has variants **Rhianedd** and **Rhianydd** based on the plural form of the word; **Rhianwen** or **Rhiainwen** combines the word for 'maiden' with that meaning 'white' or 'fair'.

Rhoda

Rhoda is from the Greek meaning 'rose' and is another example of an apparently pagan name being made 'respectable' by being that of a minor New Testament character. It was very popular at the turn of the century, but is not much used now.

Rhodri: see RODERICK

Rhona, Rona

This is a difficult name. It may be from a Scottish island, in which case it means 'rough island'; it may be a short form of ROWENA; or it may be a feminized form of **Ronan**, the name of a fifth-century Irish saint, which probably comes from the word for 'seal'. It seems to have been in use only since about 1870, and became fashionable in the 1930s when is was given glamour by the successful 'Rhona Roy' fashion clothes.

Rhonda

Rhonda is probably a respelling of the Welsh Rhondda valley, which takes its name from its river. The word means 'noisy'.

Rhonwen: see ROWENA

Rhydderch: see RODNEY

Rhys

A Welsh masculine name, Rhys means 'ardour' and so implies 'fiery warrior'. It was the name of two twelfth-century warriors who fought successfully against the English invaders of Wales. It is sometimes found in the forms **Rees** and **Reece**, more common as surnames.

Ria: see MARY

Richard

Richard comes from a Germanic root meaning 'strong ruler'. It was in use among the Anglo-Saxons in the form Ricehard, but the modern form was introduced by the Normans. It has long been a popular name, as can be seen from the number of pet forms it has developed, including **Dick, Dickie, Dicky, Diccon** or **Dickon; Rick** and **Ricky** (see also ERIC, FREDERICK), **Rich** and **Richie**. Attempts at forming feminines have been less successful, but **Ricarda, Richenda** and **Richelle** are all used.

Rick, Ricky: see ERIC, FREDERICK, RICHARD

Ringan: see NINIAN

Riona: see REX

Rita: see MARGARET

Robert

A Germanic name, Robert is formed from elements meaning 'fame' and 'bright'. Like Richard, it has long been part of the basic stock of English names and has consequently developed a large number of pet forms. Dod, Dobbin, Hob and Hobbie were all used in the past but are now obsolete, but that still leaves **Bert** and **Bertie; Bob** and **Bobbie** or **Bobby; Rob, Robbie, Robo**, and in Scotland **Rab** and **Rabbie**. **Robin** (sometimes **Robyn** in Wales) is now often used as a separate name, but started life as a French pet form of Rob. **Roberta** and **Robina** are the older feminine forms, and more recently **Robyn** and **Bobbie** have become fairly common for girls. In Germany the 'o' of Robert became a 'u' and the 'b' changed to 'p', and the name became **Rupert**. The name was introduced into this country by Prince Rupert of the Rhine (1618–92), a romantic figure who showed great flair and bravery while fighting on the side of his uncle King Charles I during the English civil war and, later, as a naval commander in the Dutch wars. Anthony Hope's swashbuckling romance *Rupert of Hentzau* (1898) added a further romantic gloss to the name.

Rochelle: see RACHEL

Roderick

Roderick comes from two Germanic name-elements meaning 'fame + power' and has the short forms **Rod** and **Roddy**. It is also used as the English equivalent of two ancient Welsh names, **Rhodri**, meaning 'circle (possibly implying a coronet) + ruler', and **Rhydderch** ('exalted ruler'). The Welsh patronymic 'ap (son of) Roderick' developed into the surname **Broderick**, which is sometimes used as a first name. In Scotland Roderick has also been used as the equivalent of the Gaelic **Ruairi** (see RORY).

Rodge: see ROGER

Rodney

This is a surname which came to be used as a first name in honour of Admiral George Rodney (1718–92), an outstanding commander who was instrumental in bringing much of the West Indies under British rule. It has the same short forms as Roderick.

Roger

Derived from the Germanic elements 'fame + spear', Roger is the French form of the name of the Danish King that appears in the great Anglo-Saxon epic *Beowulf* as Hrothgar. **Hodge** and Hodgekin were used as diminutives in the past and became typical names of rustic labourers. **Rodge** is now sometimes used as a short form.

Roisin: see ROSE

Roland, Rowland

This is a Germanic name meaning 'fame + land' (Rowland being the commoner form for the surname). The *Song of Roland* is the great epic of medieval France in which Roland, brave and honourable above all, but lacking the wisdom of his close friend OLIVER, is betrayed by his step-father Ganelon and killed by the Saracens, but is afterwards avenged by his uncle, Charlemagne. This character became the hero of later stories in Italy, where his name became **Orlando**, a form that has been growing in popularity in recent years.

Rolf, Rollo: see RALPH

Roma

This is one of a group of names connected with the city of Rome, although none of them is very common. Roma is simply the Italian form of the city's name. **Romaine**, more common on the Continent, is the feminine of **Roman**, 'a citizen of Rome', and the same name as the Italian **Romeo**. **Romola**, the eponymous heroine of George Eliot's novel (1863), is a feminine form of the name **Romulus**, the legendary founder of Rome. **Romilly**, a surname now occasionally used as a girl's name, comes from a French place name, but this in its turn would have come from a founder whose name derived from Romulus.

Romy: see ROSEMARY

Ron: see REGINALD

Rona: see RHONA

Ronald, Ronnie: see REGINALD

Ronan: see RHONA

Rory, Rorie

This is the anglicized form of the Gaelic **Ruairi** or **Ruairdhri** ('the red-haired one'), originally a nickname. In Scotland it is still very much a Highlander's name, and its spread to England is probably from Ireland rather than Scotland (see also RODERICK). **Roy** is from the same root, the Gaelic *ruadh* ('red').

Rosaleen: see ROSE

Rosalind

Rosalind is originally a Germanic name made up of elements long interpreted as meaning 'horse' and 'serpent'; but now philologists seem to prefer the meaning 'fame + shield'. However, like BELINDA, the name has been treated as if it came from a Romance language, and analysed as 'rose + beautiful'. Variants are **Rosalyn**, **Rosaline**, **Roslyn** and **Rosalinda**. In the same way **Rosamund** ('horse (or fame) + protection') has been thought of in terms of the Latin *rosa munda* ('pure rose') or *rosa mundi* ('rose of the world'), both of which are images that have been used to describe the Virgin Mary. It has **Rosamond** as a variant and the two groups of names share **Roz** as a short form.

Rose

Historically, Rose may not be the simple plant name that it appears but a Germanic name from the same root as ROSALIND and **Rosamund**. However, there can be little doubt that since the Middle Ages it has been thought of as a flower name, despite the fact that such names were unusual at that time. The rose is symbolic of so many things – the Virgin Mary, love, England and much else – that it is hardly surprising the name has enjoyed such long use. Although in recent decades it has been out of favour, in the past few years it has enjoyed a sudden burst of popularity with parents. It has developed a large number of pet forms, compounds and elaborations, many of them based of the Latin form of the name, **Rosa**. Thus we find: **Rosabel, Rosabella, Rosalia** and **Rosalie** along with **Rosetta, Rosie, Roseanna, Roseanne, Rosina**, and **Rosita**. In Ireland the name became **Roisin** or **Rosheen** ['rohsheen] or [ro'sheen], which is anglicized to **Rosaleen**.

Rosemary

One of the nineteenth-century flower names, Rosemary is an obvious elaboration of Rose. The plant's symbolism – rosemary for remembrance – is well known thanks to the mad OPHELIA's speech in *Hamlet*. In the past this strongly-scented herb was used to make crowns and garlands as well as to scent clothes and protect them from moths. The true meaning of the name has nothing to do with the rose, but comes from its Latin name *ros marinus* ('sea-dew'), so called from the plant's liking to grow near the sea, and the misty blueish colour of its leaves. **Rosemarie** is a variant, and **Rose** is used as a short form. The name **Romy**, made popular in recent years by the actress Romy Schneider, is a Germanic pet form of the name.

Rosetta, Rosheen, Rosie, Rosina, Rosita: see ROSE

Ross

This is a surname used as a first name. The surname has a number of different origins, but is particularly common in Scotland and Ulster, where it has been used as a first name since at least the sixteenth century, and in these cases it comes from the Gaelic meaning 'a promontory'.

Rowan

As a masculine name this comes from the Irish name **Ruadhán** ('little red one'), and thus like RORY and RUFUS would have started life as a nickname for someone with red hair. As a feminine name it could be a transferred use of the masculine, but just as probably refers to the plant name, which is the alternative name for the slender and graceful mountain ash. As a boy's name its use is old, but for girls it is recent, and no doubt its similarity to the already well established ROWENA has helped its spread. **Rowann** or **Rowanne** [roh'an] are also found.

Rowena

According to the traditional history of Britain, Rowena was the daughter of the Saxon invader Hengist, who used her beauty (and some say witchcraft) to persuade the ruler of Britain, Vortigern, to give large areas of the country to the Saxons in return for marriage to Rowena. It is possible to construe the name as Anglo-Saxon, composed of such elements as *hrod* + *wynn* ('fame + joy'); but the name appears in very early sources as Renwein or Ronnwen, and since most of the early accounts come from the British side, the name is most probably a form of the Welsh **Rhonwen**, made up of the elements *rhon* ('a pike or lance', thus figuratively 'tall, slender'), and *gwen* ('fair, blessed'). Rowena came into general use after Sir Walter Scott used it as the name of his heroine in the novel *Ivanhoe* (1819).

Rowland: see ROLAND

Roxana, Roxanne, Roxane

This was the name of an Asian princess who was married to ALEXANDER the Great after he defeated her father in 327 BC. According to the Greek biographer Plutarch (*c.* 46–120), the marriage took place not for political ends but because Alexander had seen Roxana and fallen in love with her. Her son by him, Alexander IV, was at one time joint ruler of his father's empire, but both he and his mother were murdered in the power struggles that followed Alexander's death. Her romantic story was turned into a play in the late eighteenth century, which dealt with the rivalry between her and Statira, her co-wife, and stories circulated about how various actresses playing the two women carried the stage rivalry over into their own lives, so that the conflict between the two women became proverbial. The name was given a further boost by the publication of a novel called *Roxana* by Daniel Defoe in 1724, and more recently by Edmond Rostand's play *Cyrano de Bergerac* (1897), in which the heroine is called Roxane. It is not clear where the name comes from. It is traditionally said to be from the Persian for 'dawn', but it may be connected with the name Roshan, an old hill-state in the Hindu Kush. **Roxy** is used as a short form.

Roy: see RORY

Roz: see ROSALIND

Ruairdhri, Ruairi: see RODERICK, RORY

Ruben: see REUBEN

Ruby

Ruby is another of the gem names so popular in the nineteenth and first part of the twentieth century. It is used only occasionally now.

Rudi, Rudolf, Rudolph, Rudy: see RALPH

Rufus

Rufus comes from the Latin word used as a nickname for someone with red hair, and thus has the same meaning as the names under ROY and ROWAN. It is particularly associated with the assassinated Norman king William Rufus (William II), but his unsavoury reputation did not stop nineteenth-century parents adopting it as a first name. The Old French equivalent of Rufus was **Russell**, which became first a surname and later a first name. **Russ** is a short form also used as an independent name.

Rupert: see ROBERT

Russ, Russell: see RUFUS

Ruth

Ruth is a Hebrew name of uncertain meaning. The Old Testament Book of Ruth tells the charming story of Ruth's devotion to NAOMI, and of how Boaz, whom she later married, saw the poor widow gleaning in his field and ordered his men to drop grain on purpose, so that she could have more to collect.

Ryan

An Irish surname of unknown meaning, Ryan has come into use as a first name, particularly since the 1970s when the actor Ryan O'Neal made it well known.

S

Sabina

With its German form **Sabine** (pronounced in the same way), this name means 'Sabine woman'. In the legendary history of Rome told by the historian Livy, the neighbouring Sabine people refused to intermarry with the newly-founded Rome, where there was a desperate shortage of women. To avoid their city dying after one generation, the Romans invited the Sabines to a festival, ambushed them, and then carried off all the young women and married them by force. It took a long time before the Sabines could organize their revenge. When battle was finally joined, the Sabine women found themselves faced with the prospect of losing either their parents or their husbands, now the fathers of their children. To escape from this situation they forced their way between the two armies and imposed peace. For this they were greatly honoured. In Ireland the name is used to anglicize the Irish name **Sive** ('goodness') which is also anglicized as **Sabia**.

Sable: see EBONY

Sabrina

According to the mythological history of Britain, Sabrina was the daughter of Locrine, the second king of Britain. Her stepmother Guendolen (see GWEN) rebelled, killed her father, took over the government and ordered her to be thrown into the nearby river, ever since called the Severn after Sabrina. She is probably best known as the nymph of the Severn in Milton's masque *Comus* (1634) where she is addressed as:

> Sabrina fair,
> Listen where thou art sitting
> Under the glassy, cool, translucent wave,

In twisted braids of lilies knitting
The loose train of thy amber-dropping hair.

In the 1960s the name was most closely associated with a voluptuous actress, Britain's answer to the Hollywood starlet of the time.

Sacha: see ALEXANDER

Sadie: see SARAH

Saffron

This name comes from the food-flavouring collected from an
autumn-flowering crocus. The plant was at one time extensively
cultivated in Cornwall, but its use as a first name probably dates
only from the 1960s.

Sal, Sally: see SARAH

Salome: see SOLOMON

Sam, Sammy: see SAMANTHA, SAMUEL

Samantha

The origin of Samantha is not known. It appears in the eighteenth
century and it has been conjectured that it is meant to be a feminine
form of Samuel. It really took off as a name after the 1950s when the
song 'I love you, Samantha' and the character of Tracy Samantha
Lord in the film *High Society* gave the name a great deal of
exposure. TRACY seems to have increased in use at the same
time. **Sam** and **Sammy** are used as short forms, as they are for
all Sam– names.

Samson

Although the Bible claims Samson as one of the judges of Israel,
he appears in the stories about him as a violent, vengeful and
unrestrained folk-hero, notable chiefly for his strength. The name
can be interpreted as a diminutive of the Hebrew for 'sun' or as
meaning 'son of the sun-god Shamash'; and this latter, with the
similarities between his adventures and those of demigods of other
cultures such as Hercules and the Babylonian Gilgamesh, has led to
suggestions that he represents a reworking of the myths of a sun
god. The name is not much used at the moment, but has been very

popular at various times in the past. **Sampson**, an alternative form, is the usual spelling of the surname.

Samuel

One of the great Judges and Prophets of the Israelites, Samuel was instrumental in making kings of both SAUL and DAVID. The name means 'name of God', and he was destined for a holy life from birth: his mother Hannah (see ANN), desperate to have children, had vowed to God that if she had a son he would be dedicated to His service. The infant Samuel was therefore taken to the Temple and given to ELI to bring up. **Sam** or **Sammy** are short forms.

Sanchia

This is a Spanish name meaning 'holy'. **Sancha** and the German form **Sancia** can also be found. The masculine is not used in this country, but is famous thanks to the resourceful servant **Sancho** Panza in Cervantes' *Don Quixote* (1605–15).

Sander, Sandor, Sandra, Sandy: see ALEXANDER

Sapphire

One of the rarer gem names, Sapphire was no doubt kept from popularity when other gem names were current by its association with the biblical **Sapphira**, wife of the Ananias, who in the Acts of the Apostles sells some of his goods to give to the Church, but keeps back a part of the proceeds for his own use. They are both struck dead for this deception.

Sarah

Sarah is Hebrew for 'princess' and the name of the wife of the patriarch ABRAHAM in the Old Testament. The name takes the form **Sara** in the Greek New Testament. **Sadie, Sal, Sally** and even **Sallie** are short forms. In Ireland the name has been used to anglicize the native **Saraid** ('excellent'), probably influenced by the similarity of the names and by the fact that Sarah was originally called the even more similar-looking Sarai ('contentious'), before her name was changed as a sign of God's blessing.

Sasha: see ALEXANDER

Saskia

This was the name of Rembrandt's wife, who was painted by him in some memorable portraits. It was also used by John Buchan as the heroine of his adventure story *Huntingtower* which would have made the name more widely known. Its origin is not certain, but it may mean 'saxon woman'.

Saul

Saul is the Hebrew for 'asked for (child)'. The Old Testament Saul is elected the first king of Israel, but his sins lead to God's favour being taken from him and given to DAVID, at one time's Saul's favourite, but who he now persecutes. Saul was also the name of St PAUL before his conversion to Christianity (see further under STEPHEN).

Sawnie: see ALEXANDER

Scarlett

This name, which is enjoying a burst of popularity at the moment, is one of the many names brought to the attention of the public by the book (1936), and particularly the film (1939), of Margaret Mitchell's *Gone with the Wind*. In this Scarlett O'Hara is actually named from her grandmother's maiden name. The surname would have originated with someone who dealt with the costly cloth called scarlet in the Middle Ages: a cloth that was worthy of the expense of being dyed bright red, then a rare shade, and so transferred its name to the colour.

Scott

This popular name is simply a surname which would have been given to someone from Scotland, particularly a Gaelic speaker, transformed into a first name. It became widely known in the 1920s through the American novelist F. Scott Fitzgerald (1896–1940).

Seamus, Seumus: see JAMES

Sean: see JOHN

Searlait: see CHARLES

Sebastian

This name means 'man from Sebastia' a town (now Sivas) in central Asia Minor, so called from a Greek word with the same meaning as AUGUSTUS. St Sebastian was a martyr of unknown date. According to his highly dubious legend he was a Roman officer who was sentenced to be shot to death with arrows for his faith, a subject very popular with Renaissance artists. Left for dead, he was healed of his wounds by a pious widow, but on confronting his persecutors he was beaten to death. **Seb** is a short form; and, rare in this country, but popular on the Continent, are **Bastian** and **Bastien**.

Seisyllt: see CECILIA

Selina
Probably a variant of CELIA and CELESTE, Selina, too, means 'heavenly', a derivation which seems to be confirmed by the form **Celina** and the French **Céline**. However, the name looks very like a Latinate form of **Selene**, the Greek moon goddess, and is often understood in this way.

Selma
This is another of the names that came into use from the popularity of the poems attributed to OSSIAN. It is not a personal name in these poems, but the name of Fingal's castle (see FINN). However, when these poems were translated into Swedish it was not clear what 'Selma' was, and it was taken to be a feminine personal name. It then became popular in Sweden from the fame of the Selma poems of the Finno-Swedish poet Frans Mikael Franzén (1772–1849). More recently the name became well known through another Swedish writer, Selma Lagerlöf (1858–1940). The name spread from Scandinavia to the English-speaking world through Scandinavian immigration in the United States. **Zemla** is an occasional variant.

Senga: see AGNES

Seonaid: see JANE

Septimus
A Latin name meaning 'seventh', Septimus was originally given to a seventh child. The feminine is **Septima**.

Serena
Serena is the feminine form of an old Roman name meaning 'serene'. It was the name of a minor saint, but until the present century its use in Britain was mainly literary. In Edmund Spenser's *The Faerie Queen* (1590–6), Serena is a character who is gathering flowers for a garland when she is attacked by the Blatant Beast, who seizes her in

his mouth and carries her off, until her cries attract the attention of a wandering knight who comes to her rescue. **Serina** is a variant, used by the playwright Thomas Otway in *The Orphan* (1680).

Serge

The old Roman name **Sergius** became **Sergei** in Russian, but it is often found in its French form Serge, partially because at one time French was the dominant language in polite society in Russia. The enormous popularity of the name in that country is due to St Sergius of Radonezh, a fourteenth-century hermit who became the founding father of Russian monasticism. He lived in the woods and had a relationship with nature not dissimilar to that of St FRANCIS.

Seth

In chapter four of the Book of Genesis we are told, 'And Adam knew his wife again; and she bare a son, and called his name Seth: For God, said she, hath appointed me another seed instead of Abel, whom Cain slew'. This has led to the name traditionally being interpreted as 'appointed'. In fact, it means 'a setting, a cutting', the pun being on the word translated as 'seed'. It was a popular name among the Puritans, and has remained in use in the United States, but it has gradually declined in this country.

Seumas, Seumus: see JAMES

Sextus: see CECILIA

Seymour

A masculine name, Seymour is taken from the surname of a noble family. This in its turn came from the French village (now a south-eastern suburb of Paris) of St-Maur-des-Fossés, where the saint's name is the local form of MAURICE.

Shamus: see JAMES

Shane: see JOHN

Shani: see JANE

Shannon

This is a girl's name from the longest river in Ireland, the name of which means 'the old one'. Like other recent names with strong

Irish associations, such as ERIN, the name is hardly used in Ireland itself, and seems to have arisen from the sentiment of those of Irish emigrant stock.

Shantal, Shantelle: see CHANTAL

Shara, Shari: see SHARON

Sharleen, Sharley, Sharlotte: see CHARLES

Sharmaine: see CHARMAINE

Sharon
Sharon means 'the plain' and in the Bible it refers to the rich and fertile coastal plain of Palestine. In the Song of Solomon the 'rose of Sharon' is an image of beauty (although 'rose' is a mistranslation: the flower referred to may be the narcissus). At one time the name was pronounced ['sheəron] but the pronunciation ['sharən] is now almost universal. **Shara** and **Shari** are pet forms, and **Sharona** an elaboration.

Shaun, Shauna, Shawn, Shawndelle: see JOHN

Sheba: see BATHSHEBA

Sheena: see JANE

Sheelagh, Sheila: see CECILIA

Shelley
This is a girl's name with a number of sources. The actress Shelley Winters, who made the name more widely known, is really a SHIRLEY, which is probably the most important source; but other names ending in the '-shell' sound, such as Michelle (see MICHAEL) and Rachelle or Rochelle (see RACHEL), have also contributed. In addition the surname, reinforced by the fame of the poet, has contributed to the name, and the occasional masculine use of the name comes from this source. **Shelly** is a variant.

Sheralyn, Sherri, Sherry, Sheryl: see CHERYL

Shiela: see CECILIA

Shirley

Shirley is a place name, made up of the elements 'shire + meadow', which became a surname. It came into fashion as a first name in 1849, after Charlotte Bronte gave it to the heroine of her highly successful novel *Shirley*, a work which urged the public to accept a wider choice in life for women.

Sholom: see SOLOMON

Sholto

Sholto, a Scottish name, was restricted at one time to the DOUGLAS (meaning 'black water') family. It has been derived from the Gaelic for 'sower'; but Sir Walter Scott in *Castle Dangerous* (1831) gives a different story, which tells of an eighth-century king of Scotland who was aided in battle by a mysterious chieftain. After the battle he asked who his helper had been and was told, in Gaelic, 'Sholto dhu glass', which Scott translates as 'See yon dark grey man'.

Shona: see JANE

Shura: see ALEXANDER

Sian: see JANE

Sib, Sibyl, Sibylla: see SYBIL

Sidney

Sidney and its alternative spelling **Sydney** is a surname, traditionally derived from the French name Saint-Denis, used as a first name for both sexes. In the United States the name is now thought of as primarily feminine. It has been suggested this feminine use comes from the name **Sidonia** or **Sidony, Sidonie** ('woman of Sidon'), but Sidney has a long history of use as a woman's name, and there is no reason why it should not be from the surname. **Sid** is a short form of Sidney, **Siddy** of Sidonia.

Siegfried

A Germanic name, from the elements 'victory + peace', Siegfried was introduced into this country in the nineteenth century by admirers of Wagner's *Ring Cycle*. Other Germanic names which have the element meaning victory are **Sigurd** ('victory + word'), the earlier name for the hero Wagner calls Siegfried;

Sigmund ('victory + protection'), the name of Sigurd's father; and its variants **Siegmund** (the German rather than Scandinavian spelling), and **Sigismund**, a name much used by the Polish royal family. **Sigrid** ('victory + beautiful') is the only well-known feminine name with this element.

Silas: see SILVIA

Sile: see CECILIA

Silvia

Silvia and its alternative spelling **Sylvia** mean 'of the wood', and would therefore be a suitable epithet for numerous goddesses and nymphs, such as DIANA. **Silvie** or **Sylvie** is the French form, used also as a diminutive of Silvia. An early use of the name is found in Rhea Silvia, the mythical mother of Romulus (see ROMA) and Remus. However, as a Vestal Virgin her associations are with the worship of the hearth and state, and in her case the name may have been changed from some earlier form that sounded as if it came from the Latin *silva* ('a wood'). The name was given Christian respectability by being the name of a saint, the mother of GREGORY the Great. There is a large group of less frequently used names which come from the same root. **Silvius**, the masculine of Silva, does not seem to be used, and **Silvanus** is almost always found in the New Testament short form of the name, **Silas**, although the feminine **Silvana** is sometimes found. **Silvester** or **Sylvester**, the name of an outstanding early Pope, is more common, and has the feminine **Sylvestra**.

Simon

This is a name that occurs frequently in the New Testament, the best-known holder being the apostle Simon Peter. It is the Greek form of the Hebrew **Simeon**, the name of one of the tribes of Judah, and of the 'righteous and devout' old man who took the infant Jesus in his arms and blessed Him when He was presented at the temple. It probably comes from the Hebrew word for 'to listen'. **Sim, Simmy** and **Simkin** are old pet forms of Simon, but **Si** is used now. **Simone** is a French feminine that has been gaining ground in recent years.

Sindy: see CYNTHIA, LUCY

Sine, Sinead: see JANE

215

Siobhan: see JANE

Sion: see JOHN

Siriol, Sirol
This Welsh feminine name means 'cheerful'.

Sis, Sisley, Sissie, Sissy: see CECILIA

Sive: see SABINE

Solomon
The name of the Old Testament king famous for his wisdom, Solomon comes from the Hebrew *shalom* ('peace'), which, with the variant **Sholom**, has been used as a girl's name. **Sol** and **Solly** are short forms of Solomon. The better known feminine equivalent of Solomon is **Salome**, a name which was much used by the ruling family of the kingdom of Judaea, but best known as the name of the girl who danced before Herod, and when asked to name her reward demanded John the Baptist's head. However, it was also the name of one of the women who stood at the foot of the cross during the Crucifixion, and occasional uses of the name are probably inspired by her.

Somerled, Somhairle: see SORLEY

Sondra: see ALEXANDER

Sophy
Sophy is the traditional English form of **Sophia**, which comes from the Greek word for 'wisdom' used to denote the holy wisdom of God, as in the great sixth-century church of St Sophia built in Constantinople (now Istanbul). **Sophie** is the French form of the name, and **Sonia** (**Sonya, Sonja**) a Slavic pet form.

Sorcha ['sawkhə]
An increasingly popular early Irish name, Sorcha means 'bright'.

Sorley
Sorley, in Irish **Somhairle** and in the Scottish islands **Somerled**, is a name which comes not from the Celtic language but from Old Norse, for it represents a form of the words *sumar* ('summer') and

lithr ('warrior'), a term used for the Vikings who made regular raids on these areas during the sailing season. They later settled, founded new communities such as Dublin, and passed on some of their names, while at the same time Celtic names passed into the stock of Norse names.

Stacey, Stacy: see ANASTASIA, EUSTACE

Stanislaus

This is the Latin form of the Slavic **Stanislav**, a name made up of the verb 'to be' + 'glory'. **Stanislas** is the French form of the word. It is occasionally used by English speakers – for instance, Stanislaus was the name of James Joyce's brother – but usually by those of Slavic descent, in honour of St Stanislaus of Cracow, an eleventh-century Polish bishop and martyr.

Stanley

As a surname Stanley belongs to one of the oldest aristocratic families in the country, with an ancestry going back to the Norman conquest. It is the family name of the earls of Derby, who were at one time kings of the Isle of Man, and who over the centuries have produced many famous politicians. The word means 'stony field', and refers to property owned by the family. It had been used quietly from the eighteenth century as a first name, but became popular in the next century in honour of the journalist and explorer Henry Morton Stanley (1841–1904) of Dr Livingstone fame. His background was anything but aristocratic: he was born illegitimate, spent part of his childhood in a workhouse and ran away to America, where he was adopted by a family named Stanley. Despite these beginnings, he did in fact join the nobility, when he became a knight of the Order of the Bath in 1899.

Steenie, Stefan, Steffan: see STEPHEN

Stella

The Latin for 'star', Stella seems to owe its use as a first name to the poet Sir Philip Sidney (1554–86), who wrote a sonnet-sequence called *Astrophel and Stella*, using the name to show how far above her lover Stella was. However he was not the first to use the idea, for **Estelle**, which comes from the same root, was an Old French name which, along with the Latinate **Estella**, became popular in the nineteenth century.

217

Stephen, Steven

St Stephen was the first person to be martyred for his Christian faith, stoned to death as a blasphemer after accusing the Jewish Elders of rejecting the Messiah. Among those who supported his execution was SAUL of Tarsus, the young man who was later to see the light on the road to Damascus, and on his conversion take the name PAUL. Stephen's name reflects the martyr's crown he won, for it comes from the Greek for 'crown'. St Stephen's feast day is 26 December, the day on which the Bohemian King **Wenceslas** (nowadays more usually found in central Europe in the forms **Vaclav** or **Wenzel**, a name that shares Stephen's meaning, being made up of Slavic elements meaning crown + glory) looked out and saw the poor man gathering winter fuel. Continental forms such as **Stefan, Steffan** or **Stephan** are sometimes found. There is an old Scots form **Steenie**, but **Steve** or **Stevie** are the usual pet forms. **Stephanie** is the French feminine of the name which has been popular in recent years, while there is an older, rarer form **Stephana**.

Steuart, Stewart: see STUART

St John: see JOHN

Stuart, Stewart, Steuart

These are all forms of the Scottish surname and royal name. The name means 'steward' and was adopted from the title of hereditary Steward of Scotland conferred by King David I on Walter Stewart (d. 1177). His great-grandson and great-great-grandson were both regents of Scotland, and the marriage of the son of the next generation into the royal family led to *his* son becoming King Robert II (1316–90).

Sukie, Suky: see SUSAN

Suleika: see ZULEIKA

Susan

In the Apocryphal story of Susanna and the Elders, **Susanna**, whose name means 'lily', is a very beautiful woman who two old men try to blackmail into going to bed with them by threatening to say that they have seen her sleeping with a young man in a garden. Susanna defies them, and when they accuse her the Judge DANIEL takes a hand in the case. He questions the old men individually, and when they differ in their account of what species of tree the couple were making love under, Susanna's innocence is proved. **Susannah** and **Suzanna** are variants of the name; **Susan** is the English form and **Suzette (Susette)** the French pet form of **Suzanne**. **Sue, Sukie** or **Suky, Susie, Susy** and **Suzy** are the short forms.

Sybil

Sybil is now the more common spelling of **Sibyl**, the title given to the women who spoke the oracles in various religious centres in the ancient world. Collections were made of these prophecies, and in the Middle Ages some of these were interpreted as fortelling Christ, so that sibyls became associated with the biblical prophets, and it became possible for Christians to use the word for a pagan priestess as a first name. (This also explains the presence of sibyls in such a seemingly inappropriate place as Michaelangelo's ceiling in the Sistine Chapel). **Sib** is a short form and variants include **Sibylla, Sybilla** and **Sybella**, while the actress **Cybil** Shepherd has recently given publicity to another spelling of the name.

Sydney: see SIDNEY

Sylvester, Sylvestra, Sylvia, Sylvie, Sylvius: see SILVIA

Syril: see CYRIL

T

Tabitha

This is an Aramaic word meaning 'gazelle'; **Dorcas** is the Greek translation of the name. In the Bible we are told 'There was at Joppa a certain disciple named Tabitha, which by interpretation is called Dorcas' (Acts x. 36). She died, and the Apostle Peter was summoned. He went to the body and said 'Tabitha, arise. And she opened her eyes: and when she saw Peter, she sat up'. The trouble taken in this account to give the Aramaic as well as the Greek form of the name probably arises from a desire to echo Jesus's words in Mark vi, when He performs a similar miracle: 'And he took the damsel by the hand and saith unto her, Talitha cumi: which is, being interpreted, Damsel, I say unto thee, arise.' **Talitha** ('damsel'), is sometimes used as a first name. Although Tabitha is now the more frequent form of the name, Dorcas was popular in the past and Dorcas Societies were formed where women would meet to make clothes for the poor, inspired by the biblical Dorcas, who was 'full of good works and almsdeeds'.

Tadhg: see TIMOTHY

Taffy: see DAVID

Talia: see NOEL

Taliesin

An ancient Welsh bard, supposedly from the sixth century, Taliesin's name means 'radiant brow'. Much of the tradition about him is mythical, but the earliest manuscripts of Welsh poetry have works that are said to be by him. (See also EUGENE, CERIDWEN.)

Talitha: see TABITHA

Tam, Tammie, Tammy: see THOMAS

Tamara

This is the Russian form of the biblical name **Tamar**, which means 'date palm'. Thamar or Tamara was a twelfth-century queen of Georgia and her fame helped to spread the name in Russia. Tamara, along with Tamsin, is one of the sources of the name **Tammy**.

Tamsin, Tamzen, Tamzin: see THOMAS

Tania, Tanya

This is the Russian pet form of the name **Tatiana**. This popular Russian name comes from ancient Rome; it means 'belonging to the house of Tatius', a Roman family name which seems to go back to the Latin baby word for 'daddy'. Tatiana spread to Russia as the name of a martyr venerated by the Eastern Church who died *c*. 228.

Tanith

The Phoenician goddess of love and fertility, Tanith was worshipped in Carthage as the Great Goddess under the name **Tanit**. The name has come into limited use in recent years, mainly in a literary context.

Tansy: see ANASTASIA

Tara

This is the hill in County Meath where the ancient High Kings of Ireland were crowned. The remains of prehistoric earthworks can still be seen there today. Although the name was certainly in use by the end of the nineteenth century, it has been widely used only in the last half century, due largely to its use for the name of the house in *Gone With the Wind* (see further SCARLETT).

Tarquin

Tarquin was the name of two semi-legendary kings of Rome in the sixth-century BC. The second of these, Tarquin the Proud, was a murderous tyrant who tried to reverse many of the reforms that had recently been made. His conduct, together with his son's rape of LUCRETIA, led to revolt and the institution of the Republic. Despite the name's reputation, it is in limited use, (for example Sir Laurence Olivier gave it to his first child), although it is more common as a literary name.

Tatiana: see TANIA

Tavia, Tave, Tavy: see OCTAVIA

Tecla: see THEKLA

Ted, Teddie, Teddy: see EDGAR, EDMOND, EDWARD, EDWIN

Tegwen

A Welsh woman's name, Tegwen means 'fair and white'. Another name based on the word *teg* ('beautiful') is **Tegan**. The masculine equivalents are **Tegwyn** and **Tegyd** or **Tegid**.

Terence

This is the anglicized form of the name of a Roman comic playwright of the second century BC. He is said to have been a Carthaginian who was brought as a slave to Rome, where his owner freed him. There is an obscure saint of the same name, which may have helped make the name more popular, but it seems likely that the short form of the name holds the key to its spread. **Terry** is also a form of the group of names that give us DEREK, and it may well be that many a Terry was 'corrected' to Terence. The name occurs in variants such as **Terrence, Terrance**, and **Terance**. **Terrel** or **Terrell** is a form that has developed in recent years. It seems to have arisen in the United States, so it may owe something to the city of Terrell in Texas. **Tel** is a recent short form of Terence and Terry.

Teresa

A name of unknown meaning, Teresa has been derived from the Greek for 'to reap' and from the Greek island of Thera (Santorini); but since it seems to have arisen in Spain, neither of these seems very likely. The spread of the name owes much to the popularity of St Teresa of Avila, the sixteenth-century nun. Her complex and engaging personality, a combination of 'the eagle and the dove', has led to many being devoted to her. She was a gifted writer and combined great practicality with being a mystic. She has the distinction of being one of the first two women ever to be officially declared doctors of the Church, in 1970. **Theresa** is an alternative spelling; the German form is **Theresia**, and the name is shortened to **Terry** or **Terri(e)**, **Tess** and **Tessa**. **Tracy** or **Tracey**, now an independent name, started out as another pet form of

Teresa, helped by the use of the surname as a masculine first name. The surname comes from a village in the Calvados region of France, which would have come from a Gallo-Roman personal name meaning 'an inhabitant of Thrace'.

Terrel, Terrell, Terrance, Terrence: see TERENCE

Terri, Terrie, Terry: see DEREK, TERENCE, TERESA

Tess, Tessa: see TERESA

Tewdwr: see THEODORE

Thaddeus, Thaddæus
This is the name of one of the Apostles. He may be the man identified elsewhere as 'Judas, not Iscariot', and so identical with St JUDE. Thaddeus would therefore be a surname to distinguish him from the treacherous man of the same name. Its meaning is disputed. It may be from the Aramaic meaning 'praise' or 'desired', or it may be a local variant of THEODORE. In the past it was used in Ireland to render the native Tadhg (see TIMOTHY), but it was not much used elsewhere until it underwent a revival in the United States in the 1970s. There is a little evidence that the name may now be spreading here. **Thaddy** or **Thady** is sometimes found as a short form.

Thea: see DOROTHY, THEODORE

Thekla
Thekla means 'god's glory' and is the name of the first female martyr. Unfortunately, unlike St STEPHEN whose story is well authenticated, little is known for sure about Thekla, as most of her legend is highly romantic and thus dubious, and even her existence has been doubted. There was a later St Thekla, an Anglo-Saxon abbess who worked as a missionary in Germany in the eighth century, so it is surprising that this name has not been more widely used in this country. **Thecla** and **Tecla** are variants.

Thelma
This is a name invented by the writer Marie Correlli for the eponymous heroine of her novel published in 1887.

Theobald

A Germanic name, Theobald is made up of elements meaning 'people + bold'. It is one of a number of Germanic names starting with the element *theo-* ('people'), which have at times been confused with those names from the Greek *theo-* 'god' (see below). Shakespeare's **Tybalt** shows an early form of the name, reflecting the old pronunciation, and it was also found as **Tibald**, a name which was once traditional for cats, but which is now best known as a surname.

Theodore, Theodora

Of the many names that contain the Greek element *theos* ('god'), the most common are Theodore and Theodora, ('gift of god'), although the latter is more likely to appear in its reversed form of DOROTHY or Dorothea, both forms using **Thea** and **Dora** for short. The Russian form of the name is **Feodor, Fedor**, and the feminine **Fedora** is occasionally found. The Welsh **Tudor (Tudur, Tudyr, Tewdwr)**, an ancient name which eventually became the surname of the ruling family of Britain, is traditionally supposed to be a form of Theodore, but may owe something to the Welsh word *tud* ('country, tribe'). **Theodosius** and **Theodosia** are related names, meaning 'given by God'. **Theophilus** ('beloved by God' or 'loving God') and its even rarer feminine **Theophila** are little used in Britain, but in France **Théophile** is not uncommon. Although *theos* names were in use in the pagan world, they were particularly popular with early Christians, and most of the names were used by a number of saints. Since the meaning of the names is quite transparent, they have been translated literally into other languages. Thus the sense of Theodore is found in French as **Dieudonné**, and Theophilus is the Greek form of Mozart's middle name, **Amadeus**, or in German, **Gotleib**. The feminine **Amadea** has also been recorded in this country, presumably used by admirers of Mozart.

Theodoric, Theoderic: see DEREK

Theophania: see TIFFANY

Theresa, Theresia: see TERESA

Thierry: see DEREK

Thomas

This is the name of one of the Twelve Apostles. The word is Aramaic for 'twin', and sometimes appears in the Bible in its Greek equivalent, Didymus. It was probably a nickname, and although no other name for him is mentioned in the Bible, there is a tradition that his name was really Judas, in which case Thomas would have been used to distinguish him from the other Judases – Judas Iscariot and the Judas also known as THADDEUS. The popularity of the name throughout Christendom may owe something to the Apostle's character, as he is shown in the Bible as one of the more fallible and human of the Twelve. When Jesus appears after the Resurrection to the assembled Apostles, Thomas is not there, being too depressed to join them. When he is told what has happened he declares that until he has touched Christ's wounds he will not believe: whence the expression 'doubting Thomas'. When this happened and his doubts were removed, he immediately declared Jesus to be God. Thomas became a particularly favoured name in medieval England, in honour of the immensely popular St Thomas à Becket (1118–70). The name is shortened to **Tom** or **Tommy** and in the North **Tam** and **Tammie**. 'Tommy' for a soldier comes from the use of the name Thomas Atkins on sample forms for recruitment issued by the War Office in the nineteenth century.

There are a good number of feminine forms of the name. Formerly **Thomasina** or **Tomasina** was the most common, but this has now been outstripped in popularity by the Cornish **Tamsin**, with its variants **Tamzin** and **Tamzen**. This is the main source of the name **Tammy**, although it can also be a pet form of any name beginning Tam-. **Thomasa** and **Tomina** have also been used.

Thora

When the Viking raiders came to stay and settle in northern England, Scotland and Ireland they brought with them a set of names based on their favourite god Thor, the god of thunder and fighting. Thora ('dedicated to Thor') is the only feminine name to have survived, and of the many masculine names based on the god only the rare **Thurstan** or **Thurston** ('Thor's stone (altar?)'), **Torquil**, a contracted form of Thorketill ('Thor's cauldron') and **Turlough** (in Irish **Toirdhealbhach**), pronounced ['turloh] or ['turlok], meaning 'like Thor', and often replaced by TERENCE, are still found.

Tib, Tibbie, Tibby: see ISABELLA

Tiffany

Theophania is a Greek name meaning 'divine appearance', which was given to girls born around the time of the Epiphany, a word that comes from the same root. This became Tiphaine in French, and Tiffania or Tiphany in English. In medieval romance Tiphany appears as the name of the mother of the Three Kings whose gifts mark Epiphany. The name more or less disappeared from English-speaking countries, but was known as a French surname, which belonged to a jeweller who set up in New York. Tiffany's famous shop featured in the title of the very successful film, *Breakfast at Tiffany's*, (based on Truman Capote's novel, 1958), where, out of context, it could be understood as a proper name; and it is this that seems to have led to a revival of this name in recent decades.

Tilda, Tilly: see MATILDA

Timothy

This really belongs with the THEODORE group of names, for it comes from Timotheos, a Greek name meaning 'honouring God'. In the Acts of the Apostles Timothy is a young man of Asia Minor, carefully brought up in religion by his mother EUNICE and grandmother LOIS, who is chosen as an able companion and assistant by the Apostle PAUL. **Tim** and **Timmie** or **Timmy** are the usual short forms. In Ireland the name has been used to replace the native **Tadhg**, which means 'poet'.

Tina: see CHRISTINE

Titus

A Roman family name, Titus is probably of Etruscan origin and thus of unknown meaning. There was an Emperor Titus, chiefly remembered for his destruction of the Temple at Jerusalem. Like that of so many other Roman names, its use is due largely to its appearance in the Bible, borne by another follower of St Paul and, with TIMOTHY, the most trusted of his followers. The notoriety of Titus Oates, fabricator of the Popish Plot in the seventeenth century, probably helped a long-lasting decline in the name, but there are slight signs of a revival at the moment, possibly helped by the publicity given to the name by Titus Groan, hero of Mervyn Peake's *Gormenghast* books.

Toby

Toby is the English, **Tobias** the Greek form of a Hebrew name meaning 'Jehovah is good'. The name comes from the Apocryphal Book of Tobit, a highly romanticized account of how Tobias, with the help of the Archangel RAPHAEL, set out with his dog, won himself a wife and cured his father Tobit's blindness. It was a popular subject for painting, and since Tobias's dog is a notable feature of such works, Toby was transferred to the animal, and became the name of Mr Punch's dog.

Todd, Tod

A surname used as a first name, Todd is a dialect word for 'fox', and would originally have been given as a nickname to someone who either had red hair or else was known for his cunning. As a first name it has been in use from at least the latter part of the nineteenth century, for the expression 'on your tod', Cockney rhyming slang for 'on your own', refers to the American jockey Tod Sloan (1874–1933).

Toirdhealbhach: see THORA

Tom, Tomina, Tommy: see THOMAS

Toni, Tonia, Tony, Tonya: see ANTHONY

Topaz: see JEWELL

Toria: see VICTORIA

Torquil: see THORA

Tracey, Tracy: see TERESA

Travis

This is a form of the surname **Travers**, which comes from the Old French word for 'a crossing', and would have been given to someone who lived at a ford or crossroads, or possibly someone who gathered tolls at such a place.

Trevor

Trevor is the English form of the Welsh name **Trefor**. It means 'large homestead' and is the name of a number of places in Wales where it has been in use since the tenth century. It came to England in the middle of the nineteenth century, and was particularly popular in the middle years of the twentieth. **Trev** is the short form.

Tricia, Trisha: see PATRICK

Trina: see CATHERINE

Triss: see BEATRICE

Tristan, Tristram, Tristam

Sir Tristan of Lyonesse is the hero of the tragic love-story of Tristan and ISOLDA. He was famous for his skill as a huntsman, one of the best fighters in Arthurian legend, the bravest knight in Cornwall and a faithful follower of his uncle, King Mark, until he fell in love with Mark's wife. The meaning of the name is not known, but it has a complex history. In the romances his name is linked with the French word *triste* ('sorrowful'), and a story was told that when his father was captured by an enchantress his mother went searching for him, even though her baby was due to be born. She fell into labour in the forest, and died from a combination of complications and exposure. Before she died, she held her son and said to her waiting woman (in Malory's words): 'Because I shall die of the birth . . . I charge thee, gentlewoman, that thou pray my lord, King Melodias, that when he is christened let him call him Tristram, that is . . . a sorrowful birth'. This is an example of folk etymology, with the name being altered to fit a recognisable word, and a story made up to go with it. The early form of the name seems to have been Drustan, derived from Pictish name Drust. The Scottish connection is not surprising, for scholars interpret Tristan's homeland of Lyonesse as a form of the Scottish place name Lothian. There are, however, very early associations of the name with Cornwall. Near Castle Dore in Cornwall – in romance the capital of King Mark – a sixth-century tombstone was found inscribed 'Here lies Drustan son of Cynvawr', and it may be no coincidence that Cynvawr is recorded as the name, along with the later GERAINT, of one of the sixth-century Cornish kings. (See also BRONWEN.)

Trix, Trixy: see BEATRICE

Troilus: see CRESSIDA

Trudie, Trudy: see GERTRUDE

Tudor, Tudur, Tudyr: see THEODORE

Turlough: see THORA

Tybalt: see THEOBALD

Tyler

A masculine name that has been popular in the United States in recent years, Tyler is simply a surname, a respelling of the occupation of tiler, used as a first name.

Tyrone

Tyrone is the name of an Irish county which, in turn, gets its name from a person: it means 'Owen's land'. Two American actors, father and son, called Tyrone Power who appeared in films in the first half of this century did much to spread the name there. In this country the stage director Tyrone Guthrie (1900–1971) gave it fame; he was called Tony as a pet form of his name, but **Ty** is the more usual short form.

U

Ulick: see HUGH, ULYSSES, WILLIAM

Ulric

This name appears in Old English as **Wulfric** ('wolf + power'), which was the name of an English saint of the twelfth century who had been a self-indulgent parson in his younger days, devoted to hunting, but who reformed in later years, to end his days a recluse in the delightfully named Haselbury Plucknett in Somerset. It is also the name of a number of German saints, and modern use of the name is probably due to introduction from Germany. This is certainly the case for **Ulrice**, the German feminine form, also found as **Ulrica**, both forms being pronounced the the same way. Ulrica seems to have been a popular literary name in the nineteenth century, appearing, among others, as characters in two of Sir Walter Scott's novels, *Ivanhoe* and *Count Robert of Paris*.

Ulysses

The Latin form of **Odysseus**, Homer's great Greek hero, Ulysses was famous for his wisdom, cunning and eloquence – and for the faithfulness of his wife PENELOPE. It is little used in modern times, but when it occurs it is probably through an association with General Ulysses S. Grant (1822–85), commander of the Union armies in the American Civil War and 18th president of the United States. In Ireland **Ulick** is sometimes anglicized as Ulysses.

Una

This early Irish name is often found as **Oona** or **Oonagh**. In the past it has sometimes been anglicized as JUNO. Its meaning is not clear, but it has been argued that it is from the Irish word *uan* meaning 'lamb'. Another source of the name is Edmund Spenser's poem *The Faerie Queene* (1590–6), in which she is the heroine of Book

I. Here the name is based on the Latin for 'one', for Una is truth personified and is so called because Truth is one, while Error is multiform. However, it is probably no coincidence that Spenser was a resident of Ireland, and he was very possibly influenced by the Irish name. The sense of 'one' is found in another name, **Unity**, introduced as an abstract name by the Puritans but often regarded as a variant of Una.

Unice: see EUNICE

Unity: see UNA

Urban
This Latin name, meaning 'townsman', was chosen by eight medieval Popes, probably because it was the opposite of 'pagan', which originally meant 'country dweller'. It is rarely found in modern times. There is a Welsh name **Urien** which is thought to come from the same root, being a form of the Latin *urbigenus*, ('town-born'). It was the name of a leader of the Northern Britons in the sixth century, who also appears as one of King Arthur's knights in the medieval romances.

Uriah: see BATHSHEBA

Urien: see URBAN

Ursula
The means 'little bear'. St Ursula was a very popular saint in the Middle Ages and had a church dedicated to her by the late fourth or early fifth century. According to legend she and 11,000 virgin companions were martyred at Cologne by the Huns on their way back from a pilgrimage to Rome. She is said to have been a British princess fleeing from an unwanted marriage. Other than that she probably existed and that her companions were originally recorded as 10 in number, little can be confidently asserted about Ursula, for the stories about her are no less fanciful than those told about her masculine equivalent ORSON.

V

Vaclav: see STEPHEN

Val: see PERCY, VALERY

Valda, Valdemar: see WALDO

Valery

With its alternative spelling **Valerie**, this is the English form of the Roman family name **Valeria** (masculine **Valerian**), a name coming from the Latin verb *valere* ('to be strong, healthy, flourish'). From the same root comes **Valentine** the name of a third century martyr. Nothing is known about him for sure, for all the stories revolve around customs associated with St Valentine's Day, and these evolved from pagan Roman fertility customs associated with mid-February. Valentine's only connection is that his feast day falls on 14 February. In the Middle Ages the name is found in the romance of *Valentine and ORSON*, in which Valentine is a brave and doughty prince. The name is especially given to children born on or about the saint's day. It can be used for both sexes, although it is more commonly masculine, with **Valentina** being used as an alternative feminine. **Val** is used as a short form of these names for both sexes, and for women it has been elaborated into a new name, **Valene**.

Vanda: see WANDA

Vanessa

This is a name invented by Jonathan Swift (1667–1745) for a poem called *Cadenus and Vanessa* (1726), in which he declines the offer of marriage made to him by a young woman called Esther Vanhomrigh, Cadenus being an anagram of *decanus*, the

232

Latin for his ecclesiastical rank of Dean, and Vanessa a play on elements of her name.

Vanora: see JENNIFER

Vashti
Vashti is the name of the Old Testament queen whose refusal to display herself at her husband's feast leads to her replacement by ESTHER. The name probably comes from the Persian for 'beautiful'. It is still in occasional use, but mainly in literary contexts, often with rather voluptuous connotations.

Vasilie: see BASIL

Vaughan
A Welsh first and surname, Vaughan is the English form of the adjective *fychan* a form of the Welsh word meaning 'little' and would originally have been given as a nickname to someone small.

Velda: see WALDO

Velma
This name is something of a mystery. It seems to have come into use in the United States in the 1880s, at a time when names such as THELMA were also popular. It may well be that the '-elma' sound was felt to be particularly attractive by parents, in the way that certain sounds seem to become strangely fashionable for a while, and that Velma was a name invented to fit this fashion. However, it has been linked with Wilhelmina (see WILLIAM), and there may be a progression of Wilhelmina moving to the pet form **Wilma**, then becoming Vilma (the German pronunciation), with Velma as a variant.

Venetia
Although Venetia is the Latin name for the city of Venice, in the past it was more often associated with the name of Venus, the Roman goddess of fertility and love, and some uses may have been in this sense. A famous early bearer of the name was Venetia Stanley (1600–33). She was a lady of noble family and outstanding intellect, who set up house on her own in London, thereby earning the description by one contemporary of 'that celebrated beautie and courtezane'. In 1625 she secretly married her childhood playmate Sir KENELM Digby against his family's wishes. It was a love match

and a happy marriage, and after Venetia's early death Digby erected an elaborate monument to her and was so overcome with grief that he went into complete seclusion for two years. Her death was lamented in verse by numerous poets, including Ben Jonson.

Venus: see JULIA, VENETIA

Vera

Vera looks as if it is from the Latin for 'truth', which would give it the same sense as the English name **Verity**; in fact, it comes from Russian and means 'FAITH'. It is sometimes used as a short form of VERONICA. The rare spelling **Viera** is closer to the Russian original. **Vere** is sometimes regarded as a masculine form of Vera, but is actually a French place name which became an aristocratic surname and then a first name.

Verena

The name of an obscure third-century saint, Verena is probably a form of the Latin word for 'truth' (see VERA). Modern use probably owes much to Henry James having given this name to the central character of his novel *The Bostonians* (1886).

Vergil: see VIRGIL

Verity: see VERA

Vernon

This is a French place name which comes from a Gaulish word meaning 'where alders grow'. A Richard de Vernon was one of the Norman conquerors of England, and he founded a noble family. In the nineteenth century, when such practices were popular, the surname was adopted as a first name. **Verna** has been used as a feminine form of the name, but is usually traced back to the Latin *vernus* ('spring').

Veronica

The story told of Saint Veronica is that she was a witness of Christ's suffering as he carried His cross through Jerusalem to the site of the crucifixion. Moved with pity at his suffering, she used her veil to wipe the sweat from His face, and an image of His face, like that of the Turin shroud, was left on her veil and became a sacred relic. In fact, the name of the relic seems to have been transferred to the (possibly fictional) woman, for Veronica means 'true image or icon'. **Véronique**, the French form, is occasionally found. An alternative interpretation of the name links it with the Macedonian Greek name **Berenice** ('bringer of victory'). Berenice was a popular name with the third-century BC rulers of Egypt, descendants of ALEXANDER's Macedonian conquerors, and a story is told of how one Berenice dedicated a lock of her hair at a temple as an offering for the safe return of her husband from war. The lock disappeared and a new constellation was seen in the sky, ever after known as the Lock of Berenice. The Greeks would have pronounced the name [bere'niekee]; it was formerly [berə'niesee] in England, but is now often [berə'nees], while the spelling **Bernice** ['bernis] or [ber'nees] shows a further reduction. **Bunnie** or **Bunny** and **Bernie** are short forms.

Vesta

This is the name of the Roman goddess of the hearth and home. The name was the stage name of the music hall-star Vesta Tilley (1864–1952), who made famous the song 'Burlington Bertie'.

Victoria

The Latin for 'victory', both Victoria and **Victor**, the masculine form, are found at an early date on the Continent, but are very rare in Britain until the nineteenth century, when Queen Victoria was christened after her German mother. **Vic** is used as a short form for both sexes, and **Vicky, Toria** and **Vita** for Victoria. Vita has been associated with the Latin word for 'life', but its most famous bearer, the writer Vita Sackville-West (1892–1962), was a Victoria. The pre-Roman British already had a name with the same meaning, used by the chieftainess and rebel leader the Romans called **Boadicea** or Boudicca, a name which has come down to us as the Welsh name **Buddug**, ['bidhig] or **Buddic**. The masculine name **Gwythyr**, found in some of the earliest surviving Welsh literature, is said to be a form of Victor.

Vida: see DAVID

Viera: see VERA

Vilma: see VELMA, WILLIAM

Vina: see DAVID, LAVINIA

Vincent

This is allied to VICTORIA, for it comes from the Latin verb for 'to conquer'. The name was popular in the Middle Ages, particularly among the French, who introduced it into this country. Later, St Vincent de Paul (1580–1660), one of many saints called Vincent, brought the name fame. He organized societies of laymen to care for the poor and neglected, as well as founding the Vincentian Fathers and the Sisters of Charity.

Violet

One of the best-known of the flower names, Violet is also found in the French form **Violette**, in the Italian **Violetta** – famous as the name of the heroine of Verdi's opera *La Traviata* (1853) – and in the Latin **Viola**, possibly influenced by Shakespeare's heroine of *Twelfth Night*. The flower and its colour seem to go back to a Greek word *ion*, which lies behind a group of less common girls' names. **Ione** means 'Violet', and is the feminine of Ion, the name of the king of Athens who gave his name to the Ionian people. Edward Bulwer–Lytton seems to have invented it for the heroine of his highly successful novel *The Last Days of Pompeii* (1834). **Ianthe** ('violet flower') is an ancient name which has a long literary history. It was taken from ancient mythology by Ovid (43 BC–AD 18), picked up by a number of sixteenth- and seventeenth-century poets and playwrights, used by Byron as the pseudonym for the dedicatee of the poem which brought him fame, *Childe Harold's Pilgrimage*, and used by Shelley for his first daughter and for a character in his *Queen Mab* (1813). **Iolanthe**, used by Gilbert and Sullivan for their opera, is probably a variant, and with the 'th' changed to a 'd' became **Yoland, Yolande** or **Yolanda**.

Virgil

This is the usual form of the name of the Latin poet (70–19 BC) which is more correctly spelt **Vergil**. It is primarily an American name, as in the composer Virgil Thomson (1896–1989), although it can also be an anglicization of the Irish FERGUS. To the Romans Virgil became almost the national poet, his epic *The Aeneid* becoming the accepted account of how Rome came to be. In the Middle Ages he was thought to have prophesied the coming of Christ in a poem which actually celebrated the birth of a grandchild of the Emperor AUGUSTUS; and from this he developed into a powerful magician in popular literature, with a magic looking-glass in which he could see whatever was happening in the world.

Virginia

The Romans told a story of a girl called Virginia whom a corrupt ruler wanted to sleep with, so he got a dependent to claim that she was actually his slave, and the ruler gave judgment in his favour. Virginia's father realised what was happening and the fate which awaited his daughter, and killed her on the spot, preferring her death to dishonour. Despite this ancient precedent, the real source of Virginia as a modern name is the American state named in honour of Elizabeth I, the Virgin Queen, by Sir Walter Raleigh when he founded a colony there. The first child born to the settlers was christened Virginia, and for long the name remained primarily an American one, although this is no longer the case. It is shortened to **Ginny** or **Jinny**.

Vita: see VICTORIA

Vivian

Derived from the Latin meaning 'lively', Vivian was originally a masculine name, with the elaborations **Vyvyan** and **Vyvian**. **Vivien** and **Vivienne** were the feminines. However, this distinction has now become blurred, and while you are unlikely to find the feminine forms used for men, woman now use all the forms, along with **Viviana** (an obscure early martyr) and **Vivianne**. **Viv** is a short form of all these.

Vonda: see WANDA

Vyvian, Vyvyan: see VIVIAN

W

Waldo

Waldo comes from a Germanic word meaning 'power' and is also a pet form of **Waldemar** or **Valdemar**, meaning 'great ruler'. **Valda**, which has a variant **Velda**, is the feminine equivalent. The word 'Waldo', as used to mean a mechanical device for handling things by remote control, comes from a science-fiction novella by Robert Heinlein, where the hero is a physically handicapped man of that name who invents devices to compensate for his inabilities. When, soon afterwards, the nuclear industry developed means of extensive remote manipulation, the name of Heinlein's fictional devices was transferred to the real ones.

Wallace

The use of this as a surname probably arose from admiration of Sir William Wallace (c. 1274–1305), the Scottish patriot who fought against the English under Edward I and temporarily drove them out of his country, until he was captured and executed by them. In contemporary accounts his name is spelt Walays, or in Latin Wallensis, which means 'the Welshman'. It comes from the Anglo-Norman word *waleis* which originally meant 'foreign' but came to be given to all the Celtic minorities in the British Isles, including those living in the Scottish border area from which Wallace is thought to have been descended.

Walter

A Germanic name, Walter was brought to England by the Norman conquest. It is made up of elements meaning 'rule + army'. In the past the pet forms were **Wat** and **Watty**, reflecting the old pronunciation which swallowed the '1'; but now **Wally** and **Walt** are used.

Wanda

It has been asserted that Wanda is a form of 'Vandal', the wandering Germanic tribe that so devastated Europe in the Dark Ages that their name has become a part of the language; but this is not well-supported. Wanda is a Slavic name, found in Poland from the nineteenth century, but seems to have come to this country only when Ouida published a novel called *Wanda* in 1883. The variants **Vanda** and **Vonda** reflect the German pronunciation of the name.

Warren

This is a surname used as a first name. Unlike the majority of such names, which came into use only in the nineteenth century, Warren has been a first name since the seventeenth. The name has a number of different sources. There was a Germanic name Varin, meaning 'to watch, guard', which the Normans brought over as Guerin and which became Warren in English; it can be from the French place-name La Varenne (near Nantes), meaning 'warren'; or it can be a name given to someone who lived near a warren or was a warren-keeper.

Warwick

Warwick is a surname and place name used as a first name. The town of Warwick, to judge by its meaning, was originally a suburb which grew up by a weir. Guy, Earl of Warwick was a popular hero of medieval romance. There were also two real-life earls of Warwick in the fifteenth century whose lives could have come from the story-books – one model of knightly courtesy and prowess, the other so influential in the Wars of the Roses that he has come down to us as Warwick the Kingmaker. The pub sign of the Bear and Ragged Staff is taken from the Warwick coat of arms. **Warrie** is used as a short form.

Wat, Watty: see WALTER

Wayne

A twentieth-century first name, Wayne owes its use to the popularity of the film star John Wayne. The surname derives from 'wain', the old word for a cart or wagon, and would have been given to a carter or cart-maker.

Wenceslas: see STEPHEN

Wendy

This has one of the best-recorded histories of any first name. It was introduced by J.M. Barrie in 1904 for the girl in *Peter Pan*. He said that he took it from the nickname that a child called Margaret Henley used for him: she regarded him as her friend, so called him 'Fwendy-Wendy'. *Peter Pan* was enormously successful and the name spread rapidly. Its spread must have been helped by its similarity to the Welsh names starting with GWEN which had been popular shortly before. With variants such as **Wenda** it is difficult to draw a line between Wendy and the Welsh Gwenda.

Wenonah: see WINONA

Wenzel: see STEPHEN

Wesley

Another name with a clear history, Wesley was introduced as a first name in honour of John Wesley (1703–91), the founder of Methodism, and his brother Charles (1707–88), evangelist and hymn writer. **Wes** is the short form. The surname means 'west meadow'.

Whitney

Whitney is an English place name meaning 'white island'. In the United States, Mount Whitney, one of the highest peaks in the Rockies, is named after Josiah Dwight Whitney (1819–96), the geologist who surveyed the Rockies and established the height of many of the range's peaks, and this is probably the main American source of the name. Whitney has been used as a first name for both sexes, but is best known in Britain through the singer Whitney Houston.

Wilbert

An old English name meaning 'will + bright', Wilbert is little used now, but it is known to generations of *Thomas the Tank Engine* fans as the first name of the Rev. Awdrey who created him.

Wilbur

This is a surname, probably from the Old English meaning 'will + fortress', used as a first name. It is popular mainly in the United States, where it is used to honour Wilbur Wright (1867–1912), who with his brother **Orville** (which appears to have been a surname invented by Fanny Burney for her novel *Evelina* of 1778) was a pioneer of aviation.

Wilfred

With its variant **Wilfrid**, this is an Old English name made up of the elements 'will + peace'. It was the name of an outstanding Northumbrian bishop in the seventh century, but it died out after the Norman conquest until revived in the saint's honour by High Church Anglicans in the nineteenth century. **Wilf** and **Fred** are the short forms.

William

A Germanic name, William is compounded from elements meaning 'will + helmet', which literally came over with the Conqueror, who was better known in his own time as William the Bastard. It rapidly became popular, and has remained among the favourite boy's names to this day. It is shortened to **Will, Willie** or **Willy** and its variants are **Bill, Billie** or **Billy**. In Welsh the name became **Gwilym** or **Gwillym**, with a short form **Gwil**; in Ireland **Ulick** (see HUGH) may be a form of the name, while **Liam**, the Irish short form of William, has become popular as a name in its own right and spread to this country. **Wilhelmina** is the basic feminine form, taken from German. This has evolved a large number of short forms such as **Elma, Willa, Wilma** or **Vilma, Mina, Minna, Minnie** and **Minella** which, along with the masculine pet forms, are used as independent female names (see also VELMA).

Winifred

This is the English form of the Welsh name Gwenfrewi ('blessed reconciliation': see further under GWEN). St Winifred was a seventh-century Welsh maiden who, according to legend, rejected the advances of a prince who then decapitated her in fury. When her head was restored to her body she miraculously came back to life, and was allowed to end her days as a nun. Her relics were moved to Shrewsbury in 1138, which accounts for the name developing an English form. Short forms are **Win, Winnie** and **Freda**. The name was very popular at the end of the nineteenth century and beginning of the twentieth.

Winona

This first name comes from the name of a number of places in the United States, including a city and county in Minnesota. It is the Sioux word for 'first-born daughter', so is particularly suited to be a first name. The name occurs as **Wenonah**, the mother of Hiawatha, in Longfellow's poem (1855).

Winston

Winston owes its modern popularity as a boy's name to Sir Winston Churchill (1874–1965), but was a traditional name in his family. The first Sir Winston Churchill, father of the first Duke of Marlborough, was born in 1620. He was named Winston in honour of his mother, who was born Sarah Winston. The surname came from a place name made up of Old English elements meaning 'joy + stone'.

Wulfric: see ULRIC

Wyn, Wynn, Wynford: see GWEN

Wyvonne: see YVONNE

X

Xan, Xandra, Xandrine: see ALEXANDER

Xanthe ['zanthi]
The Greek for 'yellow', Xanthe is thus the equivalent of the Latin names FLAVIA and Fulvia. Although Dunkling suggests that the name is obsolete or at least obsolescent, it is still being used by parents even if it is not the most common of names.

Xavier ['zaveeə]
St Francis Xavier (1506–52), the patron saint of missionaries, got his name from the Spanish-Basque village where he was born. He was one of the founding members of the Jesuits and devoted his life to spreading Christianity in the Far East, particularly in India, China and Japan. He is buried in Goa (India), where his tomb is still a popular place of pilgrimage. Xavier is most often found as a second name, often following Francis. It is occasionally spelt **Zavier**, and there are feminine forms **Xaviera, Xavia** or **Zavia, Xaverine** and **Xavière**.

Xenia ['zeeniə]
This is the full form of a name more often found as **Xena, Zena** or **Zina**. It comes from the Greek word for 'hospitable'.

Y

Yasmin, Yasmine: see JASMIN

Yehudi: see JUDE

Ynyr: see HONORIA

Yoland, Yolande, Yolanda: see VIOLET

Yseult, Yseut, Ysold, Ysolda, Ysolde: see ISOLDA

Yvonne

Yvonne is the most common form of a group of names which come from a Germanic root meaning 'yew', the tree used for making longbows. **Yves**, the French form of Ivo (see IVOR), a name popular in France but rare here, developed two feminine diminutives, Yvonne and **Yvette**. There are a number of spelling variants, of which **Yvone** and **Evonne** are the most common. In the United States in the 1930s and 1940s it was considered a rather exotic name, and some users were not sure how to pronounce it, others how to spell it. This led to some extraordinary variations in both spelling and pronunciation, of which the most extreme were **Javonne** [ya'vohn], as if the name were Slavic, and **Wyvonne** [wie'vohn], giving the alphabetical name to the original first letter.

Z

Zac: see ISAAC, ZACHARY

Zachary

The English form of the Hebrew name **Zachariah** (**Zacharias** is Greek), Zachary means 'God has remembered'. It is probably the most used of the masculine 'Z' names, particularly in its short form **Zac**. **Zach, Zack, Zacky** and **Zaz** have also been recorded as short forms. The name is attached to eight different people in the Bible, the most prominent of whom was the father of John the Baptist, who was punished with dumbness when he did not believe what the Angel Gabriel told him of his future son, and on the restoration of his voice was inspired to compose the hymn of praise known as the 'Benedictus'.

Zandra: see ALEXANDER

Zara

An Arabic name meaning 'brightness, splendour of the dawn', Zara was introduced by William Congreve as the name of an African queen in his play *The Mourning Bride* (1697). It was then used by Aaron Hill in 1735 as the title and name of the heroine of his translation of a melodramatic tragedy by Voltaire, in the original French called *Zaïre* (1733). However, it was rarely found in real life until the 1960s. Surprisingly, although its use by The Princess Royal for her daughter in 1981 brought the name to the attention of the general public, it does not seem to have led to any marked increase in the name's use.

Zavia, Zavier: see XAVIER

Zebedee

The father of the Apostles James the Great and John 'the disciple whom Jesus loved', Zebedee was a successful fisherman, working on the Sea of Galilee. His name means 'my gift'. However, the modern associations of this name are not biblical, for generations of children grew up linking the name with the spring-based puppet of television's *The Magic Roundabout* and the catch-phrase 'Time for bed, said Zebedee'.

Zeke: see EZEKIEL

Zelma: see SELMA

Zelda: see GRISELDA

Zena: see XENIA

Zenaida: see ZINAIDA

Zenobia

Zenobia was a queen of Palmyra in Syria, famous for her intellect and beauty. When her husband Odenathus died in AD 267 (some say by her hand) she took over the throne. At first the Roman emperors supported her, but she became over-ambitious, and when she invaded the Roman territories of Asia Minor and Egypt she was captured and deposed and her city-state and its unique culture obliterated. The name is interpreted as the Greek for 'force of Zeus', but this is probably an adaptation (which at that time could go a long way from the original) of her native name found in local inscriptions, which was Septimia Bathzabbai, meaning something like 'dowry of God'.

Zillah

This is a Hebrew name meaning 'shadow'. In Genesis she is the mother of Jabal and Jubal, co-wife of Lamech with ADAH. The name was used by the poet laureate Robert Southey (1774–1843) in a tale he took from a medieval source about the origin of the rose, in which a fair maiden of Bethlehem called Zillah rejects the advances of a sottish brute, is accused by him of having dealings with the devil, and is condemned to be burned at the stake. The flames destroy her false accuser, but she is unharmed and from the stake white roses blossom, 'the first ever seen on earth since paradise was lost'.

Zilpha

More correctly spelt **Zilpa**, Zilpha is a biblical name from the Arabic meaning 'with the little nose'. She was a slave girl given to LEAH by her father Laban, and by her to her husband JACOB as a concubine to be a sort of surrogate mother for Leah. Zilpa became the mother of Gad and Acher, from whom two of the 12 tribes of Israel descended.

Zina: see XENIA

Zinaida [zinie'eedə]

This is the Russian form of a Greek name meaning 'daughter of Zeus'. It is the name of two early martyrs, but its introduction to the English-speaking world is probably due to its use for the heroine of Ivan Turgenev's novella *First Love* (1860). **Zenaida** is an alternative form.

Zinnia

Zinnia is a modern flower-name, the genus to which these plants belong being named after J.G. Zinn, a German botanist.

Zita

This seems to come from an Italian dialect word for 'child'. It was the name of a Tuscan saint of the thirteenth century, who at the age of 12 started work as a domestic servant. Her care over her work and her habit of giving food to the poor brought her into conflict with both her fellow-servants and her employer, but her devotion and meek patience won her respect in the end, and she spent most of her later life in good works. She became the patron saint of domestic servants, with a bunch of keys as her emblem; but despite these lowly associations Zita was the name of the last empress of Austria, who lost the throne after the dissolution of the Austro-Hungarian empire at the end of the First World War, but who lived on in retirement until 1989.

Zoe, Zoë

The Greek word for 'life', Zoe was used by Greek-speakers for the Hebrew EVE. It was introduced to this country in the nineteenth century and has become rather popular, and has developed a phonetic spelling, **Zowie**.

Zola

Although the name has recently been most closely associated with the South African runner Zola Budd, it has been in use, particularly in the United States, for many years. For example, the lead singer of the Black American pop group The Platters, who had a hit record in 1956, was called Zola Taylor. It must be assumed that the name is a use of the surname of the French writer Emile Zola (1840–1902). His father was Italian and the name comes from a dialect word meaning 'bank, mound of earth'.

Zowie: see ZOË

Zuleika

This is a Persian name meaning 'brilliant beauty'. It is traditionally the name of both Joseph's and Potiphar's wives, but it first gained fame in this country when Byron used it for the tragic heroine of his poem *The Bride of Abydos* (1813). Its greatest fame, however, comes from Max Beerbohm's comic novel *Zuleika Dobson* (1911). When this was broadcast on the radio and his heroine's name was, in his view, mispronounced, Beerbohm sent an angry telegram to the producer, which ran 'ZULEIKA SPEAKER NOT HIKER BEERBOHM'; but although the pronunciation rhyming with speaker is the traditional one, that rhyming with hiker is now the more common. **Suleika** is a variant.